The Pizza Gourmet

Shea MacKenzie

Avery Publishing Group

Garden City Park, New York

Cover Design: William Gonzalez
Original Text Illustrations: Shea MacKenzie
Interior Color Photographs: John Strange and Associates
In-House Editor: Marie Caratozzolo
Typesetter: Bonnie Freid
Printer: Paragon Press, Honesdale, PA

Library of Congress Cataloging-in-Publication Data

MacKenzie, Shea.
   The pizza gourmet : simple recipes for spectacular pizzas / by
Shea MacKenzie.
     p. cm.
   Includes index.
   ISBN 0-89529-656-X
   1. Pizza   2. Cookery, International.   I. Title.
TX770.P58M27   1995
641.8'24—dc20

                            95-4860
                            CIP

10 9 8 7 6 5 4 3 2 1

Preface

izza has become such a staple of our culinary culture that there rages ongoing controversy as to which civilization first created it. We know that early Neolithic tribes created bread from wild grains, which they cooked on the hot stones of their campfires. It was but a small step that took them from eating this bread unadorned to filling or topping it with other foods. The first great bakers of bread, however, were the Egyptians, who taught their baking methods to the Greeks. In turn, the Greeks advanced baking further than their teachers by creating methods for refining many different kinds of flours, and by designing new types of ovens and breadmaking molds.

At this point, history becomes confusing when trying to assign credit for the creation of pizza. We know that the ancient Greeks were more sophisticated than most of their contemporaries in breadmaking. And since they occupied the southern regions of Italy for over six hundred years, there is logic to the theory that the Greeks introduced the Italians to the idea of using bread as an "edible plate for a meal." Volumes of Greek history refer to breads flavored and topped with oils, spices, seeds, vegetables, olives, and cheese. Most cultures are receptive to outside culinary influences and it seems logical that the southern portions of Italy would also be.

On the other hand, we know the Etruscans arrived in Italy from Asia Minor and introduced one of their staples—a cornmeal cake that was baked on stones beneath a fire. This bread was then seasoned with oil and herbs and eaten with other foods. The Romans incorporated this cake into their cuisine and called it focaccia (from a Latin word meaning "fireplace floor bread"). The Neopolitans of Italy topped this flatbread with oils, herbs, and sometimes cheese. When Peruvian tomatoes were introduced in Italy by Christopher Columbus, they quickly appeared on these circles of dough. In time, the tomato took over as a popular pizza-topping ingredient.

Pizza, in its primitive form, served as the springboard for a myriad of pizza dishes. One of these dishes—the calzone—is definitely Neapolitan. Also known as "mezzaluna" and "fiadone" in Italy, and "chaussons" in France, the calzone is a pizza turnover that is filled with any of a variety of pizza toppings. Calzones can be sandwich-sized and eaten as a meal or tart-sized for cocktail fare.

Another pizza variation is the double-crust type that is stuffed with a filling. Pies, tortes, and quiches are likely descendants of this filled double-crust pizza. Deep-dish double-crust pizzas are also perfect for holding fillings that tend to be messy.

A third member of the pizza family is the stromboli, a jelly-roll affair in which the dough surrounds a filling. Also called "bonata" and "pizza roll," a stromboli looks like a long crusty loaf that, when sliced, reveals a filling that is spiraled within the rolled bread. Stromboli is perfect party fare since it can be served at room temperature, sliced as thinly or thickly as desired, and easily reheated.

Whatever its origin, pizza is undeniably one of America's most popular foods. A few basic pizza types are found in the United States. In the East, the New York-style, traditional Neopolitan pizza predominates with its light, thin crust. This style pizza is the one most often sold by the slice in shopping malls and fast-food eateries up and down the East Coast. The Midwest region swears by the deep-dish Chicago-style pizza—a hearty thick Sicilian-style crust that is laden with heavy toppings. The West Coast, with its progressive and healthy attitude toward food, has inspired lighter, sophisticated pizza versions with an emphasis on fresh vegetables and whole grains. A number of other regional pizza styles come from areas such as New England and the Southwestern United States. *The Pizza Gourmet* includes pizza creations from all of these areas, as well as pizzas that reflect culinary cultures of countries throughout the world. Some recipes are authentic, others have been inspired, but all have been created with the hope of intriguing and enticing you to make your own pizza.

What began as a simple bread, made to sustain life, pizza has evolved into a variety of dishes, some basic and unassuming, others intriguing in their sophistication and creativity. Whatever the form, pizza definitely has a significant place in the eating habits of most Americans.

As most people buy pizza from restaurants or pizzarias, or rely on commercially prepared frozen products, *The Pizza Gourmet* gives you another option—create your own! Whether it is a pizza you make by digging your fingers deep into yeast dough or one you create from ingredients on hand, keep in mind that pizza is a fun food. It really doesn't matter whether it is planned in advance or whipped up on a whim. In either case, the idea of loading oozing fragrant toppings on a bit of crisp crust is one that begs for creativity and experimentation. The recipes in this book are designed to captivate your interest and excite your sense of culinary adventure. They will, hopefully, urge you to create this satisfying food that is adored by both young and old . . . pizza!

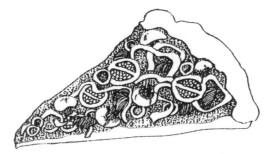

1

Getting Down to Basics

Like most people, you are probably already familiar with pizza. Personally, I have enjoyed this food for over thirty years and, even before beginning this book, considered myself somewhat of a connoisseur on the subject. Isn't everyone? This familiarity with how pizza is made and how it should taste will help when you prepare it yourself.

This opening chapter is a primer that includes a variety of basic information to help ensure a successful outcome to your pizza-making efforts. It includes a list of important basic kitchen equipment, as well as a glossary of the ingredients called for in this book. Basic techniques for preparing pizza pans and paddles, and for assembling and baking the different types of pizza are also found here. (Preparing and working with

pizza dough is presented in Chapter 2, "Pizza Doughs and Crusts.") Tips for storing and reheating pizza are also provided.

Think of this as your reference chapter. Turn to it when you come across an unfamiliar term, are uncertain about a procedure, or if you need, perhaps, some measurement information or an ingredient substitution. It's all here.

BASIC PIZZA-MAKING INFORMATION

Before diving in and trying out the recipes in *The Pizza Gourmet*, I urge you to take a few minutes to read through the following section. It provides useful guidelines on how to properly assemble pizzas, important information on baking and grilling, and helpful tips on storing and reheating. (Information on preparing pizza dough is found in Chapter 2.)

Assembling Your Pizza

Once you are ready to assemble your pizza, the following guidelines should be followed. They will help you to create a pizza that is a masterpiece, rather than a mess.

- For all thin- and medium-crust pies (not deep-dish) add toppings to within 1 inch of the edge. This rim of dough will keep the toppings from bubbling over the edge of the pizza. It will also provide a handle to make picking up a cooked slice easier.

- As the center of the pie always takes longest to cook, place the thickest amount of topping toward the edges of the pizza, rather than in the middle. If there is a heavy concentration of ingredients in the center of the pie, the outer edges may overcook before the center is done.

- When the first topping on the dough is sauce or another moist filling, any remaining topping ingredients should be on hand, so the pizza can be assembled quickly and placed in the oven immediately. This will prevent any moistness from seeping into the dough, resulting in a soggy crust.

Baking Pizza in the Oven

If you are using a conventional oven to bake your pizza, the following tips will help to ensure perfect results.

- Throughout this book, I suggest baking yeast-raised pizzas at an oven temperature of 450°F. This will produce golden crusts that are light yet crisp on the bottom; crusts that are crisp enough to support the toppings, but not so crisp that they are hard to cut with a knife. Oven temperatures do vary significantly, however, and you may need to increase or decrease yours to achieve the desired results.

- Be sure to preheat the oven for at least thirty minutes. Without this lengthy preheating, the pizza will first get warm (and probably soggy) before it begins to cook.

- Whether you use pizza pans, stones, or tiles, always bake the pizza on the lowest point of the oven possible. This means that optimally, pizza stones or tiles should be placed on the oven floor, and pizza pans should be placed on an oven rack that is set in the lowest position. This placement allows the underside of the dough to quickly firm and cook, preventing it from becoming soggy due to the toppings. (For more information on pizza stones and tiles, see page 7.)

- In the recipes, a range of baking times has been given for each pizza. Again, keep in mind that temperatures do vary from oven to oven. The first time you prepare a pizza, be sure to monitor it as it bakes. This will prevent you from overcooking or burning it.

Baking Pizza on a Grill

Just as pizza can be baked in a variety of ovens, so can it be baked atop a gas or charcoal grill. The only requirement is a cover on the grill and the ability to keep the fire or temperature at a fairly constant level. There are two ways to grill pizza—in a pan or directly on the rack. In both cases, prepare the dough as directed in the master recipe and preheat the grill to a medium temperature. (The grill has reached the appropriate temperature when you cannot hold your hand 5 inches above the heat source for more than three or four seconds.) Then, depending on whether you want to cook the pizza in a pan or directly on the grill, do one of the following:

- **Grilling in a pan.** Place the prepared dough in an oiled pan that has been dusted with cornmeal. Add the desired toppings to the crust, then place the pan on a rack in the center of the grill. Close the lid and bake the pizza for 18 to 23 minutes or until the crust is golden. As the pizza bakes, check it periodically to ensure the underside of the crust does not burn. (If it appears to be browning too quickly, reduce the temperature to low and move the pizza to a cooler part of the grill.)

- **Grilling directly on the rack.** Lightly oil the grill's rack. On an oiled inverted baking sheet, shape the dough into a rectangle or circle about 1/8 inch thick. Once the grill is hot, carefully slide the dough off the pan and drape it onto the rack. Cook the dough for 1 to 2 minutes until it puffs slightly and the bottom begins to harden. Using tongs, carefully flip the dough over and move it to a cooler portion of the grill. Brush the surface liberally with oil and add the desired toppings. Drizzle the top with more oil, then slide the pizza back near the flame, but not directly over it. Cook, rotating the pizza frequently, for 6 to 8 minutes, or until the top is bubbly and any cheese has melted.

Freezing and Reheating Pizza

I love leftover pizza. (Matter of fact, it is one of my favorite breakfasts!) When you find yourself with leftover pizza that you want to save and enjoy in the near future, wrap it tightly in foil and store in the refrigerator for up to five days. Reheat the pizza, loosely wrapped in the foil, in a preheated 400°F oven for 15 to 20 minutes. Open the foil during the final 5 minutes, and cook the pizza until it is hot and the crust is crisp.

Cooked and partially cooked pizza can be frozen then reheated at a later time. To freeze your cooked pizza, let it cool thoroughly before wrapping it tightly in foil and placing it in the freezer. To reheat, place the frozen pizza, still wrapped in foil, in a preheated 400°F oven. Cook 30 to 35 minutes for thin crusts, 45 to 50 minutes for medium-crust pizzas, and 50 to 60 minutes for thick-crust pies. Open the foil during the last 10 minutes of baking time to remove any moisture.

Partially cooked pizza may be frozen then reheated with wonderful results. Bake the pizza as directed for half of the suggested cooking (until the dough has risen and has begun to brown). Because cheese tends to become rubbery when frozen, it is best to leave it off when precooking the pizza. Add the cheese when the pizza is reheated. Allow the partially baked pizza to cool, remove it from the pan (if one has been used), then wrap it in aluminum foil and freeze. To finish baking, remove the frozen pizza from the foil and place it in a pizza pan. Cover the pizza loosely with foil and allow it to thaw for 1 hour. Bake the thawed pie in a preheated 400°F oven for 15 minutes. Remove the foil, and continue to bake the pizza until the crust is golden brown and crisp. Thin-crust pizzas will require an additional 8 to 12 minutes, medium-crust pies will take 12 to 15 minutes, while thick-crust pizzas will need another 15 to 20 minutes. If you are using cheese, add it during the final 5 minutes of baking time.

MAKING CALZONES

One of the more intriguing versions of pizza is a Neopolitan-inspired turnover called the calzone. The most common type of calzone consists of a circle of yeast dough folded in half over a savory filling. This "half-moon" is then sealed and baked. Another type of calzone is formed by wrapping rectangular pieces of yeast dough around lengths of sausage or pepperoni. The panzerotti is yet another calzone variation. Panzerotti are small circles of flaky pastry dough (not yeast dough) that are folded in half over a dab of filling, sealed, and then deep-fried.

Calzones can be more versatile than a single-crust pizza. As their filling is encased in a sealed crust, calzones are portable, convenient, and easy to eat. For this same reason, moist, oozing ingredients are easier to manage in a calzone than on a flat slice of pizza. Calzones can be made in large family-sized versions, individual portions, and small appetizer-sized morsels.

When creating calzones, keep in mind that almost any pizza topping found in this book can be used as a filling for these delicious turnovers. However, avoid very wet fillings, which can make the crust soggy. And never overstuff them. Too much filling can make the calzones impossible to seal properly, causing leaks.

Assembling and Baking Calzones

Once your dough and filling are ready, the following steps will help guide you through assembling and baking perfect calzones. Each of the dough recipes in Chapter 2 will create 4 large, 6 medium, or 8 mini calzones.

1. Preheat the oven to 450°F for 30 minutes.
2. Divide the dough into the desired number of calzones.
3. With a floured rolling pin, roll each piece of dough into a ¾-inch-thick circle.

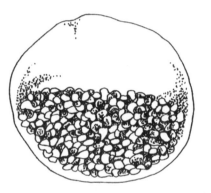

4. Place some filling on half of each circle, leaving a ½-inch border.

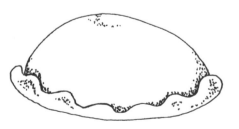

5. Fold each circle in half and press the edges together.

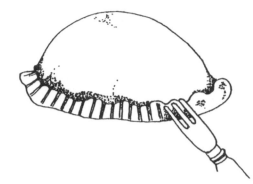

6. Seal the edges with the tines of a floured fork.
7. With a spatula, transfer the calzones to the prepared pan or paddle.
8. Brush the tops of each calzone with a mixture of beaten egg yolk and a tablespoon of oil. Bake as directed in the recipe.

Whether you use pizza pans, stones, or tiles, always bake calzones at the lowest point of the oven possible. This placement allows the bottom of the calzones to firm quickly and cook, which prevents them from becoming soggy from the fillings. (For more information on pizza stones and tiles, see page 7.)

Keep in mind that temperatures do vary from oven to oven. The first time you prepare calzones, monitor them as they bake. This will prevent you from overcooking or burning them.

Freezing and Reheating Calzones

Calzones can be eaten piping hot from the oven, at room temperature, or cold. If you do not plan to eat the freshly baked calzones immediately, allow them to cool completely before wrapping them individually in foil and refrigerating them for up to four days. You can also freeze calzones until needed.

To reheat refrigerated calzones, remove their foil wrappers and arrange them on an ungreased baking sheet. Place them in a preheated 400°F oven until the filling is very hot and the crusts are golden (15 to 18 minutes). To reheat frozen calzones, leave them in their foil wrappers and arrange them on a baking sheet.

Place in a preheated 400°F oven for 30 minutes, remove the foil, and continue to bake until the filling is hot and the crusts are crisp and golden (18 to 22 minutes).

If you are making calzones with the intention of refrigerating or freezing them to eat later on, you may want to shorten the initial baking time. This will prevent the crust from getting too dark or crisp when reheated.

DOUBLE-CRUST PIZZAS

Like calzones, the double-crust pizza is a perfect choice for enclosing a moist, savory filling. Each dough recipe in Chapter 2 will yield one 8-inch double-crust pie. Keep in mind that just about any pizza topping found in this book can also be used as a filling for these delicious covered pies.

Assembling Double-Crust Pizzas

Once your dough and filling are ready, the following steps will help guide you through assembling and baking an 8-inch double-crust pie.

1. Preheat the oven to 450°F for 30 minutes. Brush 1 tablespoon of oil over the surface of an 8-inch deep-dish pizza pan and sprinkle with cornmeal, shaking out the excess.

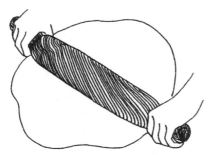

2. Roll out or stretch ⅓ of the dough to a 9-inch circle and set aside (this will be the top crust). Roll out or stretch the remaining dough to a 13-inch circle.

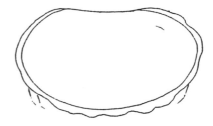

3. Fit the larger circle of dough into the prepared pan, allowing the excess to hang over the sides.

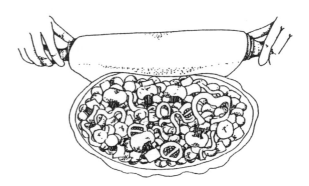

4. Add the filling, and top with the reserved circle of dough.

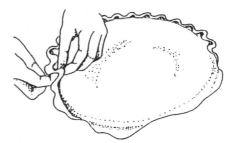

5. Fold and crimp the hanging edges of dough.
6. Brush the top crust with beaten egg. Bake until the crust is golden (18 to 22 minutes).
7. Before serving, allow the pie to sit for 10 to 15 minutes. This will allow the filling to set a bit.

As with calzones and single-crust pizzas, double-crust pies should be baked at the lowest point of the oven possible. This placement allows the bottom of the crust to firm quickly and cook properly.

KITCHEN EQUIPMENT

Working with the proper equipment will help you create perfect pizzas every time. While your kitchen probably contains most of the equipment needed for pizza making, there are a few extremely useful items that you may not have. I have listed these, plus other items I find useful (though not absolutely necessary).

Cheese grater. Although a food processor is better for shredding large amounts of cheese, a small hand-held grater is ideal when a small amount is called for. A good grater has at least two different-sized holes: small holes for grating and larger holes for shredding.

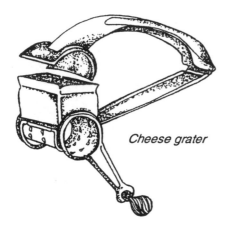

Cheese grater

Cutting wheel. A cutting wheel is the most effective tool for slicing a freshly baked pizza. When choosing a pizza wheel, select one that is strong and sharp. Professional wheels have sturdy handles, usually of metal, and blades that are 3 to 4 inches in diameter. Many professional-quality cutting wheels have replacement blades, so you do not have to buy a new wheel each time the blade gets dull.

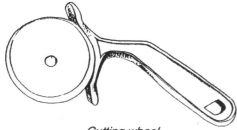

Cutting wheel

Dough scraper. A small, flexible hard rubber or stainless steel strip with a wooden handle, this scraper is perfect for dividing dough into portions. It is also great for cleaning up work surfaces.

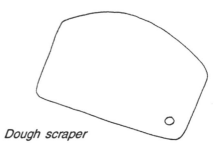

Dough scraper

Measuring cups. There are two types of measuring cups: one for measuring dry items like sugar and flour, and another type for measuring liquid ingredients. Dry measuring cups are made of plastic or metal and come in a set. A basic set includes measurements for $\frac{1}{4}$, $\frac{1}{3}$, $\frac{1}{2}$, and 1 full cup. A liquid measuring cup is generally made of glass or plastic and has a 1- to 4-cup capacity.

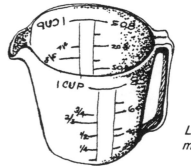

Liquid measuring cup

Measuring spoons. A basic set of measuring spoons includes measurements for $\frac{1}{4}$, $\frac{1}{2}$, and 1 full teaspoon, as well as a measurement for 1 tablespoon.

Food processor. The food processor chops, minces, shreds, beats, and purées foods. In addition, most models knead dough.

Knives. Though probably the most vital kitchen utensil, the knife is often the most neglected. Without at least one good-quality knife, you will find yourself mashing or bruising the food, rather than chopping or cutting it. The best knives are made of forged carbon steel and have hardwood handles. The part of the blade that extends into the handle should be forged from the same steel as the blade and should be securely fastened inside the handle with rivets. The most useful all-purpose knife is the French chef's knife. A good-quality paring knife and a knife with a serrated edge are also essential.

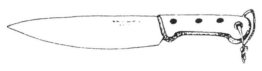

French chef's knife

Mixing bowls. Bowls can be made of stainless steel, glass, or stoneware and should come in a variety of sizes. Be sure to have a very large bowl with sufficient room for homemade dough to double in size.

Pizza stones and quarry tiles. The closest alternative to baking pizza in a wood-fired oven, is baking it on a large pizza stone or unglazed quarry tiles in a conventional oven. Most kitchen stores carry round pizza stones that are designed to conduct oven heat in the same manner as the bricks in a wood-fired oven. If you purchase one of these stones, I suggest buying the largest size available (minimum of 14 inches in diameter). Unglazed quarry tiles are found in tile stores and home-improvement centers. Do not buy sealed or glazed tiles for this purpose. Quarry tiles, which can be cut to size, should be fitted into a large rectangular baking sheet. The pizza stone or pan containing the tiles should be placed either on the oven floor or an oven rack that is set in the lowest position. There is a significant temperature difference between

the oven floor and its lowest rack, so pizza baked on the oven floor will cook quickly and must be watched carefully. Only thin-crusted pizzas and calzones (pizza turnovers) should be baked on these stones or tiles. Medium-crust, thick-crust, and deep-dish pizzas must be baked in pans that support the weight of the pizza and its topping.

Pizza paddle

Pizza paddles and screens. When baking on pizza stones or tiles, you will need a large wooden paddle that is made especially for pizzas. The round paddle, the type I prefer, is the surface on which you form your pizza before transferring it to the oven. You should buy the largest size you can find. Using a pizza screen also requires a paddle. This screen is a piece of heavy wire mesh edged with wire tape. You form the pizza on the screen, then slide the paddle beneath it. Transfer the paddle to the oven and slide the pizza onto the stone or tiles. The screen supports the dough while letting it make direct contact with the pizza stone or tiles while baking. These inexpensive screens come in 8-, 10-, 12-, 14-, 16-, 18-, and 24-inch diameters.

Pizza pans and baking sheets. You do not have to run out and purchase pizza stones to have delectable homemade pizza. All of the recipes in this book can be easily baked in pizza pans or baking sheets. There are many good-quality pizza pans on the market today. I am especially partial to black steel pans as I feel their dark color and heavy consistency retain the oven's heat best and produce golden, crisp crusts. The pan should be thick enough to keep from warping when exposed to intense heat. Aluminum pans can also be used, but they need more oil before baking because their surface reflects heat rather than absorb it.

While round is the traditional shape, pizza pans can come in many contours. Round or square pans are excellent for thin- or medium-crust pizzas. Their low rims (about ½ inch high) make the hot pizza easy to remove. Round pans usually come in 10-, 12-, 15-, and 16-inch diameters. Square pans come in 12- and 14-inch sizes. Rectangular pans generally measure 9-x-12 and 12-x-16 inches. Pans with 1-inch rims are excellent for medium- to thick-crusted pizzas. The best deep-dish pans are made of black steel, rather than aluminum. Deep dish pans have 1½- to 2-inch sides and are available in diameters of 6-, 8-, 10-, 14-, and 15-inch rounds, or in 12- and 14-inch squares.

Rolling pin. The rolling pin is a smooth cylinder, usually of wood, with a handle at each end; it is used for rolling out dough. A few pizza crust recipes in this book call for rolling out the dough to a desired thickness. Generally, patting out the dough with your hands is an acceptable substitute.

Spatula. Also called a pancake turner, an 8-inch long, heavy duty spatula may already be a fixture in your kitchen. If not, acquire a good-quality spatula that does not bend when lifting a whole pizza from the pan to a plate.

Thermometer. This little tool can be quite helpful for determining the correct water temperature when proofing yeast.

Wooden spoons. Wooden spoons, which come in assorted shapes and sizes, are so inexpensive it is affordable to have a variety on hand. In addition to being a more natural alternative to metal spoons, wooden spoons do not scratch cookware.

Brick-Oven Pizzas

Have you ever dined in an establishment that offers "brick-oven pizza"—pizza that is cooked in a huge wood-burning brick or stone oven? If so, consider yourself lucky, as this baking method is believed to be the one that produces the best pizzas, breads, and calzones.

By cooking a pizza directly on the floor of a wood-fired brick or stone oven, the intense heat of the wood fire raises the oven temperature to 500°F or more. When the pizza is slid onto the hot oven floor, the underside of the pizza bakes at the same rate as the top. Also, the wood fire gives the dough a wonderful smoky flavor.

Unfortunately, brick or stone ovens are not usually found in American kitchens; but you can come close to turning your conventional oven into a "brick oven" affair. How? By cooking your pizza on quarry tiles or pizza stones, which are placed on the floor of your conventional oven. When baking a pizza, these stones are designed to conduct heat in the same manner as the bricks in a wood-fired oven. (For more information on pizza stones and quarry tiles, see page 7.)

GLOSSARY OF INGREDIENTS

The following glossary has been compiled to help you identify many of the items called for in this book. A brief description of each ingredient is provided.

Anchovies. These small Mediterranean saltwater fish of the herring family are salt-cured and noted for their intense fishy flavor. Packed in oil or brine, anchovies are available in cans or bottles. Anchovy paste (fillets that have been boned, pounded, and blended) is available in tubes.

Appenzeller cheese. Deriving its name from the canton of Appenzell in eastern Switzerland, this superb cheese has been made since the days of Charlemagne. A full-fat cheese made from whole cow's milk, Appenzeller has a subtle, well-rounded, mildly piquant flavor. Its wrinkled, yellowish-brown skin covers a mellow inner hue of golden flesh that is filled with a scattering of small holes. Aged for a few days or a week at most, Appenzeller's delicate flavor makes it a delicious table or cooking cheese.

Artichoke. This large round vegetable has thick, green triangular-shaped leaves that emerge from its base in layers. A truly fresh artichoke has a tight plump head with bright green leaves. The base portion of each leaf and the heart of the artichoke, which lies under the leaves, are edible once cooked. Very small artichokes, when steamed, are so tender they can be eaten in their entirety. Cooked artichoke hearts and bottoms come in jars and cans.

Arugula. Arugula is a tender, spicy, mustard-flavored green with narrow leaves.

Asiago cheese. Hailing from Italy and originally made from sheep's milk, Asiago is now made from the milk of cows. When properly aged, Asiago is golden in color and has a sharp, nutty flavor. When young, it has a semi-hard texture and can be used as a table cheese. It is, however, best when used as a grating cheese. For this, the cheese must be at least three years old.

Arugula

Asparagus. Tasty asparagus spears are at their peak of freshness from May to June. Choose stalks that are very green with firm, closed tips. Fresh asparagus is quite perishable and should be eaten within two days of its purchase.

Bamboo shoots. The tips of various species of bamboo, these shoots are flat and crisp. Commonly used in Oriental-style dishes, bamboo shoots are found canned, although Far Eastern markets sell them fresh.

Bacon. A cut of meat from the side or back of a hog, bacon can be sugar-cured, maple-cured, or hickory-smoked. Each type has a distinctive aroma, color, and flavor. Most bacon is sold presliced and prepackaged in thin-, regular-, or thick-sliced varieties. Unsliced bacon is called slab bacon. *See also* Pancetta.

Balsamic vinegar. This pungent, sweet vinegar has been made in Modena, Italy for more than a thousand years. It is made solely from the cooked-down juice of white grapes, which is then aged for decades in wooden barrels. The best balsamic vinegar comes from Italy. Balsamic vinegar from other countries is usually a blend of wine vinegar, reduced grape juice, and caramel coloring.

Basil. A sweet herb originally discovered in India and tropical areas of Africa, basil was imported centuries ago into Mediterranean Europe where it became a staple herb. Basil has a pleasant pungent aroma. Its flavor enhances robust foods such as beans, pastas, and stews, yet it is delicate enough to sprinkle over garden-fresh tomatoes, pizzas, and Italian flatbreads. If you are fortunate enough to have the room to grow a pot of basil, you are in for a treat. There is nothing that compares to the flavorful taste and aroma of this freshly picked herb.

Basil

Beef. Meat from cattle that have been been raised for human consumption, beef comes in many forms and grades. In the market, you can find fresh beef in a variety of cuts, as well as ready-to-eat processed beef that has been cured, canned, frozen, precooked, freeze-dried, and vacuum-sealed. The U.S. Department of Agriculture inspects and determines the quality of the beef and applies a grade to the cuts. *Prime* refers to the highest grade; it is the most tender and the most expensive. *Choice*, though a lesser grade than prime, has enough marbling to be tender when properly cooked. *Select* grade contains the least marbling and requires slow, moist cooking to be tender. The most tender cuts of beef come from the area along the upper back of the animal (rib, short loin, and sirloin). The less tender cuts come from areas near the front and back end (chuck and round).

Bel Paese cheese. Made from cow's milk, this modern, commercially prepared Italian cheese was first marketed in the 1920s. Satiny smooth and mild, ivory-colored Bel Paese has a semi-soft texture that yields to the touch and to the palate. Suitable as a table cheese, it also melts smoothly, making it a good substitute for mozzarella.

Bergkäse cheese. An interesting hard cheese dotted with holes of all sizes, Austrian-produced Bergkäse comes in various shades of gold. Its flavor varies from very mild to pungent, and it is excellent when combined with other, softer cheeses in cooking.

Bitto cheese. A firm cheese riddled with shiny holes, Italian produced Bitto can be made from ewe's, cow's, or goats's milk. Once fully aged, Bitto is most suitable as a grating cheese.

Black bean garlic sauce. An Oriental bean paste, this thick black sauce consists of fermented black beans, garlic, water, salt, sugar, soybean oil, monosodium glutamate (MSG), and rice wine; it adds a strong, salty flavor to Asian-style dishes.

Black beans. Also called turtle beans, these tiny, kidney-shaped black-skinned legumes are a staple in their native Cuba and in South and Central America. They are also grown in the southern United States. Black beans have a prominent flavor and smooth, slightly mealy texture; and they can be purchased dried in one-pound bags or canned in salt and water.

Black beans, fermented. *See* Fermented black beans.

Blue cheese. A semi-soft cheese made of cow's milk, blue cheese has greenish blue mold and a flavor similar to Roquefort cheese. Blue cheese, which is made in a number of countries, includes such popular varieties as Bleu de Bresse, Danablue, Maytag Blue, Mycella, Norwegian Blue, Pipo Crem,' Roquefort, Saga Blue, Stilton, and Wesleydale.

Bok choy. A Chinese vegetable with a white base and pale green leaves, bok choy is sweet and juicy. It is commonly shredded and added to stir-fried dishes.

Bonbel cheese. Small rounds of buttery Bonbel come encased in yellow paraffin and wrapped in cellophane. Made in France, this cheese is creamy and mild with a slightly sour tang and a soft, pliable texture.

Bouquet garni. This traditional combination of parsley, bay leaf, and thyme is commonly added to soups, stews, and sauces.

Bread flour. Rich in gluten, this flour comes from hard wheat and is ideal for making dough for breads and pizza crusts.

Brick cheese. A native American cheese, Brick has a caramel-colored rind that encases a white to cream-colored interior. The strong, bitter-tasting rind must be removed before eating this cheese. Made from cow's milk, Brick has a firm, open texture and full-bodied flavor. When very young, this cheese can be sweet, mild, and even bland. As it ages, however, its aroma and flavor acquire strength.

Brie cheese. The best-known of the cheeses that are imported from France, Brie is made from the whole milk of cows. It is the color of heavy cream and is encased in a reddish-brown crust. With a superlative flavor and aggressive bouquet, Brie oozes slightly at room temperature.

Broccoli. This versatile member of the cabbage family is dark green in color with a slightly purple cast. It has a firm, compact cluster of small flower buds, which can be separated into flowerets. Broccoli can be eaten raw or cooked.

Bufalina cheese. *See* Mozzarella cheese.

Cabbage, green. This common type of cabbage has a firm, tightly compacted head and a distinct flavor.

Caciocavallo cheese. Similar to Provolone, straw-colored Caciocavallo is one of Italy's oldest cheeses. When young, it is slightly salty; as it matures, a spicier, piquant flavor develops. Like Provolone, this cheese has a delicious, distinctive taste that is difficult to describe. Both are good table cheeses when young and good grating cheeses when fully matured. *See also* Provolone cheese.

Camembert cheese. Bearing the name of the village in Normandy where it is reputed to have first been made, Camembert is one of Europe's best-known French cheeses. Made from whole cow's milk, each small round cheese weighs about eight ounces and comes in a little round chipboard box. A speckled, floury, moldy-looking crust encases Camembert's creamy yellow flesh with its smooth, softly melting consistency. A perfectly ripe Camembert is six weeks old and possesses a fruity, slightly tangy fragrance. It should be served at room temperature, when it is silky, spreadable, and aromatic. Camembert that has been cut before it is fully ripened will never reach its full potential. That is why buying this cheese from a reliable source is so important.

Capers. Capers are the tiny olive-green flower buds of the caper plant, which grows wild throughout the Mediterranean region of Europe. Blanched then pickled in vinegar, capers are used to flavor many dishes including salads, sauces, and pizzas.

Caraway seeds. A popular European spice, caraway seeds are widely used to add flavor and crunch to breads, stews, and cheeses. These flavorful seeds are also commonly added to dishes that include cabbage and sauerkraut.

Carrots. The edible part of this tuber is its fleshy orange root. A fresh carrot should be firm, smooth, and evenly shaped with a vibrant orange-yellow color and a green fern-like top.

Cayenne pepper. The powdered spice known as cayenne comes from the very hot fruit of the capsicum plant. Unfortunately, cayenne pepper loses a lot of its punch when left too long on the spice rack. In its full bloom, this spice has quite a kick and can liven almost any dish.

Cellophane noodles. Also called bean threads or mung bean vermicelli, cellophane noodles are actually a vegetable product made from mung bean starch. They must be soaked in water for thirty minutes, then cut into shorter lengths before cooking.

Chard. *See* Swiss chard.

Chayote. A relative of the squash family, chayote is a pale green, smooth-skinned vegetable with deep grooves running down its sides. It has a faint pleasing sweetness and a texture that falls somewhere between a potato and a zucchini. Remove and discard the thin skin and almond-shaped seed before boiling, frying, sautéing, baking, or broiling chayote. `

Cheddar, American. Wisconsin, New York, and Vermont produce the best American Cheddars, which range in flavor from mild to very sharp. New York, once the primary Cheddar producer, prides itself on a dry, crumbly variety with a sharp, full flavor. Vermont's well-cured version is sharp and almost white in color. Unlike Wisconsin Cheddar, both New York and Vermont's cheeses are made exclusively from raw milk. Today, Wisconsin produces more Cheddar than any other state. The flavor and consistency of Wisconsin Cheddar varies significantly from producer to producer.

Because many domestic Cheddars are prepackaged, you may have to rely on previous experience with a brand before buying. A good Cheddar should have a mellow, slightly sharp flavor, and a firm, smooth texture. It should be aged at least sixty days.

Cheddar, English. A matured English Cheddar made from unpasteurized milk is one of the finest cheeses to use for cooking. There are two kinds of English Cheddar: farmhouse and factory-made (the farmhouse version being far superior to the factory-produced product). This cheese grates easily and melts beautifully.

Cheese. See individual cheese types.

Chervil. A native of Eastern Europe, chervil is a member of the parsley family and one of France's best-loved herbs. Minced and sprinkled in soups, salads, and sauces, it is equally delicious in egg dishes. Chervil is often used in combination with other fresh herbs such as parsley and tarragon.

Chèvre cheese. Also referred to simply as goat cheese, French-produced Chèvre comes in a great number of shapes and flavors. Varieties that are made with the addition of cow's milk have a creamier consistency and milder flavor than the traditional goat's-milk type. All Chèvre is dipped in brandy before it is left to age. In one aging method the cheese is wrapped in chestnut or grape leaves, or coated with ash to prevent any mold from forming. The other method allows the cheese to develop a heavy mold that coats its soft inner flesh. Chèvre can be plain or laced with herbs and spices. Characteristically, Chèvre has a buttery consistency and a prominent "goaty" bouquet. When young, the cheese is soft and has a gentle aroma. With age, Chèvre becomes drier and its flavor becomes more dominant.

Chick peas. *See* Garbanzo beans.

Chicken. A broad category for a domestic bird raised for food, chicken is found in supermarkets and labeled as broilers, fryers, capons, roasters, and stewers. Known for its tender white meat and moist dark meat, fresh chicken can be purchased whole or in pieces. In addition, frozen and canned varieties are available.

Chiles. The little peppers called chiles come in many guises, but all contribute color, flavor, piquancy, and a degree of heat to food. Chiles range from mild to very hot, from sweet to acidic, and from fresh to dry. Although there are over a hundred varieties of chile peppers, only a few are readily available in supermarkets. Fresh green and red chiles have a crisp, grassy taste, while the dried ones are musky and a bit fruity. The most available varieties of fresh chiles are the Anaheim, jalapeño, poblano, and serrano.

Chili powder. Created from a blend of chile peppers and other spices, chili powder, depending on whether it is mild or hot, will give your Mexican-influenced dishes either a subtle flavor or a real jolt. Mexican grocery stores sell powdered *chile de arbol*, which has a great deal more flavor than most supermarket varieties.

Chili sauce. A thick, tangy sauce made from tomatoes, sweet and hot peppers, onions, celery, and spices, chili sauce is found in varying degrees of hotness. It is used as a condiment and recipe ingredient.

Chili oil. An Asian sesame oil that is flavored with hot chili peppers, chili oil adds a spicy jolt to Oriental-style sauces. Use it sparingly.

Chinese five-spice powder. This mustard-colored spice consists of equal parts of finely ground Chinese pepper, cinnamon, cloves, fennel seeds, and star anise.

Chive. A member of the onion family, the chive has small, slender, hollow leaves and a mild taste. Very delicate and easily bruised, chives should be snipped with scissors or minced with a very sharp knife. Since the chive's subtle flavor is easily lost, it is best added to cold dishes or sprinkled over food just before serving.

Chorizo. This Spanish sausage is made of pork that has been flavored with garlic, oregano, paprika, red wine, and chili pepper. Some varieties also include coriander and cumin. Chorizo is sold fresh in Spanish markets; it also comes dried in small cans or jars, which are found in the foreign-food sections of most supermarkets.

Cilantro. This herb, with its short stem and thin, round, slightly fringed leaves, has a pungent, peppery smell and taste. *See also* Coriander.

Clams. While there are hundreds of species of clams, two basic varieties are indigenous to our coastlines: hard-shell and soft-shell. Hard-shell clams, found embedded along the coasts, include butter clams, quahogs (also known as cherrystones or littlenecks), razor clams, pizmo clams, and Pacific butter clams. Soft-shell clams, or longnecks, are found along the coast of Cape Cod and in the Chesapeake Bay.

Clams are sold live, shucked (shelled), or canned. A live clam should be firmly closed and odorless. If it is slightly open, pinch it closed. If it stays closed on its own, it is alive. If it remains open, discard it. Soft-shell clams may be slightly open because of the long neck extending from inside their shells. When buying shucked clams, choose those that are plump with a fresh clear surface. Store all fresh clams, shucked or unshucked, in the refrigerator until you are ready to prepare them. Do not store them for longer than twenty-four hours.

Cloves. Cloves are the dried flower buds of a tropical evergreen tree. In its bud form, cloves are used to flavor soups, broths, and stews, while its powdered form is often used to spice up fruit dishes.

Coconut milk (unsweetened). Unsweetened coconut milk, available in cans, bears little resemblance to the sweet variety that is commonly used in tropical drinks. The unsweetened milk is created by processing grated coconut with water or milk. This flavorful liquid is a delicious addition to sauces.

Colby cheese. Made mostly in the midwestern United States, Colby is a version of Cheddar that has a softer, more porous texture, a higher moisture content, and a very mild, pleasant flavor.

Coriander. Aromatic coriander seeds are actually the dried, ripe berries of the cilantro plant. With a flavor of lemon peel and sage, coriander is added to many baked goods and sauces.

Corn. The high sugar content of fresh corn accounts for its sweetness. When buying fresh corn, select ears with bright green, tight-fitting husks. The silk should be moist and butter-colored, and the kernels should be plump and in even rows.

Cornmeal. Cornmeal comes in three colors: yellow, white, and blue, and is labeled either "stone-ground" or "water-ground." Look for stone-ground meals, which contain the flavorful germ that is lost in many of the processed supermarket varieties. Although yellow cornmeal retains more carotene than the white and is generally more flavorful, for the most part, the two are interchangeable. Blue cornmeal is gaining popularity particularly in the Southwest and is now available in the East. Use it as you would yellow or white cornmeal.

Cottage cheese. Made from skim milk, with cream occasionally added, cottage cheese's most noticeable characteristic is its texture. Its soft curds create a slightly lumpy consistency, yet it is firm enough to hold its shape. Creamy white with a pleasant, slightly acidic flavor, cottage cheese has a delicate aroma. It is best served at room temperature for its fullest flavor.

Crab. A valuable resource on both coasts of the

United States, there are many varieties of crab. The Pacific coast gives us the king, snow, and Dungeness crab, while the Atlantic waters offer blue, red, rock, and Jonah crabs. Modern canning and freezing procedures make crabmeat available all year round. When purchasing fresh crabmeat, be sure it has a glistening white to off-white color, a texture that is firm but fragile, and a mild aroma. Claw meat will have a brownish color and a distinct nutty flavor. Pasteurized crabmeat should be firm-textured; its color may be slightly darker than the fresh variety (a very light bluish tint is common). Fresh crabmeat has a shelf life of ten to fourteen days from its packaging date. Pasteurized crabmeat, if unopened and properly refrigerated, can be stored up to six months. When purchasing live crabs, pick active, lively ones.

Crab

Creole seasoning. This spicy blend of salt, red pepper, garlic, chili powder, and other spices is used to add zip to many foods. Since it has a high concentration of salt, it should be used sparingly.

Crimini mushrooms. Often marketed as Italian brown mushrooms, flavorful Crimini mushrooms are similar to the white button variety but are slightly larger with a light brown cap.

Cumin. A member of the parsley family, cumin hails from Egypt where it grows as a small plant bearing umbels of small rose or white flowers and produces fruit and seeds. A sharp, strong earthy spice, cumin was once found only in Middle Eastern-style dishes. Today, it is used more frequently to add range and depth to vinaigrettes, a simple hummus, or a more elaborate ratatouille.

Curry. Curry is a mixture of many spices including turmeric, cumin, and cardamom. Commercially made curry powder is often stale and uninspiring. When purchasing curry powder, look for imported brands, which are fuller flavored. Once opened, curry should be used within three to four months for maximum potency.

Dill. Originally found in southern Europe, dill has since been transplanted over the centuries to more northern climates. A member of the very large parsley clan, the dill plant has bitter seeds, skinny aromatic leaves, and a subtle licorice taste. This herb is available fresh in most supermarkets during summer months. Dill goes especially well with yogurt, potatoes, and salad vinaigrettes. The seeds, while less commonly used than the leaves, can be found in breads, pickling marinades, and some soups.

Double Gloucester cheese. Made in England, this centuries-old favorite is formed into a "millstone" of 16 inches in diameter from which wedges are cut. A fairly strong-tasting semi-hard cheese that comes in either a delicate buttercup or a pale red color, Double Gloucester is most often served as an appetizer or with dessert. When aged sufficiently (six months to a year), its texture is hard and satiny, and it has a ripe, mellow flavor with an indescribable pungency.

Edam cheese. Produced in Holland, this somewhat bland-tasting cheese is made from partly skimmed cow's milk. Edam's deep yellow, firm grainy body comes shaped in a ball that is encased in red wax. It is too soft for grating but is well suited as a table cheese or for use in cooking.

Eggplant. This vegetable, with its purplish-black

skin, can be large and plump or small and slender. The sweetest eggplant is usually 3 to 6 inches in diameter, symmetrically shaped, and deep in color; its unblemished, firm skin should not have any soft spots. An eggplant can be prepared with or without its skin. It can be cooked whole or cut up, and steamed, baked, broiled, fried, grilled, or stewed.

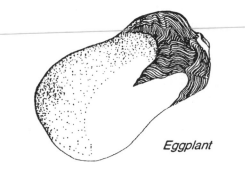

Eggplant

Emmenthaler cheese. This is one of Switzerland's two great cheeses for melting (Gruyère is the other). Made in the valley of Emmenthal in the canton of Bern since the sixteenth century, Emmenthaler is formed into huge wheels that weigh at least 145 pounds. It is a true Swiss cheese with a full, nutty flavor and a delicate, creamy golden color. Riddled with holes (or eyes), this cheese grates well and melts into characteristic long strings. When buying Emmenthaler, be sure the rind is stamped in red with the word "Switzerland" to prove its authenticity.

Farmer cheese. Once sold only in bulk, this part-skim cow's-milk cheese can now be found packaged in smaller quantities. Made in different locations throughout the United States, farmer cheese should always be milky clean and slightly sour. Its texture should be that of a slightly crumbly cream cheese. Avoid any farmer cheese that has a firm slicing texture.

Fennel. With its celery-like look, fennel's strong licorice flavor is found in its feathery leaves and bulb. The bulb, which is edible raw, can also be braised for a milder taste.

Fermented black beans. These are very small black beans that are usually preserved in salt and packed in jars; they are found in the foreign-food section of most supermarkets. Primarily used in sauces, these tiny beans are commonly added to stir-fried dishes to which they add a spicy, piquant flavor. As these beans are very salty, be sure to rinse them well before using.

Feta cheese. Originally made by Greek shepherds, this sheep's-milk cheese is soft, salty, and strong flavored. It is white and crumbly yet firm enough to hold its shape when cooked. Essential in the cuisines of Greece and the Balkans, Feta comes packed in brine. To retard the aging process, the brine should be replaced with a mixture of equal parts water and milk that has been boiled and then cooled. To date, domestic Feta cannot compete with the flavor and consistency of imported varieties.

Fish sauce. A thick brown sauce made of fish and seasonings, this Asian paste adds a distinct fishy flavor to dishes.

Five-spice powder. *See* Chinese five-spice powder.

Flour. *See* Bread flour; Graham flour; Rice flour; Rye flour; Semolina; and Whole wheat flour.

Fontina cheese. Made in the Alpine pastures of Val d'Aosta, Fontina is made from whole, unpasteurized cow's milk. It is a straw-colored, medium-textured cheese with a subtle nut-like flavor. Formed into large wheels, then covered with a reddish-brown rind, Fontina is a tender, gently savory cheese that melts well when cooked. It is often used as a substitute for Gruyère. While its taste is delicate and mild, it is not without character. There is a Danish version of Fontina, but it does not, at this point, compare to the Italian cheese.

Fontinella cheese. An American variation of Fontina, this grating cheese has a full, pronounced flavor with a drier consistency than the Italian version.

Garbanzo beans. These round, tan-colored beans come from the Mediterranean region and the Middle East. As each bean has a small peak that resembles a chicken's beak, garbanzos are also known as chick peas or ceci beans. Very versatile, garbanzo beans, with their nutty, earthy flavor, can be ground into paste and used in dips, or tossed in their entirety into soups, stews, and salads.

Garlic. Used properly, garlic imparts a gentle aroma and taste to foods, and acts as a support to other more prominent ingredients in a dish. Once, garlic was available only in fresh and powdered forms. Today, jars of fresh-tasting chopped or minced garlic that has been preserved in oil is also available. When buying fresh garlic, pick out heads that are plump and firm with papery skin that is firmly attached. Do not refrigerate fresh garlic, rather store it in a cool, dry place that has good ventilation. An earthenware jar with holes in its sides is an ideal storage spot for garlic, where it will keep for up to a month. Once fresh garlic begins to sprout, discard it, as this is a sign that most of its pungency and flavor are gone.

Ginger root. An absolute necessity in Asian-style dishes, fresh ginger root is found in the produce section of most supermarkets. Fresh roots have smooth outer skins and can be peeled and used immediately or preserved for later use.

Ginger root

Goat cheese. *See* Chèvre cheese.

Gorgonzola cheese. Together with Roquefort and Stilton, Gorgonzola has dominated the world of veined cheeses for centuries. Produced in Italy, Gorgonzola is rich, sweet, and velvety with pale green veins instead of blue. Of all the veined cheeses, Gorgonzola is the softest and creamiest with a smooth, melt-in-your-mouth quality. A good Gorgonzola has a ripe, prominent aroma and a moist texture with no visible dry patches. Made from whole cow's milk, Gorgonzola may vary in texture from very moist to somewhat dry, and it can have a flavor that ranges from sharp to luxuriously mellow.

Gouda cheese. A satiny Dutch cheese made from whole cow's milk, straw-colored, firm-textured Gouda comes encased in a rind of the same color. Usually shaped like a flattened ball, it has a mild, smooth taste with a slightly acidic quality.

Graham flour. Coarsely ground from hard wheat, graham flour may be used instead of whole wheat in recipes.

Grana Padano cheese. A very popular grating cheese in Italy, Grana Padano is grainy in texture, savory in flavor, and somewhat moister than Parmesan.

Ground beef. Also called "hamburger," ground beef describes meat that is commonly made by grinding less-tender cuts of beef together with fat trimmings.

Gruyère cheese. Gruyère is one of Switzerland's great cheeses for melting. Made only in the summertime, this cow's-milk cheese has a higher fat content than Emmenthaler (the other significant Swiss cheese) and is made in smaller 80-pound wheels. Its name comes from the Gruyère Valley in the canton of Fribourg, where it was first made in the twelfth century. Gruyère has a brown, wrinkled skin that covers a deep ivory-colored flesh. It has holes scattered throughout, but they are fewer and smaller than those found in Emmenthaler. Gruyère is deep, nutty, and full-flavored with a hint of sweetness and a distinct smell of ammonia. It melts in characteristic long strings.

Ham. Meat from the hind leg of a hog, ham may be fresh but is usually cured and smoked. Ranging in color from pink to red, its flavor also varies from salty to slightly sweet.

Hamburger. *See* Ground beef.

Havarti cheese. Made in Denmark from cow's milk, this exciting creamy cheese has small irregular holes dotting its interior. Mild yet tangy, rindless Havarti comes either plain or flavored with dill, chives, caraway, or other herbs or spices.

Hickory smoke flavoring. The flavorful essence of smoked foods can be duplicated by using a small amount of this dark brown seasoning made of vinegar, molasses, corn syrup, natural hickory flavor, and garlic.

Hoison sauce. A very thick, very dark brown sauce, hoisin is made from soybeans, garlic, sugar, and chiles. Used exclusively in Oriental-style dishes, jars of hoison sauce are found in the foreign-foods section of most supermarkets.

Honey. Honey ranges in color from ash white to dark amber with flavors from mild to quite pronounced. When substituting honey for granulated sugar in a recipe, use half the amount and adjust according to taste. The amount of liquid called for in a recipe should be reduced by ¼ cup for each cup of honey used. In cakes, cookies, and other baked items, add ½ teaspoon of baking soda for each cup of honey used.

Horseradish. A member of the mustard family, horseradish is grown for its white, fleshy root, which is shredded or grated and used as a condiment. Jars of minced horseradish are readily available in most supermarkets, but a much fresher, more pungent version can be easily prepared at home. Fresh horseradish is generally found year round in the produce section of many supermarkets. Simply scrape off the brown skin from the roots with a knife or potato peeler, then cut the roots into chunks. Place the pieces in a blender or food processor and finely chop. (A word of caution: do not lean over the bowl and inhale deeply. The fumes from the horseradish are hot and can sear the inside of your nostrils.) Transfer the chopped horseradish to a jar with a tight-fitting lid, cover with white wine vinegar, and store in the refrigerator. Preserved this way, the horseradish will keep up to a year.

Italian sausage. Fresh Italian sausage is generally made from pork that is seasoned with salt, pepper, and spices. Northern Italy produces sausage that is usually sweet and mild, often flavored with fennel seed. Sausage from southern Italy is often hot, flavored with flakes of dried chile pepper. *See also* Sausage.

Jarlsberg cheese. A Norwegian hard-pressed cow's-milk cheese, Jarlsberg has many characteristics of Gruyère and Emmenthaler. Dotted with large holes, Jarlsberg is straw-colored and has a smooth elastic texture.

Jicama. A brown-skinned root vegetable that resembles a turnip, jicama is a crisp, delicious cross between a juicy pear, a crunchy water chestnut, and a starchy potato. Once peeled, it can be eaten raw or cooked. Jicama is available in Asian markets and some supermarkets.

Kasseri cheese. Made in Greece, Kasseri is a firm sheep's-milk cheese with a light, winey flavor. When young, it is mild, aromatic, and pliable. As it ages, it becomes drier and firmer, and its taste strengthens (although it never becomes overwhelming).

Kefalotiri cheese. A strong-flavored goat's-milk cheese from Greece, Kefalotiri is popularly used for grating and cooking.

Kielbasa. This sausage is generally associated with Poland, although it is common throughout central Europe and the former Soviet Union. Kielbasa comes in many forms—smoked, raw, and precooked. Although its ingredients may vary, kielbasa generally contains beef, pork, and garlic, combined with spices such as paprika, marjoram, and savory.

Lamb. Meat from sheep that are less than a year old, lamb has a mild flavor and a rose-tinged flesh. Lamb undergoes a system of quality grading similar to that of beef; it is also subject to a certification program used to identify its quality. Certified American lamb comes from sheep that are less than a year old with ¼ inch or less trimmable fat. This is the highest quality available. Yearling, meat from older sheep (one to two years old), is not very tender. Mutton, rarely found in the United States, comes from sheep that are over two years old. It has a very pronounced flavor. Most lamb raised in the United States is marketed fresh. The frozen varieties are usually from New Zealand and Australia.

Lancashire cheese. Made in England, Lancashire is the softest of the hard-pressed cheeses and is especially noteworthy when melted. When this cheese is young, it is so buttery soft that it can be spread on bread like a cream cheese. As it ages, Lancashire's texture becomes crumbly. For all its softness, however, this cheese is not mild. It has a full and rich taste, stronger than a Cheddar or a Cheshire. Lancashire becomes custardy and bubbly when melted. It is delicious when crumbled over crusty bread or pizza crust and broiled.

Leeks. These large onion-like vegetables are actually members of the lily family. Leeks are often more than 12 inches long with flat green leaves that taper only slightly to a white bulb of about 1½ inches in diameter. They have a sweet, mild taste and can be served hot or cold. Leeks are filled with sand and grit, and must be properly cleaned before they are prepared.

Leek

Leicestershire cheese. The most noticeable characteristic of this full-bodied English cheese is its outrageous bright golden-orange color. The second thing is the slight tang that is faintly detectable in its rich, silky flesh. Leicestershire is not a particularly mild cheese, nor is it aggressive. It does have a pleasing taste and bouquet, and it is ideal for melting. Because of its high moisture content, Leicestershire is best eaten young (between three and nine months of age). Avoid buying this cheese if it has white streaks in the flesh. These are dry patches, which mean the cheese is too old and will have an unpleasant strong flavor.

Lemon zest. *See* Zest.

Lemongrass. Also called citronella root, lemongrass is an aromatic tropical grass that characterizes Vietnamese and Thai cuisines. Only the bulb-like base of the stalk is used to impart a compelling balm-like flavor to food. To prepare fresh lemongrass, cut the bulb portion up to the point where the leaves begin to branch, and discard the loose leaves. Fresh lemongrass can be stored in a plastic bag and frozen. Dried lemongrass is shredded and must be soaked in warm water for one hour before it can be chopped and added to dishes.

Lobster. There are three main species of lobster: the Maine lobster, the spiny lobster, and the lobsterette. The most popular type in the United States is the Maine lobster with its delicious claw and tail meat. No less delicious is the clawless spiny lobster, often called rock lobster or langouste. The spiny lobster is found in tropical waters and off the coast of Florida. Its only edible portion is its delicious tail meat, which is slightly coarser than that of the Maine lobster. Lobsterettes, also referred to as langostinos, rock shrimp, scampo, and prawns, are the smallest lobster variety. Like the spiny lobster, the edible meat comes from the tail, which is about 4 inches long. Lobsterettes are harvested in Florida and parts of South America.

Generally, the colder the water of its habitat, the tastier the lobster. When purchasing fresh lobster, touch its shell, which should be hard and thick. Soft shells indicate that either the lobster has recently shed its shell (indicating the meat could be skimpy), or that it comes from warm waters. Female lobsters are more flavorful and tender than the males, especially when broiled. Whenever possible, buy fresh lobsters as close to cooking time as possible.

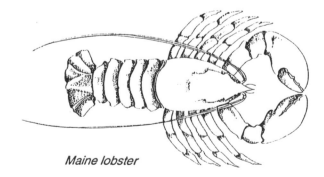

Maine lobster

Maple syrup. A simple sugar, maple syrup is the boiled

down sap of the sugar maple tree. Not quite as sweet as honey, this syrup has a more distinctive flavor and about 15 percent less calories. When substituting maple syrup for sugar, use ¾ cup of syrup for each cup of sugar called for in the recipe. When maple syrup is substituted for sugar in baking, use ¾ cup syrup for each cup of sugar, and reduce the other liquid called for in the recipe by 3 tablespoons for every cup of syrup substituted.

Marjoram. A sweet member of the mint family, marjoram has a Far Eastern ancestry and is grown as an annual for its aromatic leaves. With a sweeter, more delicate flavor than oregano, marjoram should be purchased in small quantities and discarded when age gives it a musty odor. Used interchangeably with oregano, marjoram adds subtle interest to many dishes that include tomato sauce.

Mint. A sprig of fresh mint is a delightful garnish for fruit cups, mint juleps, and a variety of vegetable and grain dishes. This almost indestructible plant is able to grow under deplorable conditions, and it keeps coming back year after year. Since it is so easily grown, there is little excuse for using dried mint, which has a decidedly bitter taste. If growing your own mint is not an option, look for fresh mint in the supermarket.

Monterey Jack cheese. Made in the United States, Monterey Jack, a distant relative of cheddar, is a young, semi-soft, pliable mild cheese. Rindless, jack cheese is smooth and spongy with a sweet, rather undistinguished flavor, which prompts its use in cooking. Monterey Jack also comes flavored with jalapeño chiles, which add a bit of spice to its otherwise unremarkable flavor.

Mozzarella cheese. Until you have tasted fresh Mozzarella, you cannot realize how truly uninspired and undistinguished most of today's Mozzarella is. The next best thing to fresh Mozzarella is Bufalina, which is made from the milk of the water buffalo. Bufalina is mild and sweet-tasting with a graceful silky texture. At one time, Mozzarella was made solely from buffalo's milk, and in some parts of southern Italy it still is. Another type of Mozzarella is Scamorza, which has a mild, pleasant flavor and is often smoked.

Today, the majority of Mozzarella, whether fresh or prepackaged, is made from cow's milk. Served as a table cheese or in salads, versatile Mozzarella is most often used as a topping on pizza and breads. It is commonly added to casseroles, where it melts into a rubbery sauce with characteristic long strings.

Mung beans. These small round green beans are wonderful for sprouting or cooking. Commonly used in Asian and Indian dishes, mung beans are a good source of vitamins A and C and some B vitamins.

Muenster cheese. Created by the Benedictine monks during the eighth century, this rich and creamy cheese was first made in the French city of Muenster. It is now produced in Germany and the United States, as well. Creamy white in color with an orange rind, this smooth and mellow cheese is fairly mild in both flavor and aroma when it is young. As it ages, it turns a buttercup yellow and develops a more distinctive air. Once used only for appetizers and desserts, Muenster is now used for cooking, as well.

Mushrooms. *See* Crimini mushrooms; Oyster mushrooms; Portabella mushrooms; Shiitake mushrooms; White mushrooms.

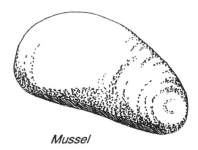

Mussel

Mussels. A bluish black shell encases the tender, smoky-colored meat of a mussel. Its flesh contains high-quality proteins, vitamins, minerals, and virtually no fat. Mussels can be substituted for clams and oysters in most recipes. You can purchase mussels fresh, frozen, or canned. When buying mussels in their shells, select those that close tightly when tapped and are odorless. If a mussel is slightly open, pinch it closed. If it remains closed on its own, it's alive. If it remains open, discard it. Mussels should be consumed soon after they are purchased. If necessary, you can store mussels for a short time (about twenty-four hours) in the refrigerator.

Neufchâtel cheese. Neufchâtel is a cow's-milk cheese that is produced in the United States and France. The version produced in the United States has a texture and appearance similar to cream cheese. It comes in rectangular blocks and contains less butterfat than the French type. Its smooth texture makes it easy to spread. French Neufchâtel, on the other hand, is slightly salted and covered with a white silky down. When young, French Neufchâtel is soft with a velvety texture and subtle flavor. With age, it becomes firm and acquires a distinct, piquant taste and bouquet. When buying a mature French Neufchâtel, look for "Neufchâtel affine" on the label. For a young version, find one marked "Neufchâtel fleuri."

Olive paste. Imported Greek olive paste is made from ground olives that have been blended with olive oil and spices.

Orange zest. *See* Zest.

Oregano. Mediterranean influence comes through loud and clear in the lusty, potent impact of this very popular herb. A traditional flavoring in tomato sauces, oregano is equally at home in salad dressings and marinades, as well as in bean, grain, and pasta dishes.

Oyster mushrooms. Available fresh or dried, the ruffle-capped oyster mushroom is a pale, pearly gray color. Its delicate flavor calls for simple preparation.

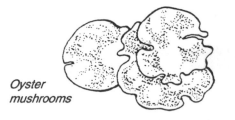

Oyster mushrooms

Pancetta. An Italian bacon, pancetta is a cured meat that is prepared in a different manner from American bacon. Rather than being smoked, pancetta is salted, lightly spiced, and rolled up tightly into a salami-like shape. Since it is cured, pancetta can be eaten without cooking.

Parmesan cheese. Parmesan, named for the city of Parma where it was created, is Italy's premier grating cheese as well as a premier flavoring agent. Made from cow's milk that is produced each year between April 1 and November 11, Parmesan requires a long aging process (a minimum of eighteen months) to obtain a distinct pungency. It will not be sold before this time. After aging for eighteen months, the cheese will be straw colored and will have a rich, mellow, slightly salty taste. It will be soft and moist enough to be gently shaved or cut, making it a perfect table cheese. As Parmesan continues to age, its flavor becomes more distinct, and its texture becomes drier.

Be aware that authentic Parmesan has "Parmesan-Reggiano" tattooed on its rind in small dots. If the word *becchio* appears on its package, the cheese is considered old, which means two years old; *stravecchio* (extra old) means the cheese is a full three years old; *stravecchione* indicates the cheese is four years old—the finest for grating.

Parsley. Parsley has two faces. One is the Italian face, which is flat-leafed and more flavorful than its curly-leafed cousin. Curly-leaf parsley is mild and commonly used as a garnish. Both parsley types are decorative and add flavor to most dishes.

Pecorino cheese. Most commonly available in the United States as Romano or Sardo, this hard, vigorous grating cheese comes from Rome. Like Parmesan, it is an excellent and savory table cheese when young. Made from ewe's milk, Pecorino starts out with a supple texture and a mild flavor and aroma. As it matures, its flavor sharpens and its consistency becomes hard and dry. At this stage, Pecorino is used for grating and is commonly substituted for Parmesan.

Pepperoni. A type of salami sausage, pepperoni is made from fresh meat that has been cured and dried during processing. The use of a bacterial fermentation during processing concentrates the flavor and acts as a preservative. It is a highly seasoned sausage that comes in firm, long links and can be eaten without cooking. Thinly sliced circles of pepperoni are popular for topping pizzas.

Peppers, bell. Bell peppers are classified as sweet peppers. There was once a time when green was the only color of bell pepper. Today, bell peppers come in a spectrum of colors—gold, red, purple, bright yellow, and even chocolate. The warm-hued varieties are sweeter, softer, and more perishable than the darker ones; they are also more expensive. When purchasing bell peppers, select smooth ones that are firm, shiny, and heavy. Store bell peppers loosely wrapped in the refrigerator for up to five days.

Peppers, roasted. Sweet red bell peppers that have been roasted, then packed in brine have a pungent, distinctive flavor and firm texture. In addition to adding a spark of color and variety to antipasto platters, roasted peppers are popularly used for topping pizzas.

Pesto. A sauce generally consisting of fresh basil or parsley, garlic, pine nuts, olive oil, and grated cheese.

Pignoli nuts. *See* Pine nuts.

Pimientos. The red pimiento is a fully ripened sweet pepper that has been cooked. Rich in vitamin C, pimientos do not have a great deal of taste, but they are useful in adding a spark of color to a dish.

Pine nuts. Pine nuts, also known as pignoli nuts, are white pellet-shaped nutmeats that come from pine cones. They possess a sweet, pine taste and are commonly used in Mediterranean-style dishes and pesto sauces.

Pork. Hogs raised for food provide pork, a light pink meat. With a finely grained texture and full yet mild flavor, pork is marketed both fresh and processed. Fresh pork is generally sold as chops and roasts. Cured and smoked pork is either fully cooked or requires some cooking before eating. *See also* Bacon.

Port du Salut cheese. Also called Port Salut, this cheese was originally made by French Trappist monks. It is a mild-flavored, subtle cheese with a russet surface, a creamy yellow interior, and a texture similar to Bel Paese. That is, however, where the comparison stops as Port du Salut's flavor, though mild, is more robust than that of Bel Paese. It is this edge that sets it apart from other bland cheeses. Since it is relatively slow ripening, Port du Salut is quite dependable and enjoys a rather long prime. Its mellowness blends well with sweets, fruits, or hearty dark breads. With its low butterfat content and fine and subtle taste, Port du Salut is best served simply. Danish Port Salut is an exceptionally delectable cheese that is more powerfully flavored than its French cousin.

Portabella mushrooms. Considered the grown-up brother of the Crimini mushroom, the Portabella has a longer growing cycle, which produces a large-capped mushroom with substantial texture and deep, meaty flavor.

Potatoes. This vegetable comes in a variety of colors, sizes, and textures. The most common potatoes are the high-starch Idaho or russets, which have a mealy texture. They are best-suited for baking, mashing, and frying. For dishes in which it is important for the potato to hold its shape, a firm, waxy "new" potato or red bliss potato is a good choice. Always choose smooth, firm potatoes, and avoid those with soft or greenish spots. Store potatoes unwashed and un-wrapped in a dark, dry spot for several weeks.

Prosciutto. Prosciutto is aged Italian ham. The famous prosciutto di Parma is cured, not cooked, and is produced under strict rule of the Parma Ham Consortium. Aged from ten months to two years, this salted, air-cured ham has a sweet, slightly nutty flavor, and is encased in a layer of fat. Once sliced, prosciutto dries out and loses its flavor, so it should be used within a day of its purchase.

Provolone cheese. Made in Italy, Provolone is similar in taste and texture to Dutch Gouda. It is a cow's-milk cheese with a noticeable milky flavor and a soft, satiny consistency. When young, this cheese has a subtle taste and a semi-soft texture, making it a good table

Shiitake have broad fleshy caps, tough inedible stems, and a pronounced woodsy flavor.

Shiitake mushrooms

Shrimp. Most shrimp sold in the United States is frozen. Flash-frozen shrimp can be delicious when handled and stored properly. When purchasing packages of frozen shrimp, inspect the shells for signs of freezer burn. A shrimp's shell color depends on its age, size, harvest season and location, and diet. Despite variations in shell color, a shrimp's flesh color should be white. Occasionally, small discolorations on the meat called blackspots are found. While unattractive, blackspots are harmless and do not indicate spoilage. Spoiled shrimp have an ammonia-like smell. Some shrimp, depending on their species, harvest location, and time of harvest, have an iodine flavor. Again, this does not indicate spoilage. The number of shrimp per pound varies with size: colossal—under 10 per pound; jumbo—10 to 15 per pound; extra-large—16 to 20 per pound; large—21 to 30 per pound; medium—31 to 40 per pound. Shrimp that yield more than 40 per pound are considered small.

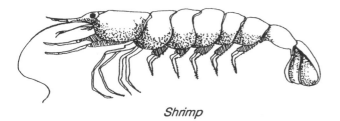

Shrimp

Soy sauce. A dark liquid with a rich fragrance and salty, slightly tart flavor, soy sauce is used to enhance dishes that range from soups to stir-fries. Tamari and shoyu are the two types of natural, traditionally made Japanese soy sauces. Both types are made with water, whole soybeans, and sea salt. In addition, shoyu contains wheat. While shoyu and tamari can be used interchangeably in most recipes, tamari is more concentrated and, therefore, its influence on dishes is more pronounced.

Soybean sauce. A traditional light brown sauce prepared from ground soybeans, roasted rice powder, and salt, soybean sauce is sold only in Vietnamese grocery stores. Vietnamese vegetarians commonly use soybean sauce.

Spinach. A most versatile green, fresh spinach has a bright green color and subtle lemony taste. Some varieties have smooth leaves while others produce leaves that are more crinkled. Fresh spinach is gritty and must be soaked several times in water before it is served fresh or cooked. Quite perishable, even when refrigerated, spinach will stay fresh only three or four days.

Stilton cheese. Without a doubt, Stilton is one of the finest of the many delectable British cheeses. Very seasonal, Stilton is made only from May to September. It is a double-cream cow's-milk cheese, which means it is made from the finest and richest milk to which the cream of other milk has been added. It has a creamy, buttercup-colored interior with blue veining, and its brownish wrinkled rind is covered with a velvety white down. Stilton's flavor is a cross between an aged English Cheddar and a French Roquefort. It has an intense, moist taste with a semi-hard, somewhat crumbly yet silky texture.

Swiss chard. A member of the beet family, this green can be found all year. There are two chard varieties: white and red. The white-ribbed variety with its vivid green leaves is the more common. The stems of chard have a mild, delicate celery-like flavor while its leaves have a more noticeable spinach taste. Mild-flavored chard can be substituted for fresh spinach, although its thicker leaves will take a little longer to cook. Swiss chard should be washed in cold water, patted dry, and stored in a plastic bag lined with paper towels. Wrapped this way, chard can be stored in the refrigerator for up to three days.

Swiss cheese The universal success of Switzerland's Emmenthaler has inspired virtually every country that makes cheese into creating its own domestic Swiss cheese variation. Many types are uninspiring and not worth mentioning. Others, such as the Swiss cheese that is produced in Wisconsin, are worthy of consideration. The major problem with most Swiss cheese is a lack of sufficient aging. A good Swiss should be aged for at least six months, and it should be white or a slightly glossy cream color. Riddled with shiny holes, Swiss cheese should have a mild, nutty sweet taste. *See also* Emmenthaler cheese; Gruyère cheese; Jarlsberg cheese.

Sun-dried tomatoes. Adding a unique quality to many dishes, sun-dried tomatoes possess an unusual, intense flavor that is far removed from that of a fresh tomato. The best sun-dried tomatoes, which are packed in olive oil, come from Italy. Since domestic farmers are beginning to produce them, dry sun-dried tomatoes are popping up in the produce section of many supermarkets.

Tahini. A smooth paste made from ground hulled sesame seeds, tahini has the consistency of peanut butter and can be found in natural foods stores and in the foreign-food section of many supermarkets. Tahini is a good source of protein but is quite high in fat. The oil from the seeds floats to the top of the jar from time to time. For the creamiest texture, the oil should be stirred back into the paste before using. Pouring off half the oil and stirring the remainder back into the paste reduces the fat content without altering the consistency. Once opened, the jar of tahini must be refrigerated. Tahini is most commonly used in hummus and other Middle Eastern-style dishes.

Taleggio cheese. Made in Italy, this fruity cow's-milk cheese dates back to the tenth century. Then, as now, it was ripened in caves for at least forty days. Taleggio, which comes in flattened squares, has a rose-colored crust that encases its buttery yellow interior. Smooth,

satiny, and even-textured, Taleggio has a full yet delicate flavor and aroma. With age, it becomes stronger tasting and develops a hint of tartness.

Tarragon. Delicate and versatile, tarragon is often seen floating around the inside of gourmet vinegar bottles. Flavoring vinegar is just one of the many ways this herb is used. Fresh tarragon is also a flavorful addition to salads, sauces, and omelets.

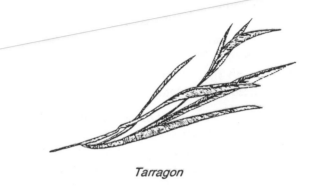

Tarragon

Tempeh. Originally from Asia, tempeh is made from partially cooked split and hulled soybeans that have been injected with bacteria and allowed to ferment for twenty-four hours. During fermentation, a white mold forms that binds the beans together in a cake. Tempeh has a firm knobby texture and mild flavor. It is the richest known source of vitamin B_{12}.

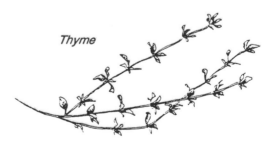

Thyme

Thyme. During the summer months in France, hillsides are fragrant with an abundance of thyme. An essential ingredient in French cuisine, thyme has crossed the ocean to add a sharp, warm, and pungent addition to American dishes, as well. Sauces, stews, stuffings, soups, and breads all benefit from just a pinch of thyme.

Tilsiterkäse cheese. Often referred to as Tilsit, this is Germany's most popular cheese. Made from cow's milk, its flavor is similar to Denmark's Port du Salut. Tilsiterkäse has a firm, solid flesh of pale yellow that is dotted with many tiny holes. Its flavor is smooth and constant and can vary from mild to sharp.

Toasted sesame oil. This dark amber-colored Oriental oil with its strong nut-like taste and aroma is made from toasted sesame seeds; it should be used sparingly to flavor dishes. Toasted sesame oil should not be confused with light-colored, cold-pressed sesame oil, which is used for cooking.

Tofu. Once found only in Oriental restaurants, tofu is no longer the sole possession of the Far East. This soybean curd has the consistency of Ricotta cheese that has been pressed into a dense cube. Tofu is low in fat, high in protein and calcium, and contains no cholesterol. In addition, tofu contains all eight essential amino acids. Having very little taste and even less character, tofu is attractive mainly because of its wonderful nutritional qualities. In all its forms—silken, firm, extra-firm, and snow-dried—tofu has a chameleon-like ability to adapt to its surrounding ingredients. Having no special flavor of its own, tofu absorbs the flavors of its companions.

Tofu is found in natural foods stores, and in the dairy case or produce section of most supermarkets. It may be labeled tofu, bean curd, bean cake, or soybean curd. Refrigerated, tofu will stay fresh for about one week. It will stay fresher for a longer period of time if you place it in an air-tight water-filled container and change the water every other day. Although tofu can be frozen, when thawed, its consistency will be soft and spongy.

Tomatoes. Technically a fruit, fresh tomatoes come in three varieties: round slicing, pulpy plum, and tiny cherry. Slicing tomatoes, like the mighty beefsteaks, are juicy and bright to dark red in color. They are ideal to eat raw. Plum tomatoes are oval, true red in color, and excellent for making sauces, ketchup, and chutneys. Little cherry tomatoes are the size of Bing cherries and are ideal in salads. Select firm, unbruised tomatoes that are plump and rich in color. Store them at room temperature until fully ripened. Once ripe, tomatoes can be refrigerated up to three days.

Tomatoes, sun-dried. *See* Sun-dried tomatoes.

Turkey. A heavy-bodied domestic bird known for its large quantity of mild, tender meat, the turkey is native to the United States. Once sold only as a whole bird, individual turkey parts are now available, as well as ground turkey and turkey sausage.

Vidalia onions. From the rich soil of Vidalia, Georgia, sweet Vidalia onions come in two varieties: green and dry. Green Vidalias are sold in bunches of three or four and resemble giant scallions. Dry Vidalias are bulblike and are similar in form to large yellow onions; their high sugar and water content gives them a crisp texture and a sweet, nutty flavor. When choosing green Vidalias, look for ones with crisp, fresh-looking tops and clean white bottoms. The dry variety should have papery outer skins and firm yet moist interiors. Refrigerate the whole onion, unwashed, in a plastic bag for up to one week. Both green and dry Vidalias are susceptible to bruising and have a shorter shelf life than other onions.

Water chestnuts. The crunchiest of vegetables, this pale, almost translucent tuber, with its erect, cylindrical leaves, grows in dense clumps in mud and water. Once washed, peeled, and sliced, water chestnuts are an attractive addition to many dishes. They are prized for their ability to stay crunchy.

White mushrooms. The most recognized and available variety of mushrooms in the United States, the white mushroom has a smooth white cap and a crisp yet delicate texture. Purchased fresh, white mushrooms should have unblemished caps and undersides that are white. The edges of the cap should fit tightly against the stem. Canned white mushrooms, which are tasteless, soggy, and have no nutritional value, should be avoided.

Whole wheat flour. This medium-fine flour is the ground bran and germ of the whole wheat berry and is used primarily to make yeasted doughs for breads and pizza crusts. It has the same texture and weight as bread flour, but its gluten content is much lower, resulting in a denser bread. Often a dough recipe with whole wheat flour also calls for the addition of gluten flour to lighten the final product.

Worcestershire sauce. A thin, pungent liquid made from soy sauce, vinegar, anchovies, garlic, tamarind, onions, molasses, and various seasonings, Worcestershire sauce was once found only in the dark brown variety. Today, a white variety, which has a lighter flavor, is also available.

Yeast. Yeast is a simple one-celled organism that is the leavening agent for cakes and breads. When added to certain ingredients under proper conditions, yeast grows rapidly, forming the gas that makes breads and cakes light and airy.

Yeast for baking comes in two forms: compressed cakes and active dry. Before purchasing the active dry type (most commonly used), check the expiration date found on the package. Avoid buying dry yeast within three months of its expiration. Fresh compressed cake yeast is found in the refrigerator section of supermarkets. Quite perishable, cake yeast should be used within a week of purchase.

Yellow bean sauce. This thick, spicy sauce is a fermented mixture of yellow beans, flour, and salt. Quite salty, yellow bean sauce adds a distinctive flavor to Chinese-style sauces. This sauce comes in two forms: whole beans in a thick sauce, and mashed beans. Of the two varieties, the whole bean type is slightly less salty.

Zest. Lemon and orange zest is actually the coarse outer rind of the fruit. (Only the colored part contains the flavor, not the inner white portion, which is bitter.) Zest should be grated and used whenever the distinct flavor of lemon or orange is desired. Dried zest, which is found in the spice section of most supermarkets, should be kept on hand for emergencies. Freshly grated zest has no equal. When lemons or oranges are in season, buy a large quantity to make your own zest. Cut the fruits in half and squeeze out the fresh juice, reserving it for another use. With a sharp knife or potato peeler, remove the outer rind from the fruit and coarsely grind it in a blender or food processor. Place the ground zest in a heavy duty plastic bag and keep in the freezer, where it will stay fresh-tasting for up to a year.

Zucchini. A type of summer squash, zucchini is tender and versatile, and can be eaten raw or cooked. Choose zucchini that are firm and smooth with unblemished skin and an even color.

Table of Measurements

For the most accurate recipe results, use only standard measuring cups and spoons (see *Kitchen Equipment* beginning on page 6). The handy table below provides equivalent weights and measures. When calculating, be sure to use level measurements.

MEASUREMENT	EQUIVALENT AMOUNTS			
Pinch or dash	= less than ⅛ teaspoon			
1 teaspoon	= ⅓ tablespoon			= ⅙ fluid ounce
1 tablespoon	= 3 teaspoons			= ½ fluid ounce
2 tablespoons	= ⅛ cup			= 1 fluid ounce
4 tablespoons	= ¼ cup			= 2 fluid ounces
8 tablespoons	= ½ cup			= 4 fluid ounces
12 tablespoons	= ¾ cup			= 6 fluid ounces
16 tablespoons	= 1 cup	= ½ pint		= 8 fluid ounces
⅛ cup	= 2 tablespoons			= 1 fluid ounce
¼ cup	= 4 tablespoons			= 2 fluid ounces
½ cup	= 8 tablespoons			= 4 fluid ounces
¾ cup	= 12 tablespoons			= 6 fluid ounces
1 cup	= 16 tablespoons	= ½ pint		= 8 fluid ounces
2 cups	= 1 pint			= 16 fluid ounces
4 cups	= 2 pints	= 1 quart		= 32 fluid ounces
8 cups	= 4 pints	= 2 quarts		= 64 fluid ounces
16 cups	= 8 pints	= 4 quarts	= 1 gallon	= 128 fluid ounces
½ pint	= 1 cup			= 8 fluid ounces
1 pint	= 2 cups			= 16 fluid ounces
2 pints	= 4 cups	= 1 quart		= 32 fluid ounces
4 pints	= 8 cups	= 2 quarts		= 64 fluid ounces
8 pints	= 16 cups	= 4 quarts	= 1 gallon	= 128 fluid ounces
½ quart	= 2 cups	= 1 pint		= 16 fluid ounces
1 quart	= 4 cups	= 2 pints		= 32 fluid ounces
2 quarts	= 8 cups	= 4 pints		= 64 fluid ounces
4 quarts	= 16 cups	= 8 pints	= 1 gallon	= 128 fluid ounces
½ gallon	= 8 cups	= 4 pints	= 2 quarts	= 64 fluid ounces
1 gallon	= 16 cups	= 8 pints	= 4 quarts	= 128 fluid ounces

Cheese Equivalency Amounts

Since you may purchase cheese in chunks and grate it yourself, or buy packages marked in ounces when the recipe calls for cups, it is useful to understand that the conversion of cheese from ounces (weight) to cups (volume) varies depending on the texture of the cheese.

The main cheese textures are *soft*, *semi-soft*, *semi-firm*, and *hard*. Soft cheeses, such as Ricotta and cottage, measure approximately 8 ounces per cup, while 8 ounces of many semi-soft cheeses like Muenster and Mozzarella, measure 2 cups in their commonly used shredded form. For hard cheeses like Parmesan and Pecorino-Romano, which are most often grated, 8 ounces is equal to approximately 2 cups.

Refer to the table below to determine the *approximate* volume (cup) measurement for 8 ounces of the following popular cheeses. These measurements are based upon each cheese's most commonly used form (grated, shredded, diced, crumbled, etc). Note: all measurements are for loosely packed cheese.

CHEESE	TEXTURE	APPROXIMATE VOLUME FOR 8 OUNCES
Appenzeller	Semi-firm	2 ¾ cups shredded or diced
Asiago	Hard	2 cups grated
Bel Paese	Semi-soft	1½ cups diced
Bergkäse	Hard	2 cups grated
Bitto	Hard	2 cups grated
Blue	Semi-firm	2 cups crumbled
Boursalt	Semi-soft	1½ cups crumbled
Boursin	Semi-soft	1½ cups crumbled
Brick	Semi-firm	2 ¾ cups shredded or diced
Brie	Semi-soft	2 cups
Caciocavallo	Semi-soft	1½ cups diced
Camembert	Semi-soft	2 cups
Cheddar	Semi-firm	2 ¾ cups shredded or diced
Colby	Semi-firm	2 ¾ cups shredded or diced
Cottage	Soft	1 cup
Cream	Soft	1 cup
Edam	Semi-soft	1½ cups diced
Emmenthaler	Semi-firm	2 ¾ cups shredded or diced

CHEESE	TEXTURE	APPROXIMATE VOLUME FOR 8 OUNCES
Farmer	Semi-soft	1½ cups crumbled
Feta	Semi-firm	2½ cups crumbled
Fontina	Semi-soft	1½ cups diced
Goat	Semi-soft	1½ cups crumbled
Gorgonzola	Semi-soft	1½ cups crumbled
Gouda	Semi-soft	1½ cups diced
Grana Padano	Hard	2 cups grated
Gruyère	Semi-firm	2 ¾ cups shredded or diced
Havarti	Semi-firm	2 ¾ cups shredded or diced
Jarlsberg	Semi-firm	2 ¾ cups shredded or diced
Kasseri	Hard	2 cups grated
Kefalotiri	Hard	2 cups grated
Neufchâtel	Soft	1 cup
Monterey Jack	Semi-soft	2 cups shredded or diced
Montrachet	Semi-soft	1½ cups crumbled
Mozzarella	Semi-soft	2 cups shredded or diced
Muenster	Semi-soft	2 cups shredded or diced
Parmesan	Hard	2 cups grated
Pecorino-Romano	Hard	2 cups grated
Port du Salut	Semi-soft	1½ cups diced
Provolone	Semi-soft	1½ cups shredded or diced
Ricotta	Soft	1 cup
Roncal	Semi-soft	1½ cups diced
Roquefort	Semi-firm	2 cups crumbled
Sardo	Hard	2 cups grated
Stilton	Semi-firm	2 cups crumbled
Swiss	Semi-firm	2 ¾ cups shredded or diced
Taleggio	Semi-soft	1½ cups diced
Tilsiterkäse	Semi-soft	1½ cups diced

Ingredient Substitutions

Missing a recipe ingredient? The following is a list of suggested ingredient substitutions. Don't be afraid to experiment. Please note that dairy-based milk and cheeses can be substituted for soy-based products. For those who are lactose-intolerant, be aware of the growing availability of lactose-free milk and cheese products.

INGREDIENT	AMOUNT	SUBSTITUTE INGREDIENT
Arrowroot	1 tablespoon	= 2 tablespoons flour = 1 tablespoon cornstarch

Baking powder	2 teaspoons	= ½ teaspoon baking soda
		   plus 1¼ teaspoon
		   cream of tartar

Buttermilk	1 cup	= 1 cup plain yogurt
		= 1 tablespoon vinegar or
		   lemon juice and enough
		   milk to make 1 cup. Let
		   curdle (5 minutes).

Cocoa powder		= equal amount carob powder
Cracker crumbs	¾ cup	= 1 cup whole grain bread crumbs
Eggs	1 whole	= 2 egg whites = ¼ cup egg substitute
Flour	1 tablespoon	= 1½ teaspoons cornstarch = 1 tablespoon quick-cooking tapioca
Garlic	1 clove	= ½ teaspoon minced or crushed = ⅛ teaspoon garlic powder
Herbs, fresh	1 tablespoon	= 1 teaspoon dried
Lemon juice	1 teaspoon	= ½ teaspoon cider vinegar

Milk (dairy)	1 cup	= equal amount of soy or
		   cashew milk
		= ½ cup evaporated milk
		   plus ½ cup water

Mustard, dried	1 teaspoon	= 1 tablespoon prepared mustard
Salt	1 teaspoon	= 4 tablespoons soy sauce = 2 tablespoons miso
Shallots		= equal amount scallions

INGREDIENT	AMOUNT	SUBSTITUTE INGREDIENT
Sugar	1 cup	= ½ cup honey = ¾ cup maple syrup = ½ cup molasses = ¾ cup fruit purée = ¾ cup barley malt = 1¾ cups rice syrup
Tomatoes, chopped	1 cup	= ½ cup tomato sauce plus ½ cup water

2

Pizza Doughs & Crusts

Homemade pizza is an amazingly uncomplicated affair once your kitchen contains the necessary ingredients and some basic equipment, and you have mastered a few elementary skills. One of these skills involves making your own pizza dough. Although it is not mandatory that you make your pizza dough from scratch (see *Underneath It All* beginning on page 38), creating your own delicious crust can be wonderfully satisfying and relatively simple. This chapter outlines the basic techniques necessary to make your own pizza dough. It includes information on working with yeast, instructions for properly

kneading dough, and guidelines for shaping your pizza crust.

In addition to basic information on making dough, also included in this chapter is a wide variety of pizza dough recipes. You will find recipes for basic whole wheat, rye, and semolina crusts, as well as instructions for more creative affairs such as *Cheese Dough, Greek Garlic Dough,* and *Basil-Rosemary Dough*. There is even a recipe for *Speedy Dough*, which can be ready for the oven in thirty minutes! The wide selection of doughs found in this chapter is sure to fire your imagination and inspire you to create wonderful pizza masterpieces.

CREATING SUCCESSFUL
YEAST DOUGHS

Keep in mind that making your own pizza dough from scratch is not an exact science, but rather a labor of love. And the more you love creating something, the more skilled you will become in your attempts. There will be those times, however, when no matter how carefully you have followed a recipe or how lovingly you have kneaded the dough, something goes wrong, resulting in a less-than-perfect product. To help create successful pizza dough, read the following guidelines carefully.

Accurate Measuring

More pizza crusts fail due to careless measuring than for any other reason. While it is possible to compensate for not enough liquid or too much flour while you are kneading the dough, it is easier to simply start out with the proper proportions. Using the right utensils is critical.

When measuring dry ingredients, use measuring cups that are designed for this purpose. Scoop the dry ingredient into the cup and gently mound it over the rim. Do not tap the bottom of the cup or otherwise settle the ingredients. Use the flat side of a knife or spatula to level the top. Measure liquid ingredients in a proper liquid measuring cup. For more information on measuring utensils, see *Kitchen Equipment* beginning on page 6.

Freshness of Ingredients

If you have gone through the time, labor, and expense of making your own pizza crust, only to have it come out heavy and leaden, you have probably used ingredients that were past their prime. Yeast is one of the biggest culprits in this area, yet any of the following ingredients can contribute to the failure of a crust. Also, unless otherwise instructed, all ingredients should be used at room temperature.

- **Yeast.** The two forms of active yeast for baking are the compressed cake yeast and the dry granulated

type, which comes in small square packages. All of the yeast dough recipes in this chapter call for the dry granulated yeast, as it is the one most readily available.

Yeast, when mixed with flour and liquid, creates an alcoholic fermentation that converts its starch to carbon dioxide. The gluten in the flour captures the gas and stretches, causing the dough to rise. Depending on the recipe, the dough will rise once or twice before it is baked, with the yeast fermenting one last time before dying.

When buying yeast, it is difficult to determine freshness with any certainty. The expiration date on the package is a fairly reliable indicator, but it cannot tell you if the yeast was subjected to extreme temperatures during storage or transport. For this reason it is important to check, or *proof* the yeast to be certain of its freshness.

Proofing yeast is easy. Simply fill a cup with some warm water (110°F to 115°F) and add the yeast. Within five minutes, the water should become foamy, signifying the yeast is fresh. If the water does not foam, you can be sure the yeast is past its prime and will not cause the dough to rise. It should be discarded.

When dissolving yeast, be sure the water is neither to hot nor too cold. Water over 120°F will kill the yeast. If the water is too cold, the yeast will not activate quickly enough.

Cake yeast, which is more perishable than the dry type, will stay up to two weeks in the refrigerator and up to two months in the freezer. Active dry yeast should be stored in the refrigerator (even if the package is unopened), where it will keep for several months.

- **Eggs.** While eggs should be used at room temperature, they should be kept refrigerated until twenty minutes before they are used. Eggs should always be very fresh.

- **Flours.** All flour should be placed in airtight containers and stored at a cool temperature. If you have the space, refrigerate or freeze the flour to keep it fresh. Allow the flour to come to room temperature before using it. In areas of the country where weevils are a problem, freeze the flour for at least a week before opening the package. This will kill any larva that might be present.

Whole wheat flour, unlike bread flour, is very perishable and must be fresh to make a good dough. Each package should have a "pull" date, indicating when it should be removed from the shelf. Avoid wheat flour that has been on the shelf more than two months.

Room Temperature

High humidity or extreme cold can have a negative effect on your finished product. For the best results, it is best to reserve your dough making for those days when the room temperature is between 67°F and 77°F.

Kneading the Dough

Kneading the dough is essential for producing a fine, even-textured pizza crust. Kneading causes the ingredients to become thoroughly distributed. The gluten produces an elastic webwork that traps the tiny air bubbles that are produced by the yeasting action.

Before you begin, it is important to prepare a clean, level work surface. Sprinkle the surface with flour, keeping the open container at your elbow. Place the dough on the floured surface and flatten it with your hand. You are now ready to knead.

Using floured hands, fold the dough in half towards you (see Figure 2.1a). With the heels of your hands, press into the dough, pushing it away from you. Give it a quarter turn and repeat the folding, pressing, and turning (see Figure 2.1b). During this process, you will need to reflour the work surface and your hands from time to time, as the moisture from the dough will absorb the flour rapidly.

Continue kneading until the dough becomes smooth and elastic (8 to 12 minutes). You will know you have kneaded enough when you push your finger into the dough and the hole fills up quickly.

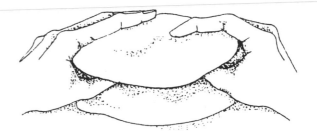

a. Fold the dough in half.

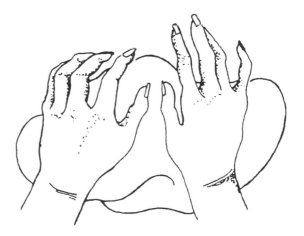

b. Push the dough with the heels of your hands.

Figure 2.1 Kneading Dough.

Rising

Once kneaded, it is time for the dough to rise. Choose a very large bowl (at least a 2-quart size) that will allow the dough ample room to expand. Brush the interior of the bowl with vegetable or olive oil and set the dough in the bottom, turning it once to coat all sides with oil. Cover the bowl with wax paper and a clean kitchen towel, and set it in a draft-free, warm place (80°F to 85°F) until it has doubled in size. The length and number of times the dough must rise will be different for each recipe, so follow the individual instructions carefully. In all cases, however, you can tell if the dough has risen enough by poking two fingers into it. If the indentation remains, the dough has doubled.

Shaping the Dough

Once the dough has risen for the final time, punch it down with your floured fist and turn it onto a well-floured work surface. Knead it for a minute to soften the dough, then form it into a ball. Cover the dough with a clean towel and allow it to rest for 15 minutes (times will vary with individual recipes). This resting period relaxes the dough for easy shaping.

There are three easy ways to shape your pizza dough—patting, stretching, and rolling. Each method has its own advantages and some are more suitable to certain crusts than others.

Patting the dough works well with medium- and thick-crusted pizzas. On a floured work surface, flatten the dough with floured hands in the general desired shape. Transfer the dough to the prepared pan or paddle, and continue to pat and push the dough, from the center toward the edges, until the dough is the desired size or has covered the surface of the pan (see Figure 2.2a). The dough at the edges should be slightly thicker than the dough in the middle, thus forming a rim. The thickness of the dough should be as consistent as possible.

Stretching the dough requires some coordination (and short fingernails). To stretch the dough, first form it into a flat circle about 1 inch thick. Dust your hands and the work surface with flour, then, starting from the

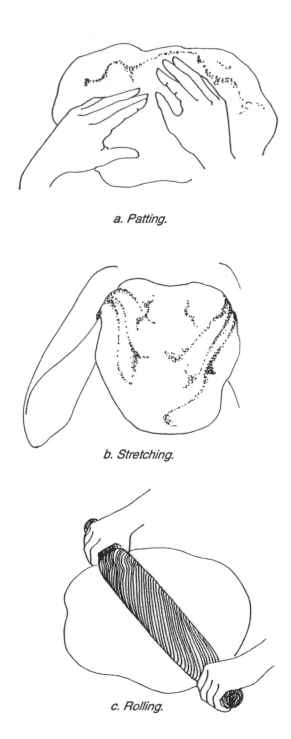

a. Patting.

b. Stretching.

c. Rolling.

Figure 2.2 Dough-Shaping Techniques.

center, press the dough outwards with your fingertips, working it into a circle. Once the dough has thinned to a ½ inch, lift the dough, and let it drape over your fists, which must be positioned close together. Gently move your fists apart, stretching the dough as you do so. Rotate the dough as you move your fists together once more, then repeat moving your fists apart and stretching the dough (see Figure 2.2b). Continue this procedure, taking care not to stretch the dough too thinly at the outer edges, as this area will serve as the rim. Transfer the stretched dough to the prepared pan or paddle, and pat it in place.

Rolling the dough creates the thinnest crust of all and is most suitable for whole grain and vegetable doughs. Form the dough into a flattened round and dust it liberally with flour. Using a well-floured rolling pin and work surface, roll out the dough until it is about 1 inch larger than the pan size (see Figure 2.2c). Place the dough on the prepared pan or paddle.

Preparing Pizza Pans and Paddles

Pizza pans must be properly prepared to ensure easy removal of the cooked pizza. Before assembling the pizza, generously brush oil over the bottom and sides of the pan, then liberally sprinkle it with cornmeal and shake out the excess.

Depending on whether your pizza is to be thin-, medium-, or thick-crusted will largely determine how you form your dough and on which utensil it will be baked. Thin-crusted pizzas and pizza calzones can be baked directly on pizza stones or tiles. A thin pizza crust can also be formed on a pizza screen before it is baked on the hot stone or tiles. It is not necessary to prepare a pizza screen before shaping the dough on its surface. Once the dough is on the screen and the toppings have been assembled, slide the pizza paddle under the screen. To transfer the screen from the paddle to the oven, give the paddle a short forward jerk to start the screen sliding onto the stone or tiles. When the pizza is cooked, lift one edge of the screen, slide the paddle underneath, and remove it from the oven.

Yield

Unless otherwise indicated, all of the doughs in this chapter will make any one of the following:

- 16-inch thin crust (8 slices).
- 14-inch medium crust (6 slices).
- 12-inch thick crust (6 slices).
- 8-inch double crust (4 slices).
- 9-x-13-inch rectangular crust (8 slices).
- 4 large calzones (8 inch).
- 6 medium calzones (6 inch).
- 8 mini-pizzas or calzones (4 inch).

Underneath It All—
Pizza Crust Alternatives

If you have neither the time nor the inclination to make a pizza dough from scratch, don't worry! Almost any leavened or unleavened bread, cracker, roll, or biscuit can be used as support for a fast and easy pizza. Today's supermarkets and bakeries abound with bread products that can be used as pizza crusts. Listed below are some of the most common ones. There are many, many more!

Bagels. A bagel is a doughnut-shaped roll made of raised dough that is simmered in water, then baked. With a glazed brown crust and firm white interior, a good bagel has a distinctively chewy yet tender texture. In my opinion, the best, most flavorful bagels are found in New York. The excellent quality of the city's water enhances the bagel's taste and crust. If at all possible, don't buy bagels from a supermarket. Seek out bagel shops, which usually offer a wide assortment of good-quality bagels—plain, egg, onion, garlic, salt, pumpernickel, poppyseed, sesame seed, rye, cinnamon raisin, whole wheat, oat bran, and blueberry, to name a few.

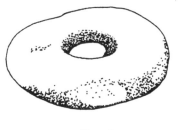

Bagel

Boboli. A type of focaccia, these Italian bread shells are small round loaves that have been strewn with cheese and then baked. Found in 6- and 12-inch sizes, Boboli make wonderful quick crusts for almost any kind of pizza.

Bread Dough. Loaves of frozen yeast dough are available in the freezer section of most supermarkets. These 1-pound raw loaves, made of flour, yeast, water, and sometimes oil, must be thawed and allowed to rise in a warm place just as you would any pizza dough. Once risen, the dough can be patted, stretched, or rolled into a pizza crust.

Crescent Rolls. Tubes of uncooked flaky crescent rolls are found in the refrigerator section of most supermarkets. The dough for these rolls can be patted onto a prepared pan and formed into a single pizza crust.

Egg Roll Wrappers. Wafer-thin sheets of dough, these Oriental wrappers can serve as crisp individual pizza shells. Simply brush the flat sheets lightly with oil and bake until crisp.

English Muffins. This light unsweetened yeast roll is baked on a griddle. The addition of baking soda to the dough results in the muffin's characteristic porous texture. When split in half, the muffin's flat, round shape and unsweetened flavor make it ideal to use as the crust for miniature pizzas.

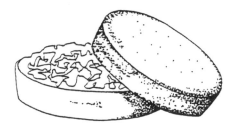

English muffin

Flour Tortilla. A thin, flat Mexican creation of flour, water, and a bit of oil, these round breads range from 6- to 10-inches in diameter and come in both white and whole wheat varieties.

Focaccia Bread. Also known as "flatbread," focaccia is a circular (6 to 10 inches in diameter) leavened bread that goes through two risings. You can buy focaccia plain, or flavored with herbs, onions, or cheese.

French Bread. Traditionally a long, cylindrical loaf, this bread is also found in round loaves called "boules." Made without preservatives, yeasted French bread contains no fat or preservatives and is very perishable. Sliced in half horizontally, French bread makes an excellent pizza crust. It can also be sliced vertically into circular crusts and used for "two-bite" pizzas.

dense bread, without the airy pocket of a pita. Naan is cooked in a clay oven called a "tandoor."

Puff Pastry. This soft pastry dough has many light, crisp layers that puff up and separate during baking. Ready-to-bake sheets of puff paste can be found in the freezer section of most supermarkets.

Pie Pastry Dough. Prepared pie crusts can be found in the refrigerator or freezer sections of most supermarkets.

Pizza Crust. Prebaked pizza crusts are available in a number of sizes and can be found in the refrigerator sections of most supermarkets. Simply add the toppings of your choice and bake.

Pizza Dough. Tubes of pizza dough are found in refrigerator sections of supermarkets. Simply remove the dough from the tube and pat, roll, or stretch into a crust.

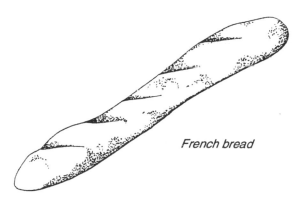

French bread

Refrigerated pizza dough

Italian Bread. There are many Italian breads on the market today, and they can be used to host pizza toppings in the same fashion as French bread. Most Italian loaves are plump. Once they have been cut in half horizontally, I suggest toasting them lightly before adding any toppings.

Naan. Similar to pita bread, naan is an Indian leavened flatbread made of flour, milk, egg, salt, sugar, baking powder, yeast, and yogurt. It is a soft,

Pita Bread. A round, flat, Middle Eastern bread, pita is also known as "pocket bread" because of the gap in its center. Pita can be split in half horizontally to create two very thin rounds or left intact to make a thicker surface upon which to build your pizza.

Roll Mix. Premixed packages of flour, shortening, yeast, and salt need only water to form a soft bread dough that can be formed into a pizza crust.

Simple Dough

Yield: *Any one of the following:*

16-inch thin crust (8 slices)
14-inch medium crust (6 slices)
12-inch thick crust (6 slices)
8-inch double crust (4 slices)
9-x-13-inch rectangular crust (8 slices)
4 large calzones (8 inch)
6 medium calzones (6 inch)
8 mini-pizzas or calzones (4 inch)

1 cup warm water

1 package active dry yeast

½ teaspoon date sugar or brown sugar

3½ cups bread flour

1 teaspoon sea salt

1½ tablespoons olive oil

This most basic of my pizza dough recipes, Simple Dough can be used for pizzas, calzones, and focaccia bread. It can also be prepared in advance. Simply punch down the dough after its second rising, seal the bowl with plastic wrap, and refrigerate. Bring the dough back to room temperature before shaping.

1. Place the warm water in a small bowl and stir in the yeast and sugar until dissolved. Cover the bowl with a clean towel and set aside until the liquid is foamy (about 10 minutes).

2. In a large bowl, combine 3 cups of the flour and the salt. Make a well in the center of the flour and add the yeast mixture and oil. With a wooden spoon, beat the ingredients together to form a soft, sticky mass.

3. Turn the dough onto a well-floured work surface. With floured hands, knead the dough, adding more flour, a little at a time, until smooth and elastic (8 to 12 minutes). (See *Kneading the Dough* on page 35.) Form the dough into a ball.

4. Place the dough in a large bowl that has been brushed with oil. Turn the dough to coat all sides with oil. Cover with wax paper and a clean towel, and place in a warm, draft-free place. Let the dough rise until doubled in size (about 1 hour).

5. With a floured fist, punch down the dough. Cover again and allow the dough to rise another 40 minutes.

6. The dough is now ready to be patted, stretched, or rolled according to the recipe.

Semolina Dough

Semolina, a grain milled from durum wheat kernels, has a fine granular texture, is high in protein, and creates an outstanding pizza dough.

1. Place the warm water in a small bowl and stir in the yeast and sugar until dissolved. Cover the bowl with a clean towel and set aside until the liquid is foamy (about 10 minutes).

2. In a large bowl, combine the semolina and ¾ cup of the bread flour. Make a well in the center of the flour and add the yeast mixture, salt, and oil. With a wooden spoon, beat the ingredients together to form a soft, sticky mass.

3. Turn the dough onto a well-floured work surface. With floured hands, knead the dough, adding more flour, a little at a time, until smooth and elastic (8 to 12 minutes). (See *Kneading the Dough* on page 35.) Form the dough into a ball.

4. Place the dough in a large bowl that has been brushed with oil. Turn the dough to coat all sides with oil. Cover with wax paper and a clean towel, and place in a warm, draft-free place. Let the dough rise until doubled in size (about 3 hours).*

5. With a floured fist, punch down the dough and turn it onto a floured surface. Cover with a damp towel and let rest 10 minutes.

6. The dough is now ready to be patted, stretched, or rolled according to the recipe.

* While most recipes indicate that the dough will double in volume in about an hour, I suggest allowing this dough to rise for 3 hours for best results. Also, whenever I use this dough, I sprinkle semolina over the surface of the oiled pizza pan instead of cornmeal.

Yield: *Any one of the following:*

16-inch thin crust (8 slices)
14-inch medium crust (6 slices)
12-inch thick crust (6 slices)
8-inch double crust (4 slices)
9-x-13-inch rectangular crust (8 slices)
4 large calzones (8 inch)
6 medium calzones (6 inch)
8 mini-pizzas or calzones (4 inch)

1 cup warm water

1 package active dry yeast

½ teaspoon date sugar or brown sugar

2½ cups semolina

1 cup bread flour

1 teaspoon sea salt

1 tablespoon olive oil

Speedy Dough

Yield: *Any one of the following:*

16-inch thin crust (8 slices)
14-inch medium crust (6 slices)
12-inch thick crust (6 slices)
8-inch double crust (4 slices)
9-x-13-inch rectangular crust (8 slices)
4 large calzones (8 inch)
6 medium calzones (6 inch)
8 mini-pizzas or calzones (4 inch)

3 cups bread flour

1 package active rapid-rise dry yeast

1 teaspoon sea salt

½ teaspoon date sugar or brown sugar

1 large beaten egg

1–1½ cups warm water

The fastest of my pizza doughs, Speedy Dough can be prepared from start to finish during the 30 minutes it takes for the oven to preheat. The recipe calls for rapid-rise yeast, and the dough is kneaded for less than a minute and rises only briefly. The result, surprisingly, is a wonderful crisp, light crust.

1. In a large bowl, combine the flour, yeast, salt, and sugar. With a wooden spoon, beat in the egg and as much of the warm water as necessary to form a soft but not sticky dough.

2. Turn the dough onto a lightly floured work surface. With floured hands, knead the dough 10 times. Cover the dough with a clean towel and let it rest about 30 minutes.

3. The dough is now ready to be patted, stretched, or rolled according to the recipe.

For a Special Touch . . .

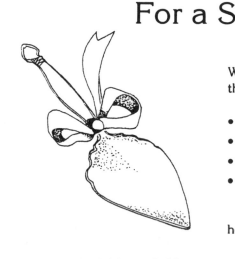

Want to "dress up" an otherwise plain-crusted pizza? Press one of the following along the edge of the dough before baking:

- Sesame seeds
- Poppy seeds
- Caraway seeds
- Seed combination

Not only will this add a visually pleasing dimension to your homemade pizza, it will give it a delightful crunch as well.

Sponge Dough

This savory crust has an intriguing light texture that works with almost any topping.

1. In a large bowl, combine the sugar, yeast, ½ cup of the flour, and ½ cup of water. Set aside in a warm place for 20 minutes.

2. With a wooden spoon, beat the oil, salt, and the remaining flour and water into the yeast mixture to form a soft, sticky dough.

3. Turn the dough onto a well-floured work surface. With floured hands, knead the dough, adding more flour, a little at a time, until smooth and elastic (8 to 12 minutes). (See *Kneading the Dough* on page 35.) Form the dough into a ball.

4. Place the dough in a large bowl that has been brushed with oil. Turn the dough to coat all sides with oil. Cover with wax paper and a clean towel, and place in a warm, draft-free place. Let the dough rise until doubled in size (about 1 hour 20 minutes).

5. With a floured fist, punch down the dough. Cover again and allow the dough to rise another 40 minutes.

6. The dough is now ready to be patted, stretched, or rolled according to the recipe.

Variation

- For a more fiber-rich crust, use equal amounts of bread flour and whole wheat flour.

Yield: *Any one of the following:*

16-inch thin crust (8 slices)
14-inch medium crust (6 slices)
12-inch thick crust (6 slices)
8-inch double crust (4 slices)
9-x-13-inch rectangular crust (8 slices)
4 large calzones (8 inch)
6 medium calzones (6 inch)
8 mini-pizzas or calzones (4 inch)

½ teaspoon date sugar or brown sugar

2 packages active dry yeast

4 cups unbleached bread flour

1½ cups warm water

2 tablespoons olive oil

1 teaspoon sea salt

Combo Dough

Yield: *Any one of the following:*

16-inch thin crust (8 slices)
14-inch medium crust (6 slices)
12-inch thick crust (6 slices)
8-inch double crust (4 slices)
9-x-13-inch rectangular crust (8 slices)
4 large calzones (8 inch)
6 medium calzones (6 inch)
8 mini-pizzas or calzones (4 inch)

1 cup warm water

1 package active dry yeast

$\frac{1}{2}$ teaspoon date sugar or brown sugar

1 teaspoon sea salt

$1\frac{1}{2}$ cups whole wheat bread flour

2 cups bread flour

$1\frac{1}{2}$ tablespoons olive oil

This slightly nutty pizza dough combines white and whole wheat flours.

1. Place the warm water in a small bowl and stir in the yeast and sugar until dissolved. Cover the bowl with a clean towel and set aside until the liquid is foamy (about 10 minutes).

2. In a large bowl, combine the salt, whole wheat flour, and $1\frac{3}{4}$ cups of the bread flour. Make a well in the center of the flour and add the yeast mixture and oil. With a wooden spoon, beat the ingredients together to form a soft, sticky dough.

3. Turn the dough onto a well-floured work surface. With floured hands, knead the dough, adding more flour, a little at a time, until smooth and elastic (8 to 12 minutes). (See *Kneading the Dough* on page 35.) Form the dough into a ball.

4. Place the dough in a large bowl that has been brushed with oil. Turn the dough to coat all sides with oil. Cover with wax paper and a clean towel, and place in a warm, draft-free place. Let the dough rise until doubled in size (about 1 hour).

5. With a floured fist, punch down the dough. Cover again and allow to rise another 40 minutes.

6. The dough is now ready to be patted, stretched, or rolled according to the recipe.

Graham Dough

Graham flour, found in natural foods stores, provides flavor and texture to this nutritious pizza dough.

1. Place the warm water in a small bowl and stir in the yeast and ½ teaspoon of the sugar until dissolved. Cover the bowl with a clean towel and set aside until the liquid is foamy (about 10 minutes).

2. In a large bowl, combine the salt, graham flour, 1¼ cups of the oat blend flour, and the remaining sugar. Make a well in the center of the flour and add the yeast mixture and oil. With a wooden spoon, beat the ingredients together to form a soft, sticky dough.

3. Turn the dough onto a well-floured work surface. With floured hands, knead the dough, adding more flour, a little at a time, until smooth and elastic (8 to 12 minutes). (See *Kneading the Dough* on page 35.) Form the dough into a ball.

4. Place the dough in a large bowl that has been brushed with oil. Turn the dough to coat all sides with oil. Cover with wax paper and a clean towel, and place in a warm, draft-free place. Let the dough rise until doubled in size (about 1 hour 15 minutes).

5. With a floured fist, punch down the dough. Cover again and allow the dough to rise another 40 minutes.

6. The dough is now ready to be patted, stretched, or rolled according to the recipe.

Yield: *Any one of the following:*

16-inch thin crust (8 slices)
14-inch medium crust (6 slices)
12-inch thick crust (6 slices)
8-inch double crust (4 slices)
9-x-13-inch rectangular crust (8 slices)
4 large calzones (8 inch)
6 medium calzones (6 inch)
8 mini-pizzas or calzones (4 inch)

1 cup warm water

1 package active dry yeast

1 tablespoon plus ½ teaspoon date sugar or brown sugar

1 teaspoon sea salt

1 cup graham flour

2 cups oat blend flour or whole wheat bread flour

1 teaspoon canola, safflower, or sunflower oil

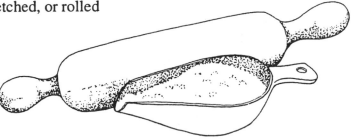

Whole Wheat Dough

Yield: *Any one of the following:*

16-inch thin crust (8 slices)

14-inch medium crust (6 slices)

12-inch thick crust (6 slices)

8-inch double crust (4 slices)

9-x-13-inch rectangular crust (8 slices)

4 large calzones (8 inch)

6 medium calzones (6 inch)

8 mini-pizzas or calzones (4 inch)

1 cup warm water

1 package active dry yeast

½ teaspoon date sugar or brown sugar

3½ cups whole wheat bread flour

1 teaspoon sea salt

3 tablespoons olive oil

Whole wheat flour produces a dough that is soft and sticky to work with and not quite as pliable as those made with white flour. Since whole wheat flour has a noticeable taste, this crust is best used with toppings that have a pronounced flavor.

1. Place the warm water in a small bowl and stir in the yeast and sugar until dissolved. Cover the bowl with a clean towel and set aside until the liquid is foamy (about 10 minutes).

2. In a large bowl, combine 3¼ cups of the flour and the salt. Make a well in the center of the flour and add the yeast mixture and oil. With a wooden spoon, beat the ingredients together to form a soft, sticky dough.

3. Turn the dough onto a well-floured work surface. With floured hands, knead the dough, adding more flour, a little at a time, until smooth and elastic (8 to 12 minutes). (See *Kneading the Dough* on page 35). Form the dough into a ball.

4. Place the dough in a large bowl that has been brushed with oil. Turn the dough to coat all sides with oil. Cover with wax paper and a clean towel, and place in a warm, draft-free place. Let the dough rise until doubled in size (about 1 hour 15 minutes).

5. With a floured fist, punch down the dough. Cover again and allow the dough to rise another 40 minutes.

6. The dough is now ready to be patted, stretched, or rolled according to the recipe.

Rye Dough

Rye, graham, and whole wheat flours combine to make the most nutritious of pizza doughs. It produces, from the very nature of the grains, a firm, robust bread, which is why I add a bit more yeast to lighten it up a bit. To lighten it even further, substitute bread flour in whole or part for the whole wheat flour.

1. Place the warm water in a small bowl and stir in the yeast and sugar until dissolved. Cover the bowl with a clean towel and set aside until the liquid is foamy (about 10 minutes).

2. In a large bowl, combine the rye flour, graham flour, 1 cup of the whole wheat flour, the salt, and the remaining sugar. Make a well in the center of the flour and add the yeast mixture and oil. With a wooden spoon, beat the ingredients together to form a soft, sticky dough.

3. Turn the dough onto a well-floured work surface. With floured hands, knead the dough, adding more flour, a little at a time, until smooth and elastic (8 to 12 minutes). (See *Kneading the Dough* on page 35). Form the dough into a ball.

4. Place the dough in a large bowl that has been brushed with oil. Turn the dough to coat all sides with oil. Cover with wax paper and a clean towel, and place in a warm, draft-free place. Let the dough rise until doubled in size (about 1 hour 15 minutes).

5. With a floured fist, punch down the dough. Cover again and allow the dough to rise another 40 minutes.

6. The dough is now ready to be patted, stretched, or rolled according to the recipe.

Yield: *Any one of the following:*

16-inch thin crust (8 slices)
14-inch medium crust (6 slices)
12-inch thick crust (6 slices)
8-inch double crust (4 slices)
9-x-13-inch rectangular crust (8 slices)
4 large calzones (8 inch)
6 medium calzones (6 inch)
8 mini-pizzas or calzones (4 inch)

1 cup warm water

4 ½ teaspoons (1 ½ packages) active dry yeast

1 tablespoon plus ½ teaspoon date sugar or brown sugar

1 cup rye flour

⅝ cup graham flour

1 ½ cups whole wheat bread flour

1 teaspoon sea salt

1 tablespoon canola, safflower, or sunflower oil

Olive Oil Dough

Yield: *Any one of the following:*

16-inch thin crust (8 slices)
14-inch medium crust (6 slices)
12-inch thick crust (6 slices)
8-inch double crust (4 slices)
9-x-13-inch rectangular crust (8 slices)
4 large calzones (8 inch)
6 medium calzones (6 inch)
8 mini-pizzas or calzones (4 inch)

2 garlic cloves, crushed

¼ cup olive oil

1 cup warm water

1 package active dry yeast

½ teaspoon date sugar or brown sugar

3½ cups bread flour

1 teaspoon sea salt

Adding olive oil to pizza dough, creates a thick, hard crust with a cake-like texture. This dough is ideal for toppings that are very moist.

1. Place the crushed garlic cloves on a work surface and mash, crush, or chop them a second time until well pulverized. Place the mashed garlic in a small bowl along with the olive oil and set aside.

2. In another small bowl, combine the warm water, yeast and sugar, and stir until dissolved. Cover the bowl with a clean towel and set aside until the liquid is foamy (about 10 minutes).

3. In a large bowl, combine 3¼ cups of the flour and the salt. Make a well in the center of the flour and add the yeast mixture and garlic oil. With a wooden spoon, beat the ingredients together to form a soft, sticky dough.

4. Turn the dough onto a well-floured work surface. With floured hands, knead the dough, adding more flour, a little at a time, until smooth and elastic (8 to 12 minutes). (See *Kneading the Dough* on page 35). Form the dough into a ball.

5. Place the dough in a large bowl that has been brushed with oil. Turn the dough to coat all sides with oil. Cover with wax paper and a clean towel, and place in a warm, draft-free place. Let the dough rise until doubled in size (about 1 hour).

6. With a floured fist, punch down the dough. Cover again and allow the dough to rise another 40 minutes.

7. The dough is now ready to be patted, stretched, or rolled according to the recipe.

Herb Dough

Adding herbs to a basic dough results in an aromatic, flavorful crust.

1. Place the warm water in a small bowl and stir in the yeast and sugar until dissolved. Cover the bowl with a clean towel and set aside until the liquid is foamy (about 10 minutes).

2. In a large bowl, combine the bread flour, $1\frac{1}{4}$ cups of the whole wheat flour, and the salt. Make a well in the center of the flour and add the yeast mixture and the oil. With a wooden spoon, beat the ingredients together to form a soft, sticky dough.

3. Turn the dough onto a well-floured work surface. With floured hands, knead the dough, adding more flour, a little at a time, until smooth and elastic (8 to 12 minutes). (See *Kneading the Dough* on page 35). Form the dough into a ball.

4. Place the dough in a large bowl that has been brushed with oil. Turn the dough to coat all sides with oil. Cover with wax paper and a clean towel, and place in a warm, draft-free place. Let the dough rise until doubled in size (about 1 hour).

5. With a floured fist, punch down the dough and turn it onto a floured surface. Knead the basil, rosemary, and thyme into the dough. Shape the dough into a ball and return it to the bowl. Cover with a towel and allow the dough to rise another 40 minutes.

6. The dough is now ready to be patted, stretched, or rolled according to the recipe.

Yield: *Any one of the following:*

16-inch thin crust (8 slices)
14-inch medium crust (6 slices)
12-inch thick crust (6 slices)
8-inch double crust (4 slices)
9-x-13-inch rectangular crust (8 slices)
4 large calzones (8 inch)
6 medium calzones (6 inch)
8 mini-pizzas or calzones (4 inch)

1 cup warm water

1 package active dry yeast

$\frac{1}{2}$ teaspoon date sugar or brown sugar

2 cups bread flour

$1\frac{1}{2}$ cups whole wheat bread flour

1 teaspoon sea salt

$1\frac{1}{2}$ tablespoons olive oil

1 tablespoon minced fresh basil, or 1 teaspoon dried

1 tablespoon snipped fresh rosemary, or 1 teaspoon dried

2 teaspoons snipped fresh thyme, or $\frac{3}{4}$ teaspoon dried

California Dough

Yield: *Any one of the following:*

16-inch thin crust (8 slices)
14-inch medium crust (6 slices)
12-inch thick crust (6 slices)
8-inch double crust (4 slices)
9-x-13-inch rectangular crust (8 slices)
4 large calzones (8 inch)
6 medium calzones (6 inch)
8 mini-pizzas or calzones (4 inch)

1 cup warm water

1 package active dry yeast

$\frac{1}{2}$ teaspoon date sugar or brown sugar

$3\frac{1}{2}$ cups bread flour, whole wheat flour, or a combination of both

1 teaspoon sea salt

6 oil-packed sun-dried tomatoes, drained and minced

$1\frac{1}{2}$ tablespoons oil from the sun-dried tomatoes

6 shallots or scallions, minced

$1\frac{1}{2}$ tablespoons snipped fresh chives, or $1\frac{1}{2}$ teaspoons dried

This exciting dough, filled with bits of sun-dried tomatoes, minced scallions, and a sprinkling of herbs, results in a heavenly scented crust that is best when simply adorned.

1. Place the warm water in a small bowl and stir in the yeast and sugar until dissolved. Cover the bowl with a clean towel and set aside until the liquid is foamy (about 10 minutes).

2. In a large bowl, combine $2\frac{1}{4}$ cups of the flour and the salt. Make a well in the center of the flour and add the yeast mixture, sun-dried tomatoes, oil, shallots, and chives. With a wooden spoon, beat the ingredients together. Continue adding small amounts of flour to form a soft but not sticky dough.

3. Turn the dough onto a well-floured work surface. With floured hands, knead the dough, adding more flour, a little at a time, until smooth and elastic (8 to 12 minutes). (See *Kneading the Dough* on page 35). Form the dough into a ball.

4. Place the dough in a large bowl that has been brushed with oil. Turn the dough to coat all sides with oil. Cover with wax paper and a clean towel, and place in a warm, draft-free place. Let the dough rise until doubled in size (about 1 hour).

5. With a floured fist, punch down the dough. Cover again and allow the dough to rise another 40 minutes.

6. The dough is now ready to be patted, stretched, or rolled according to the recipe.

Cheese Dough

This dough makes a very light crust with a hint of cheese.

1. In a large bowl, place the sugar, yeast, $\frac{1}{2}$ cup of flour, and $\frac{1}{2}$ cup of water. Stir until well combined. Cover and set aside in a warm place for 20 minutes.

2. With a wooden spoon, beat the oil, salt, and the remaining flour and water into the yeast mixture to form a soft, sticky dough.

3. Turn the dough onto a well-floured work surface. With floured hands, knead the dough, adding more flour, a little at a time, until smooth and elastic (8 to 12 minutes). (See *Kneading the Dough* on page 35.) Form the dough into a ball.

4. Place the dough in a large bowl that has been brushed with oil. Turn the dough to coat all sides with oil. Cover with wax paper and a clean towel, and place in a warm, draft-free place. Let the dough rise until doubled in size (about 1 hour).

5. With a floured fist, punch down the dough and turn it onto a floured surface. Knead in the grated cheese until well combined and shape the dough into a ball. Place the dough back in the bowl, cover, and allow to rise another 40 minutes.

6. The dough is now ready to be patted, stretched, or rolled according to the recipe.

Variation

- For a crust with a bit of heat, substitute 1 cup shredded Monterey Jack cheese with jalapeños for the grated cheese.

Yield: *Any one of the following:*

16-inch thin crust (8 slices)
14-inch medium crust (6 slices)
12-inch thick crust (6 slices)
8-inch double crust (4 slices)
9-x-13-inch rectangular crust (8 slices)
4 large calzones (8 inch)
6 medium calzones (6 inch)
8 mini-pizzas or calzones (4 inch)

$\frac{1}{2}$ teaspoon date sugar or brown sugar

2 packages active dry yeast

4 cups unbleached bread flour

$1\frac{1}{2}$ cups warm water

2 tablespoons olive oil

1 teaspoon sea salt

4 ounces (1 cup) finely grated Parmesan, Pecorino-Romano, or Asiago cheese

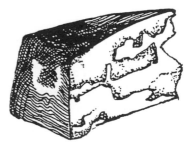

Rosy Dough

Yield: *Any one of the following:*

16-inch thin crust (8 slices)
14-inch medium crust (6 slices)
12-inch thick crust (6 slices)
8-inch double crust (4 slices)
9-x-13-inch rectangular crust (8 slices)
4 large calzones (8 inch)
6 medium calzones (6 inch)
8 mini-pizzas or calzones (4 inch)

1 cup V-8 juice

1 package active dry yeast

½ teaspoon date sugar or brown sugar

3 cloves garlic, crushed

1 tablespoon minced fresh basil, or 1 teaspoon dried

2 tablespoons olive oil

½ teaspoon sea salt

3 cups bread flour

This recipe makes a lovely rose-colored pizza crust. The dough can also be formed into delicious, flavorful rolls.

1. In a small saucepan, gently warm the juice over low heat for about 30 seconds. Transfer the juice to a large bowl and stir in the yeast and sugar until thoroughly dissolved. Cover and let stand for 10 minutes.

2. With a wooden spoon, beat the garlic, basil, oil, salt, and 2 cups of the flour into the yeast mixture until well combined. Continue adding small amounts of flour until a soft dough forms.

3. Turn the dough onto a well-floured work surface. With floured hands, knead the dough, adding more flour, a little at a time, until smooth and elastic (8 to 12 minutes). (See *Kneading the Dough* on page 35). Form the dough into a ball.

4. Place the dough in a large bowl that has been brushed with oil. Turn the dough to coat all sides with oil. Cover with wax paper and a clean towel, and place in a warm, draft-free place. Let the dough rise until doubled in size (about 1 hour).

5. With a floured fist, punch down the dough. Cover again and allow the dough to rise another 40 minutes.

6. The dough is now ready to be patted, stretched, or rolled according to the recipe.

European Milk Dough

This soft, milk dough makes a tender, light crust, suitable for simple toppings. As it has only one rising, European Milk Dough takes less time to prepare than most yeast doughs.

1. In a small saucepan, gently warm the milk over low heat for about 30 seconds. Transfer the milk to a large bowl and stir in the yeast and sugar until thoroughly dissolved. Cover and let stand for 10 minutes.

2. With a wooden spoon, beat the oil, salt, and 3 cups of the flour into the yeast mixture until well combined. Continue adding small amounts of the remaining flour until a soft dough forms.

3. Turn the dough onto a well-floured work surface. With floured hands, knead the dough, adding more flour, a little at a time, until smooth and elastic (8 to 12 minutes). (See *Kneading the Dough* on page 35). Form the dough into a ball.

4. Place the dough in a large bowl that has been brushed with oil. Turn the dough to coat all sides with oil. Cover with wax paper and a clean towel, and place in a warm, draft-free place. Let the dough rise until doubled in size (about 1 hour).

5. With a floured fist, punch down the dough. Cover again and allow the dough to rise another 40 minutes.

6. The dough is now ready to be patted, stretched, or rolled according to the recipe.

Yield: *Any one of the following:*

16-inch thin crust (8 slices)
14-inch medium crust (6 slices)
12-inch thick crust (6 slices)
8-inch double crust (4 slices)
9-x-13-inch rectangular crust (8 slices)
4 large calzones (8 inch)
6 medium calzones (6 inch)
8 mini-pizzas or calzones (4 inch)

1 cup milk

2 packages active dry yeast

1 teaspoon date sugar or brown sugar

¼ cup canola, safflower, or sunflower oil

½ teaspoon sea salt

4 cups bread flour

Pesto Dough

1¼ cups warm water

2 packages active dry yeast

½ teaspoon date sugar or brown
  sugar

1 cup firmly packed fresh basil leaves

1 clove garlic, crushed

3 tablespoons olive oil

4 ounces (1 cup) grated Parmesan or
  Pecorino-Romano cheese

1¼ cups whole wheat bread flour

½ teaspoon sea salt

2 cups bread flour

Redolent of fresh basil and sharp Italian cheese, this dough is much like that used for Italian focaccia bread. I prefer topping this pizza dough with simple ingredients, so as not to overwhelm the lovely flavorful crust.

1. Place the water in a large bowl and stir in the yeast and sugar until dissolved. Cover the bowl with a clean towel and set aside until the liquid is foamy (about 10 minutes).

2. In a blender or food processor, mince the basil leaves and garlic. Add the grated cheese and pulse until well combined. With the motor running, add the oil in a slow, steady stream and process until smooth and well combined.

3. With a wooden spoon, beat the basil mixture, whole wheat flour, and salt into the yeast mixture. Add enough of the bread flour to form a soft but not sticky dough.

4. Turn the dough onto a well-floured work surface. With floured hands, knead the dough, adding more flour, a little at a time, until smooth and elastic (8 to 12 minutes). (See *Kneading the Dough* on page 35). Form the dough into a ball.

5. Place the dough in a large bowl that has been brushed with oil. Turn the dough to coat all sides with oil. Cover with wax paper and a clean towel, and place in a warm, draft-free place. Let the dough rise until doubled in size (about 1 hour).

6. With a floured fist, punch down the dough. Cover again and allow the dough to rise another 40 minutes.

7. The dough is now ready to be patted, stretched, or rolled according to the recipe.

Greek Garlic Dough

Flavorful garlic and Greek Kasseri cheese lend a tantalizing taste and aroma to this matchless pizza dough. If Kasseri is not available, substitute it with freshly grated Kefalotiri, Bitto, Grana Padano, or Sardo.

1. Place the water in a large bowl and stir in the yeast and sugar until dissolved. Cover the bowl with a clean towel and set aside until the liquid is foamy (about 10 minutes).

2. With a wooden spoon, beat the Kasseri cheese, garlic, oil, salt, and 2 ¾ cups of flour into the yeast mixture to form a soft, sticky dough.

3. Turn the dough onto a well-floured work surface. With floured hands, knead the dough, adding more flour, a little at a time, until smooth and elastic (8 to 12 minutes). (See *Kneading the Dough* on page 35). Form the dough into a ball.

4. Place the dough in a large bowl that has been brushed with oil. Turn the dough to coat all sides with oil. Cover with wax paper and a clean towel, and place in a warm, draft-free place. Let the dough rise until doubled in size (about 1 hour).

5. With a floured fist, punch down the dough. Cover again and allow the dough to rise another 40 minutes.

6. The dough is now ready to be patted, stretched, or rolled according to the recipe.

Yield: *Any one of the following:*

16-inch thin crust (8 slices)
14-inch medium crust (6 slices)
12-inch thick crust (6 slices)
8-inch double crust (4 slices)
9-x-13-inch rectangular crust (8 slices)
4 large calzones (8 inch)
6 medium calzones (6 inch)
8 mini-pizzas or calzones (4 inch)

1 ¼ cups warm water

1 package active dry yeast

½ teaspoon date sugar or brown sugar

4 ounces (1 cup) grated Kasseri cheese

2 garlic cloves, crushed

¼ cup olive oil

1 teaspoon sea salt

3 cups bread flour

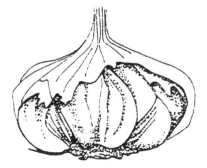

Hard Pretzel Dough

Yield: *Any one of the following:*

16-inch thin crust (8 slices)
14-inch medium crust (6 slices)
12-inch thick crust (6 slices)
8-inch double crust (4 slices)
9-x-13-inch rectangular crust (8 slices)
4 large calzones (8 inch)
6 medium calzones (6 inch)
8 mini-pizzas or calzones (4 inch)

1 cup warm water

1 package active dry yeast

$\frac{1}{2}$ teaspoon date sugar or brown sugar

$1\frac{1}{3}$ cups ground (medium-fine) hard salted pretzels

$1\frac{1}{4}$ cups bread flour or whole wheat bread flour

$\frac{1}{2}$ teaspoon sea salt

1 tablespoon olive oil

1 tablespoon honey

Ground pretzels give this splendid dough a delightful taste and crisp texture. It is an ideal crust for pizzas with heavy or moist toppings.

1. Place the water in a small bowl and stir in the yeast and sugar until dissolved. Cover the bowl with a clean towel and set aside until the liquid is foamy (about 10 minutes).

2. In a large bowl, combine the pretzels, 1 cup of the flour, and the salt. Make a well in the center of the flour and add the yeast mixture, oil, and honey. With a wooden spoon, beat the ingredients together to form a soft, sticky dough.

3. Turn the dough onto a well-floured work surface. With floured hands, knead the dough, adding more flour, a little at a time, until smooth and elastic (8 to 12 minutes). (See *Kneading the Dough* on page 35). Form the dough into a ball.

4. Place the dough in a large bowl that has been brushed with oil. Turn the dough to coat all sides with oil. Cover with wax paper and a clean towel, and place in a warm, draft-free place. Let the dough rise until doubled in size (about 1 hour).

5. With a floured fist, punch down the dough. Cover again and allow the dough to rise another 40 minutes.

6. The dough is now ready to be patted, stretched, or rolled according to the recipe.

Rich Egg Dough

This light, golden yeast dough does not require lengthy kneading, yet it makes a thick, wondrous pizza crust. It is best suited for simple toppings.

1. Place the water in a large bowl and stir in the yeast until dissolved. Cover the bowl with a clean towel and set aside until the liquid is foamy (about 10 minutes).

2. In a small saucepan, heat the milk, butter, salt, and sugar over medium heat until bubbles appear around the edges of the saucepan. (Do not boil.) Remove from the stove and allow the milk to cool to lukewarm. Stir the milk mixture and the eggs into the yeast mixture. With a wooden spoon, beat in the flour, ½ cup at a time, to form a soft, sticky dough.

3. Turn the dough onto a well-floured work surface. With floured hands, knead the dough, adding more flour, a little at a time, until smooth and elastic (8 to 12 minutes). (See *Kneading the Dough* on page 35). Form the dough into a ball.

4. Place the dough in a large bowl that has been brushed with oil. Turn the dough to coat all sides with oil. Cover with wax paper and a clean towel, and place in a warm, draft-free place. Let the dough rise until doubled in size (about 1 hour).

5. With a floured fist, punch down the dough. Cover again and allow the dough to rise another 40 minutes.

6. The dough is now ready to be patted, stretched, or rolled according to the recipe.

Yield: *Any one of the following:*

18-inch thin crust (10 slices)
16-inch medium crust (8 slices)
14-inch thick crust (6 slices)
9-inch double crust (4 slices)
9-x-13-inch rectangular crust (8 slices)
6 large calzones (8 inch)
8 medium calzones (6 inch)
12 mini-pizzas or calzones (4 inch)

½ cup warm water

1 package active dry yeast

½ cup milk or soymilk

4 tablespoons unsalted butter, margarine, or soy margarine

1 teaspoon sea salt

2 tablespoons date sugar or brown sugar

2 large eggs, beaten, or ½ cup egg substitute

5 cups whole wheat or all-purpose flour (not bread flour)

Basil-Rosemary Dough

Yield: *Any one of the following:*

16-inch thin crust (8 slices)
14-inch medium crust (6 slices)
12-inch thick crust (6 slices)
8-inch double crust (4 slices)
9-x-13-inch rectangular crust (8 slices)
4 large calzones (8 inch)
6 medium calzones (6 inch)
8 mini-pizzas or calzones (4 inch)

1 cup warm water

1 package active dry yeast

$\frac{1}{2}$ teaspoon date sugar or brown
sugar

$2\frac{2}{3}$ cups bread flour

1 tablespoon minced fresh basil, or
1 teaspoon dried

2 teaspoons snipped fresh rosemary,
or $\frac{3}{4}$ teaspoon dried

1 teaspoon sea salt

2 garlic cloves, crushed

2 tablespoons olive oil

This dough has fragrant yet unassuming flavors, and is best used for pizzas that are topped with subtle ingredients. Its flecked surface is so pretty I often use this dough for double-crusted pizzas or calzones.

1. Place the water in a small bowl and stir in the yeast and sugar until dissolved. Cover the bowl with a clean towel and set aside until the liquid is foamy (about 10 minutes).

2. In a large bowl, combine $2\frac{1}{3}$ cups of the flour, the basil, rosemary, and salt. Make a well in the center of the flour and add the yeast mixture, garlic, and oil. With a wooden spoon, beat the ingredients together to form a soft, sticky dough.

3. Turn the dough onto a well-floured work surface. With floured hands, knead the dough, adding more flour, a little at a time, until smooth and elastic (8 to 12 minutes). (See *Kneading the Dough* on page 35). Form the dough into a ball.

4. Place the dough in a large bowl that has been brushed with oil. Turn the dough to coat all sides with oil. Cover with wax paper and a clean towel, and place in a warm, draft-free place. Let the dough rise until doubled in size (about 1 hour).

5. With a floured fist, punch down the dough. Cover again and allow the dough to rise another 40 minutes.

6. The dough is now ready to be patted, stretched, or rolled according to the recipe.

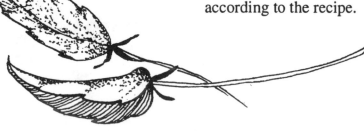

Tandir Dough

Turkish tandir dough has a lengthy preparation time. It requires a starter that must ferment at room temperature for 8 hours, and the dough itself needs a total of 5 hours rising time. The result, however, is a delectable pizza crust with a rich, yeasty aroma.

1. To make the starter, place 3 tablespoons of the warm water in a medium-sized bowl and stir in the yeast. Cover the bowl with a clean towel and set aside until the liquid is foamy (about 10 minutes). Stir in the flour and remaining water. Knead the flour in the bowl, adding more flour as necessary to form a soft, smooth dough. Cover with plastic wrap and leave at room temperature until the starter is light and bubbly (about 8 hours.)

2. To make the dough, place ¼ cup of the warm water in a large bowl and stir in the yeast and sugar until dissolved. Cover the bowl with a clean towel and set aside until the liquid is foamy (about 10 minutes). Stir in the oil, salt, starter mixture, and the remaining water until well blended. With a wooden spoon, gradually beat in the wheat flour and 2½ cups of the bread flour to form a soft, sticky dough.

3. Turn the dough onto a well-floured work surface. With floured hands, knead the dough, adding more flour, a little at a time, until smooth and elastic (8 to 12 minutes). (See *Kneading the Dough* on page 35.) Form the dough into a ball.

4. Place the dough in a large bowl that has been brushed with oil. Turn the dough to coat all sides with oil. Cover with wax paper and a clean towel, and place in a warm, draft-free place. Let the dough rise until doubled in size (about 3 hours).

5. With a floured fist, punch down the dough, and turn it onto a floured surface. Knead briefly and shape into a smooth round. Cover with a clean towel and allow to rise another 2 hours.

6. The dough is now ready to be patted, stretched, or rolled according to the recipe.

Yield: *Any one of the following:*

16-inch thin crust (8 slices)
14-inch medium crust (6 slices)
12-Inch thick crust (6 slices)
8-inch double crust (4 slices)
9-x-13-inch rectangular crust (8 slices)
4 large calzones (8 inch)
6 medium calzones (6 inch)
8 mini-pizzas or calzones (4 inch)

STARTER
8 tablespoons warm water

¼ teaspoon active dry yeast

1 cup plus 2 tablespoons bread flour

DOUGH
1¼ cups warm water

2 teaspoons active dry yeast

½ teaspoon date sugar or brown sugar

2 tablespoons olive oil

1 tablespoon sea salt

⅓ cup whole wheat bread flour

3 cups bread flour

Soft Pretzel Dough

Yield: *9-x-13-inch crust*

1 cup warm water

1 package active dry yeast

2¼ cups bread flour

1 teaspoon sea salt

1 teaspoon honey

1 tablespoon olive oil

2 tablespoons coarse sea salt

This dense, chewy dough gets its unique texture from being immersed in simmering water before it is baked.

1. Place the water in a small bowl and stir in the yeast and sugar until dissolved. Cover the bowl with a clean towel and set aside until the liquid is foamy (about 10 minutes).

2. In a large bowl, combine 2 cups of the flour and the salt. Make a well in the center of the flour and add the yeast mixture and honey. With a wooden spoon, beat the ingredients together to form a soft, sticky dough.

3. Turn the dough onto a well-floured work surface. With floured hands, knead the dough, adding more flour, a little at a time, until smooth and elastic (8 to 12 minutes). (See *Kneading the Dough* on page 35). Form the dough into a ball.

4. Place the dough in a large bowl that has been brushed with oil. Turn the dough to coat all sides with oil. Cover with wax paper and a clean towel, and place in a warm, draft-free place. Let the dough rise until doubled in size (about 1 hour).

5. With a floured fist, punch down the dough and turn it onto a floured surface. Divide the dough into thirds, then cut each third into five pieces. Roll each piece into 5-inch "logs." Cover with a clean towel and allow to rise 30 minutes.

6. Brush a 9-x-13-inch baking pan with the oil and sprinkle the surface with coarse sea salt. Set aside.

7. Bring a large shallow pan of water to a rolling boil. In batches, transfer the pretzel logs to the pan and cook, turning once, approximately 1½ minutes per side. Remove with a slotted spoon to the prepared baking pan.

8. Arrange the logs as close together as possible.

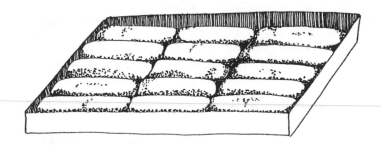

9. Bake the pretzel logs in a preheated 400°F oven for 6 to 8 minutes. This crust is now ready to be topped according to the recipe.

American Pie Dough

This pastry-like crust is flaky and delicious, and should be used for thin-crusted pizzas or calzones. Not leavened, this dough can be ready in less than 10 minutes.

Yield: *Any one of the following:*

16-inch thin-crust (8 slices)
4 large calzones (8 inch)
6 medium calzones (6 inch)
10 mini-pizzas or calzones (4 inch)

2 cups unbleached flour

1 teaspoon sea salt

8 tablespoons vegetable shortening or soy margarine

¼–⅓ cup orange juice

1. In a medium-sized bowl, combine the flour and salt. With a pastry blender or two knives, cut the shortening into the flour until it resembles small peas. With a fork, stir in enough orange juice to form a soft but not sticky dough. Shape into a ball.

2. Place the dough on a lightly floured work surface. With a floured rolling pin, roll out the dough to a circle that is 2 inches larger than the pan you will be using.

3. Transfer the dough to the ungreased baking pan. Fold the excess dough onto itself and crimp.

4. The dough is now ready to be topped and baked according to the recipe.

Scallion Pancakes

Yield: *Four 8-inch pancakes*

3 cups unbleached flour

1⁷⁄₈ cups cold water

6 tablespoons canola, safflower, or
   sunflower oil

12 scallions, finely chopped

2 teaspoons sea salt

Oriental restaurants often serve this incredible-tasting bread with a dipping sauce of soy and ginger. Scallion pancakes also make a wonderful crust for Far Eastern-style pizzas.

1. Place the flour and water in a medium-sized bowl, and beat with a wooden spoon to form a soft, sticky dough.

2. Turn the dough onto a lightly floured surface. Briefly knead, adding more flour, a little at a time, to form a soft but not sticky dough.

3. With floured hands, divide the dough into 4 portions. Pat each portion into a 12-inch circle.

4. Place 2 tablespoons of the oil in a small bowl. Brush each circle with some of the oil, and top with the scallions, pressing them lightly into the dough. Top each circle with ½ teaspoon salt, and roll them into tight cylinders.

5. Fold each cylinder into thirds and pat into a flat circle. With a floured rolling pin, roll each into an 8-inch pancake and set aside.

6. In a medium-sized skillet, heat 1 tablespoon of the oil over medium-low heat. Using a spatula, carefully transfer one of the pancakes to the skillet and cook it until the bottom is speckled brown (about 2 minutes). Turn and cook the other side until golden brown. Transfer to paper towels. Cook the remaining pancakes.

7. The pancakes are now ready to be topped and used according to the recipe.

Rice Cake Dough

This very nutritious dough contains mung beans, rice flour, and a number of spices reflective of the Middle East. It goes well with any of the Middle Eastern-style pizzas found in Chapter 11.

1. Place the mung beans in a medium-sized bowl and cover with hot water. Soak for 30 minutes.

2. Place the coconut milk in a small bowl and stir in the yeast and sugar until dissolved. Cover the bowl with a clean towel and set aside until the liquid is foamy (about 10 minutes).

3. Drain the beans and place in a blender or food processor along with the milk mixture. Purée until smooth. Transfer to a large bowl.

4. With a wooden spoon, beat the rice flour, salt, turmeric, cumin, and 1½ cups of bread flour into the puréed bean mixture. Continue to add flour, a little at a time, to form a soft but not sticky dough.

5. Turn the dough onto a well-floured work surface. With floured hands, knead the dough, adding more flour, a little at a time, until smooth and elastic (8 to 12 minutes). (See *Kneading the Dough* on page 35). Form the dough into a ball.

6. Place the dough in a large bowl that has been brushed with oil. Turn the dough to coat all sides with oil. Cover with wax paper and a clean towel, and place in a warm, draft-free place. Let the dough rise until doubled in size (about 1 hour).

7. With a floured fist, punch down the dough. Cover again and allow the dough to rise another 40 minutes.

8. The dough is now ready to be patted, stretched, or rolled according to the recipe.

Yield: *Any one of the following:*

16-inch thin crust (8 slices)
14-inch medium crust (6 slices)
12-inch thick crust (6 slices)
8-inch double crust (4 slices)
9-x-13-inch rectangular crust (8 slices)
4 large calzones (8 inch)
6 medium calzones (6 inch)
8 mini-pizzas or calzones (4 inch)

¾ cup dried yellow mung beans

1 cup warm unsweetened coconut milk

1 package active dry yeast

½ teaspoon date sugar or brown sugar

1 cup rice flour

1 teaspoon sea salt

½ teaspoon turmeric

½ teaspoon ground cumin

2 cups bread flour or whole wheat bread flour

Fruit Dough

Yield: *Any one of the following:*

16-inch thin crust (8 slices)

14-inch medium crust (6 slices)

12-inch thick crust (6 slices)

8-inch double crust (4 slices)

9-x-13-inch rectangular crust (8 slices)

4 large calzones (8 inch)

6 medium calzones (6 inch)

8 mini-pizzas or calzones (4 inch)

½ cup orange juice

½ cup dark rum

10 large dried apricots, cut into small pieces

5 large dried apple rings, cut into small pieces

5 large dried pear rings, cut into small pieces

⅓ cup golden raisins

⅓ cup chopped dried dates

½ cup warm water

1 package active dry yeast

¾ cup date sugar or brown sugar

4 cups bread flour

1 tablespoon grated orange zest

1 teaspoon ground cinnamon

1 teaspoon sea salt

1 large egg, beaten

Sweet chewy bits of dried fruit adorn this rich pizza crust, which is perfect served alone or when used as a magnificent surface upon which to pile luscious dessert toppings.

1. In a medium-sized saucepan, bring the orange juice, rum, and dried fruit to a boil over medium heat. Remove from the heat and let stand 5 minutes.

2. Place the warm water in a small bowl and stir in the yeast and a pinch of the sugar until dissolved. Cover the bowl with a clean towel and set aside until the liquid is foamy (about 10 minutes).

3. In a large bowl, combine 2½ cups of the flour, the remaining sugar, the orange zest, cinnamon, and salt. Make a well in the center of the flour and add the yeast mixture and fruit mixture. With a wooden spoon, beat the ingredients together until smooth. Stir in the egg and enough of the remaining flour to form a soft, sticky dough.

4. Turn the dough onto a well-floured work surface. With floured hands, knead the dough, adding more flour, a little at a time, until smooth and elastic (8 to 12 minutes). (See *Kneading the Dough* on page 35). Form the dough into a ball.

5. Place the dough in a large bowl that has been brushed with oil. Turn the dough to coat all sides with oil. Cover with wax paper and a clean towel, and place in a warm, draft-free place. Let the dough rise until doubled in size (about 1 hour).

6. With a floured fist, punch down the dough. Cover again and allow the dough to rise another 40 minutes.

7. The dough is now ready to be patted, stretched, or rolled according to the recipe.

Sweet Dough

This dough makes the perfect crust for sweet pizzas, such as the Country Market Apple Pizza found on page 204.

1. Place the water in a small bowl and stir in the yeast and a pinch of the sugar until dissolved. Cover the bowl with a clean towel and set aside until the liquid is foamy (about 10 minutes).

2. In a large bowl, combine 2¾ cups of the flour, the remaining sugar, the orange zest, and salt. Make a well in the center of the flour and add the yeast mixture and butter. With a wooden spoon, beat the ingredients together to form a soft, sticky dough.

3. Turn the dough onto a well-floured work surface. With floured hands, knead the dough, adding more flour, a little at a time, until smooth and elastic (8 to 12 minutes). (See *Kneading the Dough* on page 35). Form the dough into a ball.

4. Place the dough in a large bowl that has been brushed with oil. Turn the dough to coat all sides with oil. Cover with wax paper and a clean towel, and place in a warm, draft-free place. Let the dough rise until doubled in size (about 1 hour).

5. With a floured fist, punch down the dough. Cover again and allow the dough to rise another 40 minutes.

6. The dough is now ready to be patted, stretched, or rolled according to the recipe.

Yield: *Any one of the following:*

16-inch thin crust (8 slices)
14-inch medium crust (6 slices)
12-inch thick crust (6 slices)
8-inch double crust (4 slices)
9-x-13-inch rectangular crust (8 slices)
4 large calzones (8 inch)
6 medium calzones (6 inch)
8 mini-pizzas or calzones (4 inch)

1¼ cups warm water

1 package active dry yeast

¾ cup date sugar or brown sugar

3 cups bread flour

1 tablespoon grated orange zest

1 teaspoon sea salt

2 tablespoons melted unsalted butter, margarine, or soy margarine

3

Pizza Sauces

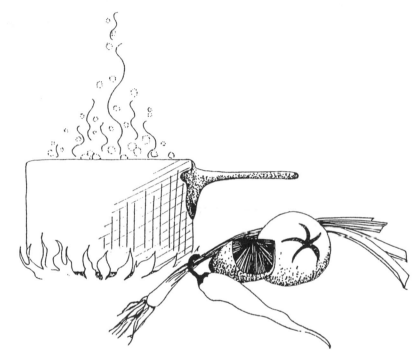

Making pizza from scratch requires a considerable investment of time and effort. Each step is important. You lovingly knead and shape the dough for your crust, search for the finest, freshest vegetables and spices, and seek out the most delectable cheeses. After going through such effort, it would be an insult to treat the sauce with less care. Especially since a fresh, well-seasoned sauce is so easy to make.

When most people think of traditional pizza, they imagine a pie topped with some type of tomato sauce. The *Fresh Tomato* and *Quick Tomato* sauces found in this chapter are two toppings that are sure to please. In addition to these simple tomato-based sauces, you will find others that are designed to lift your pizzas to creative new heights. Does a Chinese-style pizza sound interesting? Then I invite you to try my *Chinese Black Bean Sauce*. When the kids are in the mood for a barbecue, make them a pizza topped with *Zesty Barbecue Sauce*. For a sophisticated change of pace, top your pizza with the flavorful *Pizza Pesto*.

No matter what your mood, you will be sure to find the right sauce in this chapter. As an added bonus, all of the sauces are quick and easy to make.

Fresh Tomato Sauce

Yield: *2 cups*

2 tablespoons olive oil

2 cloves garlic, crushed

1 medium-sized sweet yellow onion, chopped

10 ripe plum tomatoes, skinned* and chopped

⅔ cup prepared tomato sauce

½ cup Madeira wine

2 tablespoons chopped fresh basil, or 2 teaspoons dried

1 tablespoon olive paste

1 teaspoon sea salt

1 teaspoon ground black pepper

½ teaspoon honey

* For tomato-skinning information, see inset below.

This full-bodied, lusty sauce is easy to prepare and can be easily doubled or tripled.

1. In a medium-sized saucepan, heat the oil over medium-low heat. Add the garlic and sauté until soft (about 2 minutes). Add the onions and reduce the heat to low. Sauté the onions, stirring occasionally, until they are soft and golden brown (about 8 minutes).

2. Stir in the tomatoes, tomato sauce, wine, basil, olive paste, salt, pepper, and honey. Bring the mixture to a boil, then reduce the heat to low. Cover and simmer, stirring occasionally, for 30 minutes.

3. Use immediately. To store, refrigerate in a covered container for up to 7 days, or freeze until needed.

Skinning Fresh Tomatoes

Fresh tomatoes are a common ingredient in many pizza toppings; often, they must be skinned before they are used. Once you know how, removing the skin from fresh tomatoes is really quite easy. Simply do the following:

1. Carefully drop the tomatoes in a pot of boiling water and boil for 1 minute.

2. Remove the tomatoes with a slotted spoon and place in a colander.

3. Rinse under cold water, then slip off the skin with your fingers.

Pizza Béchamel Sauce

This is a thicker variation of the classic French white sauce.

Yield: *1½ cups*

1. In a medium-sized saucepan, melt the butter or heat the oil over medium-low heat. Reduce the heat to low and whisk in the flour, blending thoroughly. Cook, while whisking constantly, 1 to 2 minutes. Do not let the mixture brown or it will become bitter.

2. While the flour mixture is cooking, gently heat the milk in a small saucepan until hot. (Do not boil.)

3. Remove the flour mixture from the stove and slowly add the hot milk while whisking constantly. Continue to whisk until the sauce is very smooth.

4. Return the mixture to the stove and bring to a boil over medium heat and cook, whisking constantly, until the sauce is very thick (about 5 minutes). Stir in the salt, pepper, and paprika.

5. Use immediately. To store, refrigerate in a covered container for up to 4 days, or freeze until needed.

4 tablespoons unsalted butter or margarine, or canola, safflower, or sunflower oil

¼ cup unbleached flour

1½ cups milk

¾ teaspoon sea salt

½ teaspoon white pepper

⅛ teaspoon paprika

Cucumber‑Yogurt Sauce

This fresh, sparkling pizza sauce also makes a wonderful dip for raw vegetables or toasted pita triangles.

Yield: *2 cups*

1. Place the cucumber halves in a colander, sprinkle with the salt, and allow to drain for 10 minutes. Rinse the cucumber, pat dry, and finely chop. Transfer to a medium-sized bowl. Stir in the rest of the ingredients and combine well.

2. Use immediately. To store, refrigerate in a covered container for up to 3 days. Do not freeze.

1 medium-sized cucumber, peeled, halved lengthwise, and seeded

1 teaspoon sea salt

2 cups plain yogurt

2 tablespoons minced fresh cilantro or parsley, or 2 teaspoons dried

1 scallion, minced

1 garlic clove, crushed

1 tablespoon fresh lemon juice

½ teaspoon ground cumin

⅛ teaspoon cayenne pepper (or to taste)

Quick Tomato Sauce

Yield: *3 cups*

3 tablespoons olive oil

2 cloves garlic, crushed

1 large sweet yellow onion, chopped

1 can (32 ounces) plum tomatoes, drained and coarsely chopped

¼ cup red or white wine, or vermouth

¼ cup chopped fresh basil leaves

2 tablespoons tomato paste

1 tablespoon chopped fresh oregano, or 1 teaspoon dried

½ teaspoon sea salt

½ teaspoon ground black pepper

¼ teaspoon crushed dried hot red chiles

While this sauce takes as long to simmer as my Fresh Tomato Sauce (page 68), it is easier to prepare.

1. In a large saucepan, heat the oil, garlic, and onion over medium heat. Add the tomatoes and wine. Bring the ingredients to a boil, then reduce the heat to low and simmer the sauce for 15 minutes.

2. Transfer half of the mixture to a blender or food processor and purée until smooth. Return this puréed mixture to the saucepan. Stir in the basil, tomato paste, oregano, salt, pepper, and chiles.

3. Bring the sauce to a boil, then reduce the heat to low. Cover and simmer 15 minutes more while stirring occasionally.

4. Use immediately. To store, refrigerate in a covered container for up to 7 days, or freeze until needed.

Guacamole

Yield: *1½ cups*

3 cloves garlic, roasted* and crushed

1⅓ tablespoons fresh lime juice

1 teaspoon lime zest

2 ripe avocados, halved and pitted (reserve pit)

1 large ripe plum tomato, chopped

4 scallions or shallots, minced

2 tablespoons minced chives or green scallion tops

1 fresh hot chile, seeded and minced

1 teaspoon sea salt

¾ teaspoon ground black pepper

Today, guacamole is as much a part of a cocktail party as was onion dip years ago. It can also be a sensational pizza topping. This basic guacamole can be brought to fiery levels by increasing the amount of chiles.

1. In a medium-sized bowl, mash together the garlic, lime juice, and zest. With a spoon, scoop out the avocado flesh, transfer to the bowl, and mash coarsely into the garlic mixture. Stir in the tomato, scallions, chives, chile, salt, and pepper.

2. Use immediately. To store, bury the avocado pit deep in the guacamole (to prevent it from turning brown), cover, and refrigerate for up to 2 hours.

* For garlic-roasting information, see page 90.

Pizza Pesto

Generally thought of as a basil-based sauce, pesto can also be made with spinach, parsley, or mint.

Yield: 1 cup

1. Place the basil, garlic, grated cheese, pine nuts, and pepper in a blender or food processor, and pulse to chop. With the motor running, add the oil in a slow, steady stream and blend the mixture until smooth.

2. Use immediately. To store, refrigerate in a covered container for up to a month, or freeze until needed.

4 cups loosely packed fresh basil leaves

4 cloves garlic, chopped

2 ounces ($\frac{1}{2}$ cup) grated Parmesan, Pecorino-Romano, or Asiago cheese

2 tablespoons pine nuts

1 teaspoon ground black pepper

$\frac{1}{3}$ cup olive oil

Variation

- For a smoother, creamier, more lavish pesto, follow the steps above, but make the following ingredient changes:

  2 cloves garlic, chopped

  $\frac{1}{2}$ teaspoon sea salt

  $\frac{1}{2}$ teaspoon ground black pepper

  1 cup olive oil

Chopping Fresh Basil

When chopped fresh basil is called for in a recipe, use the following quick and easy method to get the job done.

1. Stack the fresh leaves, then roll them into a tight cylinder.
2. With a very sharp knife, cut the roll into very thin slices.
3. Use these julienned strips as you would chopped.

Zesty Barbecue Sauce

Yield: *2 cups*

2 tablespoons canola, safflower, or sunflower oil

1 medium-sized sweet yellow onion, chopped

2 cloves garlic, crushed

2 pounds ripe tomatoes, skinned* and chopped

1 can (4 ounces) green chiles, drained and chopped

½ cup date sugar, brown sugar, or honey

½ cup chili sauce

2 tablespoons cider vinegar

1 tablespoon tamari or other soy sauce

1 tablespoon Dijon-style mustard

1 teaspoon ground ginger

1 teaspoon sea salt

¾ teaspoon ground black pepper

* For tomato-skinning information, see page 68.

This outstanding barbecue sauce really packs a punch!

1. In a large saucepan, heat the oil over medium-low heat. Add the onion and garlic, and sauté until soft (about 3 minutes).

2. Add the remaining ingredients and bring to a boil. Reduce the heat to low and simmer uncovered and stirring frequently, until the sauce is very thick (50 to 55 minutes).

3. Use immediately. To store, refrigerate in a covered container for up to 7 days, or freeze until needed.

Catalina Sauce

This spicy almond and hot pepper sauce packs quite a wallop, depending on how much hot chile you add.

1. Finely chop the almonds in a blender or food processor. Add the garlic, chiles, tomato, salt, pepper, and lemon juice, and grind to a fine paste.

2. With the motor running, slowly add the oil in a thin steady stream until the sauce has thickened and is smooth. Adjust the seasonings.

3. Use immediately. To store, refrigerate in a covered container for up to 7 days. Do not freeze.

Yield: 1½ cups

¼ cup toasted almonds

2 cloves garlic, chopped

½ teaspoon crushed dried hot red chiles

1 large ripe tomato, skinned* and chopped

1 teaspoon sea salt

½ teaspoon ground black pepper

2 teaspoons fresh lemon juice

1 cup olive or walnut oil

* For tomato-skinning information, see page 68.

Chinese Black Bean Sauce

Use this robust, authoritative sauce for pizzas with a decidedly Far Eastern flair.

1. In a shallow bowl, lightly mash together the canned black beans and fermented black beans and set aside.

2. In a medium-sized saucepan, heat the oils over medium-low heat. Add the scallions and garlic, and sauté until soft and tender (about 3 minutes). Add the mashed black beans, wine, vegetable stock, ginger, garlic sauce, and chiles. Stir well.

3. Bring the mixture to a boil, then reduce the heat to very low. Cover and simmer, stirring frequently, until the sauce is very thick (20 to 25 minutes).

4. Use immediately. To store, refrigerate in a covered container for up to 7 days. Do not freeze.

Yield: 1½ cups

1 can (16 ounces) black beans, drained

1 tablespoon Chinese fermented black beans

1 tablespoon canola, safflower, or sunflower oil

1 teaspoon toasted sesame oil

4 scallions, chopped

2 cloves garlic, crushed

½ cup rice wine

½ cup vegetable stock

1 teaspoon ginger

1 teaspoon black bean garlic sauce

¼ teaspoon crushed dried hot red chiles

Curried Tomato Sauce

Yield: *2 cups*

3 tablespoons olive oil

2 cloves garlic, crushed

1 large sweet yellow onion, chopped

2 teaspoons curry powder

6 medium-sized ripe tomatoes, skinned* and chopped

1 cup vegetable stock

½ cup dry white wine

1 tablespoon bouquet garni

1 teaspoon sea salt

1 teaspoon ground black pepper

1 tablespoon chopped fresh parsley, or 1 teaspoon dried

2 teaspoons chopped fresh cilantro, or ¾ teaspoon dried

* For tomato-skinning information, see page 68.

Use this spicy blend of tomatoes and onions on Caribbean- and Indian-style pizzas.

1. In a medium-sized saucepan, heat 2 tablespoons of the oil over medium-low heat. Add the garlic and sauté until soft (about 2 minutes). Add the onions and reduce the heat to low. Sauté the onions, stirring occasionally, until they are soft and golden brown (about 8 minutes).

2. While the onions are sautéing, heat the remaining oil in a small skillet over low heat. Add the curry powder and cook, stirring occasionally, for 2 minutes. Add this curry oil to the sautéed onions along with the tomatoes, vegetable stock, wine, bouquet garni, salt, and pepper. Combine well.

3. Bring the mixture to a boil, then reduce the heat to low. Cover and simmer, stirring occasionally, for 30 minutes. Stir in the cilantro and parsley.

4. Use immediately. To store, refrigerate in a tightly covered container for up to 7 days, or freeze until needed.

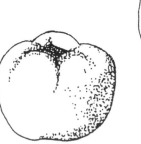
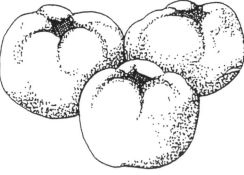

Fresh Salsa

Although there are many wonderful salsas on the market today, most contain preservatives and cannot compare to the fresh salsa you can whip up yourself.

1. In a medium-sized bowl, blend all the ingredients together until well combined.

2. Cover and refrigerate for at least 2 hours before using. To store, refrigerate in a covered container for up to 7 days, or freeze until needed.

Yield: 2 cups

3 large ripe tomatoes, diced

5 scallions, chopped

2 tablespoons minced cilantro or parsley leaves

3 cloves garlic, minced

1 jalapeño chile (or to taste), seeded and minced

1 tablespoon fresh lime or lemon juice

1 tablespoon olive oil

1 tablespoon fresh oregano, or 1 teaspoon dried

1 teaspoon honey

1 teaspoon sea salt

¾ teaspoon ground black pepper

¼ teaspoon ground cumin

Roasting Peppers

When fresh peppers are roasted, they become soft and mellow-tasting with skins that can be easily removed. Roasting peppers can be accomplished in three simple steps:

1. Rinse the peppers and slice in half. Remove the stems, membranes, and seeds. (Use rubber gloves if preparing hot chile peppers.)

2. Place the peppers cut side down on a baking sheet that has been lined with foil. Bake in a preheated 425°F oven until the skins are blistered and very dark brown (about 25 minutes).

3. Transfer the peppers to a brown paper bag and close it tightly. Let the peppers steam in the bag for 10 minutes. When cool enough to handle, gently peel the blackened skin from the peppers with a small paring knife. The peppers are now ready to be eaten or used in a recipe.

Mexican Chile Sauce

Yield: *3 cups*

2 tablespoons olive oil

1 large sweet yellow onion, chopped

3 cloves garlic, chopped

1 can (16 ounces) plum tomatoes, drained and chopped

1 can (8 ounces) tomato sauce

$2/3$ cup flat beer

2 serrano or jalapeño chiles (or to taste), chopped

$1\frac{1}{2}$ teaspoons chili powder

$1/2$ teaspoon turmeric

$1/2$ teaspoon sea salt

$1/2$ teaspoon ground black pepper

This is a simply made, south-of-the-border sauce that adds a spicy spark to Mexican-style pizzas.

1. In a large saucepan, heat the oil over medium-low heat. Add the onion and garlic, and sauté, stirring frequently, until soft (about 5 minutes).

2. Add the remaining ingredients and bring to a boil. Reduce the heat to low and simmer uncovered, stirring frequently, for 15 minutes.

3. Remove from the heat and allow the mixture to cool for 10 minutes. Transfer to a blender or food processor and purée until smooth.

4. Use immediately. To store, refrigerate in a covered container up to 7 days, or freeze until needed.

Sea Cream Sauce

Yield: *$1\frac{1}{2}$ cups*

4 tablespoons unsalted butter or margarine, or canola, safflower, or sunflower oil

$1/2$ cup unbleached flour

1 cup milk

$2/3$ cup fish stock or clam juice

$3/4$ teaspoon sea salt

$1/2$ teaspoon white pepper

$1/8$ teaspoon paprika

This pizza sauce is a divine blend of ingredients that will support any type of seafood.

1. In a medium-sized saucepan, melt the butter or heat the oil over medium-low heat. Reduce the heat to low and whisk in the flour, blending thoroughly. Cook, while whisking constantly, for 3 minutes. Do not let the mixture brown or it will become bitter.

2. While the flour mixture is cooking, gently heat the milk and fish stock in a small saucepan until hot. (Do not boil.)

3. Increase the heat to medium under the flour mixture and slowly add the hot milk and fish stock while whisking constantly. Continue to cook the sauce until it thickens (about 5 minutes). Stir in the salt, pepper, and paprika.

4. Use immediately. To store, refrigerate in a covered container for up to 4 days. Do not freeze.

Fast and Easy Toppings

Just about all of the pizzas found in this book can be prepared on a number of commercially prepared breads (see *Underneath It All* beginning on page 38.) In addition, your kitchen cabinets and refrigerator probably contain the makings for dozens of pizza toppings. The variations can be endless. The challenge is in creating ways to combine some of these on-hand ingredients. What follows is a partial list of suggested pizza toppings to keep on hand.

• Cans or jars of anchovies, artichoke hearts, prepared chili, clams, tuna, bean varieties, sardines, olives, hot peppers, mushrooms, corn, roasted bell peppers, sauerkraut, Chinese vegetables, sun-dried tomatoes, hearts of palm, capers, grated cheese, and whole and crushed tomatoes.

• Prepared sauces, such as Alfredo, taco, pizza, spaghetti, salsa, and pesto.

• Fresh meat including ground and/or other cuts of beef, pork, lamb, chicken, and turkey; bacon; and sausages.

• Cheeses that melt.

• Tofu, tempeh, and other soybean products.

• Fresh cold cuts, such as salami, prosciutto and other types of ham, corned beef, and pastrami.

• Fresh seafood, such as lobster, crabmeat, shrimp, scallops, and clams.

• Fresh vegetables such as eggplant, squash, broccoli, cauliflower, spinach, onions, shallots, scallions, leeks, tomatoes, corn, peas, bean sprouts, mushrooms, bell peppers, and hot chiles.

• Leftovers of everything imaginable.

• Dried or fresh herbs and spices.

Onion Sauce

Yield: *2 cups*

¼ cup olive oil

3 cloves garlic, crushed

2 large leeks, white bulb cleaned and thinly sliced

2 large sweet yellow onions, thinly sliced

6 scallions, chopped

4 shallots, chopped

2 tablespoons arrowroot or unbleached flour

½ cup dry white wine

2 tablespoons Cognac

1 teaspoon sea salt

½ teaspoon white pepper

This sauce is very heady stuff with a delicious blend of four kinds of onions that have been sautéed until they are almost caramelized. Not only is it a perfect sauce for topping white pizzas, it is a wonderful pasta sauce, too.

1. In a large skillet or saucepan, heat the oil over medium-low heat. Add the garlic, leeks, onions, scallions, and shallots, and quickly toss to coat well with the oil. Reduce the heat to low, cover, and sauté, stirring often, until the onions are very soft and golden brown (about 25 minutes).

2. Stir the arrowroot into the sautéed onions, and cook over low heat for 2 minutes. Add the wine, Cognac, salt, and pepper, and bring to a low boil while stirring. Reduce the heat to low and simmer the sauce until thick (3 to 4 minutes).

3. Use immediately. To store, refrigerate in a covered container for up to 7 days, or freeze until needed.

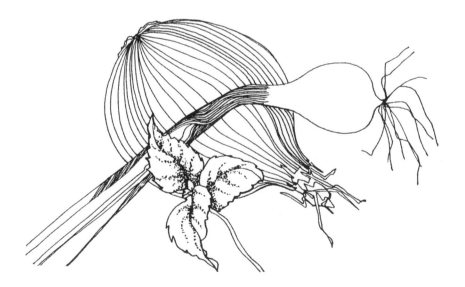

Sauce Americaine

This very simple combination of wine, brandy, and tomato sauce is delicious on pizzas that are topped with seafood.

Yield: 1½ cups

1. Place the flour in a small bowl and whisk in ½ cup of the wine until smooth. Set aside.

2. In a medium-sized saucepan, melt the butter or heat the oil over low heat. Add the scallions and sauté until soft and tender (about 2 minutes). Remove from the heat.

3. Add the remaining wine and the brandy to the sautéed scallions. Hold a lighted match to the liquid until the brandy catches fire. Shake the saucepan gently and return to the heat. When the fire dies down, stir in the reserved wine and flour mixture and the tomato sauce. Cook, stirring constantly, until the sauce is thick and smooth (about 5 minutes).

4. Use immediately. To store, refrigerate in a covered container for up to 7 days, or freeze until needed.

¼ cup unbleached flour

1 cup dry white wine

3 tablespoons unsalted butter or margarine, or canola, safflower, or sunflower oil

2 scallions, minced

¼ cup good-quality brandy

⅓ cup tomato sauce

Spanish Romesco Sauce

This sauce is a variation of a specialty of the Spanish province of Tarragona, where annual Romesco-cooking contests are held. It is a peppery sauce that gets its unique flavor from hazelnuts.

Yield: 1 cup

1. Place the tomato, chiles, garlic, and nuts in a blender or food processor and purée. With the motor running, add the olive oil in a slow, steady stream and process until smooth and thick. Add the vinegar and salt and process briefly.

2. Use immediately. To store, refrigerate in a covered container for up to 7 days, or freeze until needed.

1 small ripe tomato, skinned* and chopped

½ teaspoon crushed dried hot red chiles (or to taste)

3 cloves garlic, chopped

24 hazelnuts, toasted

¾ cup olive oil

¼ cup white wine vinegar

1 teaspoon sea salt

* For tomato-skinning information, see page 68.

4

East Coast Pizzas

When I think of the type of pizza commonly found in the eastern United States, New York City immediately comes to mind. It is where I had my first taste of pizza. I had just returned to the United States after years of living in Europe. I'll never forget that delicious "tomato pie" with its light thin crust, oozing cheese, and flavorful tomato sauce.

True New York-style pizza is a classic Neopolitan pie. Its yeasted dough is tossed into the air, then caught on two fists that stretch it into a thin circle. The dough is covered with whole-milk mozzarella, topped with crushed tomatoes or a tomato sauce, and flavored with herbs. True New York-style pizza is baked directly on the oven floor to develop its crisp, chewy crust and puffed edges. Today, most pizzerias offer these pies with various toppings to accommodate American tastes. In this chapter, I have offered some unique and, I hope, delectable variations of this classic pie. Be sure to try the *Grilled Barbecue Pizza* for an outstanding taste sensation, and the *New York Pretzel Pizza* with its unusual chewy crust.

The northeastern New England States and the southeastern coast of Florida have their own versions of New York-style pizza. Cheeses, seafood, and other popular local ingredients are added to the classic tomato pie. One taste of a *Bayside Scallop Pizza* will surely conjure images of the salty air and sea breezes of a New England fishing town, while an *Emerald Coast Pizza* will transport you to the balmy, tropical Florida coast.

Whatever your fancy, you will surely find just the right pizza in this chapter. All are distinctive and delicious reflections of the East Coast.

Grilled Barbecue Pizza

Yield: *16-inch thin-crust pizza / 8 slices*

Suggested Crusts: *Basil-Rosemary,*

California, Cheese, Combo,

Greek Garlic, Herb, Olive Oil,

Simple, Speedy, or Whole Wheat.

(See Chapter 2 for recipes.)

---

8 tablespoons olive oil

2 tablespoons cornmeal

Dough for 16-inch crust (see
    suggestions)

4 cloves garlic, crushed

$1/2$ teaspoon crushed dried hot red
    chiles (or to taste)

$2/3$ cup *Fresh Tomato Sauce* (page
    68), *Quick Tomato Sauce* (page
    70), or commercial pizza sauce

$1/2$ teaspoon liquid hickory smoke
    flavoring

$1/3$ cup *Zesty Barbecue Sauce* (page
    72), or commercial barbecue sauce

6 ounces ($1 1/2$ cups) shredded
    Mozzarella cheese

4 ounces ($3/4$ cup) diced Fontina
    cheese

1 pound fresh mushrooms, wiped
    clean

2 large sweet yellow or Vidalia onions,
    peeled and left whole

1 large red bell pepper, halved and
    seeded

1 large green or yellow bell pepper,
    halved and seeded

2 chayote, peeled, cored, and
    quartered

$1 1/2$ teaspoons sea salt

1 teaspoon ground black pepper

This creation has a sumptuous smoky flavor and is ideal when you are in the mood for a barbecue.

1. Preheat the oven to 450°F for 30 minutes. Brush 1 tablespoon of the oil over the surface of a 16-inch pizza pan and sprinkle with cornmeal, shaking out the excess. (If using pizza stones or tiles, place them in the oven before preheating, and heavily flour a pizza paddle.) Pat, stretch, or roll the dough in the prepared pan or on the paddle and set aside.

2. Preheat a gas or charcoal grill to medium.

3. In a small bowl, combine the remaining oil with the garlic and chiles, and set aside. In another bowl, combine the *Fresh Tomato Sauce, Zesty Barbecue Sauce,* and hickory flavoring. In a third bowl, combine the Mozzarella and Fontina cheese.

4. When the grill is ready, lightly brush the rack with oil. Liberally brush the mushrooms, onions, bell peppers, and chayote with the garlic oil, and grill them, turning once and basting frequently, until golden brown (12 to 15 minutes).

5. When the bell peppers have cooked, place them in a clean paper bag and close it tightly. Let them steam in the bag for 10 minutes before removing their skin and slicing them into strips. Thinly slice the mushrooms, onions, and chayote.

6. Spread the tomato-barbecue sauce over the prepared crust, and scatter the cheese mixture on top. Add the grilled vegetables and sprinkle with salt and pepper.

7. Bake the pizza until the top is bubbly and the crust is golden (13 to 18 minutes).

Bayside Scallop Pizza

The combination of artichokes, velvety goat cheese, and spices brings out the sweetness of the scallops in this outstanding pizza. This topping is also a great filling for calzones and double-crusted pizzas.

1. Preheat the oven to 450°F for 30 minutes. Brush the oil over the surface of a 16-inch pizza pan and sprinkle with cornmeal, shaking out the excess. (If using pizza stones or tiles, place them in the oven before preheating, and heavily flour a pizza paddle.) Pat, stretch, or roll the dough in the prepared pan or on the paddle and set aside.

2. In a medium-sized saucepan, bring the water, wine, thyme, and lemon zest to a boil over medium-high heat. Add the scallops and boil for 1 minute. Drain in a colander.

3. When the scallops are cool enough to handle, cut them into thin slices and place in a bowl, along with the artichoke hearts, scallions, and garlic. Stir together well.

4. In another bowl, mash together the Mozzarella, Ricotta, and goat cheese. Add the scallop mixture, garlic-pepper, salt, and white pepper. Mix the ingredients well, then spread the mixture evenly over the prepared crust.

5. Bake the pizza until the top is bubbly and the crust is golden (13 to 18 minutes). Remove from the oven, sprinkle with the grated cheese, and serve immediately.

Yield: *16-inch thin-crust pizza / 8 slices*

Suggested Crusts: *Basil-Rosemary, California, Cheese, Combo, Herb, Olive Oil, Simple, Speedy, Sponge, or Whole Wheat.*

(See Chapter 2 for recipes.)

1 tablespoon olive oil

2 tablespoons cornmeal

Dough for 16-inch crust (see suggestions)

½ cup water

¼ cup dry white wine

1 tablespoon snipped fresh thyme, or 1 teaspoon dried

1 teaspoon grated lemon zest

1 pound fresh scallops

1 can (14 ounces) artichoke hearts, drained and quartered

4 scallions or shallots, minced

2 cloves garlic, crushed

8 ounces (2 cups) shredded Mozzarella cheese

6 ounces (¾ cup) Ricotta cheese

5 ounces Montrachet or other soft mild goat cheese, crumbled

1 teaspoon garlic-pepper seasoning*

½ teaspoon sea salt

½ teaspoon white pepper

2 ounces (½ cup) grated Parmesan, Pecorino-Romano, or Asiago cheese

* Available in most supermarkets, garlic-pepper seasoning consists of a variety of spices including black pepper, garlic, salt, sugar, red bell pepper, and onion.

Balsamic Eggplant Pizza

Yield: *16-inch thin-crust pizza / 8 slices*

Suggested Crusts: *Basil-Rosemary,*

Combo, Herb, Simple, Speedy,

or Whole Wheat.

(See Chapter 2 for recipes.)

2 pounds small eggplants

1 large red bell pepper, halved and seeded

1 large yellow, orange, or green bell pepper, halved and seeded

1 large sweet yellow or Vidalia onion, peeled and left whole

1 tablespoon olive oil

2 tablespoons cornmeal

Dough for 16-inch crust (see suggestions)

4 large semi-ripe tomatoes

2 tablespoons chopped fresh basil, or 2 teaspoons dried

1 tablespoon sea salt

½ teaspoon ground black pepper

2 ounces (½ cup) grated Parmesan, Pecorino-Romano, or Grana Padano cheese (optional)

MARINADE

1 cup mayonnaise

⅓ cup balsamic vinegar

2 tablespoons olive oil

Years ago, my very dear friend Laura suggested combining mayonnaise and balsamic vinegar to use as a marinade/baste. It proved to be a divine combination.

1. Whisk together the marinade ingredients in a small bowl. Set aside.

2. Cut off and discard the ends of the eggplants. Slice the eggplants in half horizontally, and place them in a shallow baking dish, along with the bell peppers and onion. Cover with the marinade and let sit for 30 minutes.

3. While the vegetables marinate, preheat a gas or charcoal grill to medium. Also preheat the oven to 450°F.

4. Brush the oil over the surface of a 16-inch pizza pan and sprinkle with cornmeal, shaking out the excess. (If using pizza stones or tiles, place in the oven before preheating, and flour a pizza paddle.) Pat, stretch, or roll the dough in the prepared pan or on the paddle and set aside.

5. When the grill is ready, lightly brush the rack with oil. Grill the eggplant, bell peppers, onion, and tomatoes, turning once and basting frequently, until golden on all sides (5 to 15 minutes). Reserve remaining marinade.

6. When the peppers have cooked, place them in a clean paper bag and close it tightly. Let the peppers steam in the bag for 10 minutes before removing their skin and slicing them into strips. Slice the eggplants into 1-inch pieces, and thinly slice the onion. Cut each tomato into 8 pieces and place them on paper towels to drain.

7. Brush any remaining marinade over the prepared crust and arrange the eggplant, bell peppers, onion, and tomatoes on top. Sprinkle with basil, salt, and black pepper.

8. Bake the pizza until the crust is golden (13 to 18 minutes). Remove from the oven, sprinkle with the grated cheese (if using), and serve immediately.

Bush Country Pizza

Named in honor of former President George Bush, this bright, lively pizza features fresh broccoli, basil pesto, and velvety cheese.

Yield: *16-inch thin-crust pizza / 8 slices*

Suggested Crusts: *California, Cheese, Combo, Graham, Olive Oil, Rye, Semolina, Simple, Speedy, Sponge, or Whole Wheat.*

(See Chapter 2 for recipes.)

4 tablespoons olive oil

2 tablespoons cornmeal

Dough for 16-inch crust (see suggestions)

5 scallions or shallots, minced

4 cloves garlic

1 large head broccoli, separated into flowerets

¾ teaspoon sea salt

½ teaspoon ground black pepper

1 cup *Pizza Pesto* (page 71) or commercial pesto

8 ounces (2 cups) shredded Mozzarella cheese

1. Preheat the oven to 450°F for 30 minutes. Brush 1 tablespoon of the oil over the surface of a 16-inch pizza pan and sprinkle with cornmeal, shaking out the excess. (If using pizza stones or tiles, place them in the oven before preheating, and heavily flour a pizza paddle.) Pat, stretch, or roll the dough in the prepared pan or on the paddle and set aside.

2. Heat the remaining oil in a large skillet over medium heat. Add the scallions and garlic, and sauté until soft (about 3 minutes).

3. Add the broccoli to the skillet and toss to coat with oil. Sauté until tender-crisp (about 5 minutes). Sprinkle with salt and pepper, and set aside.

4. Spread the *Pizza Pesto* over the prepared crust and sprinkle with 1½ cups of the Mozzarella. Top with the broccoli mixture.

5. Bake the pizza for 10 minutes, remove from the oven, and top with the remaining Mozzarella.

6. Return the pizza to the oven and continue to bake until the cheese has melted and the crust is golden (4 to 8 minutes).

Cheese‑Onion Tart

Yield: *16-inch thin-crust pizza / 8 slices*

Suggested Crust: *American Pie*

Prepared *American Pie Dough* (page 61)

2 tablespoons canola, safflower, or sunflower oil

4 large sweet yellow onions, chopped

4 cloves garlic, crushed

8 ounces (2¾ cups) shredded Jarlsberg cheese

1 tablespoon white Worcestershire sauce

2 large eggs, beaten

¾ teaspoon sea salt

1 teaspoon ground black pepper

4 ounces (1 cup) shredded Mozzarella cheese

4 ounces (1 cup) grated Parmesan, Pecorino-Romano, or Asiago cheese

This sensuous pie is a cross between a tart and a pizza. While it can be prepared on any mild-flavored crust, I find American Pie Dough to be the best.

1. Preheat the oven to 400°F for 10 minutes. On a floured surface, roll the dough into an 18-inch circle. Place this circle of dough in a 16-inch unoiled pizza pan, allowing the edges to hang over the sides. Fold the overlapping dough onto itself, forming a ridge along the edge. With floured fingers, crimp the edge. Set aside.

2. Heat the oil in a large skillet over medium-low heat. Add the onions and garlic, and sauté, stirring frequently, until soft and pale (about 10 minutes). Transfer to a large bowl and add the Jarlsberg cheese, Worcestershire, eggs, salt, and pepper. Combine well.

3. Scatter the Mozzarella cheese over the prepared crust, and top with the onion mixture. Sprinkle with the grated cheese.

4. Bake the pizza until the cheese is bubbly and the crust is golden (22 to 30 minutes).

Emerald Coast Pizza

When you live near Gulf waters, as I do, there is ample opportunity to enjoy the seafood harvested in its emerald depths.

1. Preheat the oven to 450°F for 30 minutes. Brush 1 tablespoon of the oil over the surface of a 16-inch pizza pan and sprinkle with cornmeal, shaking out the excess. (If using pizza stones or tiles, place them in the oven before preheating, and heavily flour a pizza paddle.) Pat, stretch, or roll the dough in the prepared pan or on the paddle and set aside.

2. Heat 3 tablespoons of the oil in a large skillet over medium-low heat. Add the scallions and garlic, and sauté, stirring frequently until soft and pale (about 5 minutes).

3. Add the scallops to the skillet and sauté until they are no longer opaque (3 to 4 minutes). With a slotted spoon, transfer this mixture to a medium-sized bowl and set aside.

4. Heat the remaining oil in the skillet. Toss in the shrimp and sauté until they curl and turn pink (about 3 minutes). Add the shrimp to the scallops, and stir in the dill, salt, and pepper.

5. Spread the *Sea Cream Sauce* over the prepared crust and bake for 10 minutes. Remove from the oven, top with the seafood mixture, and sprinkle with Gorgonzola cheese.

6. Return the pizza to the oven and continue to bake until the cheese has melted and the crust is golden (4 to 8 minutes).

Yield: *16-inch thin-crust pizza / 8 servings*

Suggested Crusts: *Cheese, Combo, Greek Garlic, Herb, Semolina, Simple, Speedy, or Sponge.*

(See Chapter 2 for recipes.)

6 tablespoons olive oil

2 tablespoons cornmeal

Dough for 16-inch crust (see suggestions)

6 scallions or shallots, minced

2 cloves garlic, crushed

1 pound fresh scallops, rinsed and cut in half horizontally

1 pound medium-sized raw shrimp, peeled and deveined

3 tablespoons snipped fresh dill, or 1 tablespoon dried

¾ teaspoon sea salt

½ teaspoon ground black pepper

1 cup *Sea Cream Sauce* (page 76)

8 ounces (1½ cups) crumbled Gorgonzola cheese

New York Pretzel Pizza

Yield: *9-x-13-inch pizza / 8 slices*

Suggested Crust: *Soft Pretzel*

Prepared and prebaked *Soft Pretzel Dough* (page 60)

6 tablespoons olive oil

2 large sweet yellow or Vidalia onions, sliced into ¼-inch rounds

2 jalapeño chiles (or to taste), minced

2 cloves garlic, crushed

3 large ripe tomatoes, skinned* and thickly sliced

1½ tablespoons minced fresh basil, or 1½ teaspoons dried

2 teaspoons minced fresh parsley, or ¾ teaspoon dried

½ teaspoon ground black pepper

1 cup sliced Kalamata or other imported black olives

1½ cups sour cream (optional)

* For tomato-skinning information, see page 68.

I bought my first soft pretzel from a New York City street vendor, and I ate it right on the spot amidst the clamor of the noonday traffic. It was a memorable experience—one I have tried to recapture with this hot, chewy pretzel pizza.

1. Preheat the oven to 450°F for 30 minutes. After the *Soft Pretzel Dough* has been assembled on a lightly oiled 9-x-13-inch pizza pan and briefly baked (according to recipe instructions), brush 1½ tablespoons of the oil over its surface. Set aside.

2. Heat the remaining oil in a large skillet over medium-low heat. Add the onions, chiles, and garlic, and sauté, stirring frequently, until soft and tender (3 to 5 minutes).

3. Arrange the tomatoes over the crust, and sprinkle with half of the basil and parsley. Reserving the oil, remove the onion mixture from the skillet with a slotted spoon, and layer it over the tomatoes. Top with the remaining basil and parsley, the black pepper, and olives. Drizzle with some of the reserved oil.

4. Bake the pizza until the crust is golden (13 to 18 minutes). If desired, serve each slice with a dollop of sour cream.

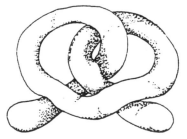
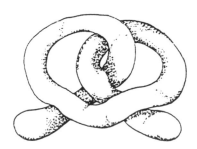
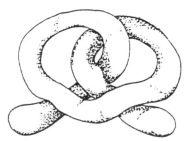

Sausage-n-Cheese Pizza

This "tomato-less" pizza has slices of sweet Italian sausage and a smooth blend of creamy cheeses.

Yield: 16-inch thin-crust pizza / 8 slices

Suggested Crusts: Basil-Rosemary, California, Cheese, Combo, Graham, Greek Garlic, Herb, Pesto, Rosy, Rye, Semolina, Simple, Speedy, Sponge, or Whole Wheat.

(See Chapter 2 for recipes.)

1. Preheat the oven to 450°F for 30 minutes. Brush 1 tablespoon of the oil over the surface of a 16-inch pizza pan and sprinkle with cornmeal, shaking out the excess. (If using pizza stones or tiles, place them in the oven before preheating, and heavily flour a pizza paddle.) Pat, stretch, or roll the dough in the prepared pan or on the paddle and set aside.

2. Heat the remaining oil in a large skillet over medium-low heat. Add the sausage and toss to coat with oil. Reduce the heat to low, cover the skillet, and cook the sausage for 4 minutes, stirring frequently. Uncover and continue cooking the sausage until it begins to brown and no pink remains (4 to 6 minutes). Transfer to paper towels.

3. In a small bowl, combine the basil, oregano, salt, and pepper. In another bowl, combine the Mozzarella and Cheddar cheese.

4. Scatter 2 cups of the cheese mixture over the prepared crust, arrange the sausage on top, and sprinkle with the herb mixture.

5. Bake the pizza for 10 minutes. Remove from the oven and top with the remaining cheese.

6. Return the pizza to the oven and continue to bake until the cheese has melted and the crust is golden (4 to 8 minutes).

3 tablespoons olive oil

2 tablespoons cornmeal

Dough for 16-inch crust (see suggestions)

1 pound sweet Italian sausage, cut into ½-inch slices

2 tablespoons chopped fresh basil, or 2 teaspoons dried

2 teaspoons chopped fresh oregano, or ¾ teaspoon dried

¾ teaspoon sea salt

½ teaspoon ground black pepper

6 ounces (1½ cups) shredded Mozzarella cheese

6 ounces (2 cups) shredded sharp Cheddar cheese

Roasting Garlic and Shallots

Responsible for adding fragrance and flavor to many luscious dishes, garlic and shallots are usually crushed, minced, or chopped before they are used. Recently, an interesting preparation method has emerged—slow-roasting. When a garlic or shallot clove is slow-roasted, it becomes a meltingly honeyed morsel that adds a caramelized sweetness to the dish. The soft, roasted cloves can also be spread on crusty bread in place of butter.

Method 1

After using this method to roast garlic or shallots, be sure to reserve the fragrant oil and use it to flavor other dishes.

15 garlic or shallot cloves, unpeeled

⅓ cup extra-virgin olive oil

1. Bring a small saucepan of water to a boil. Add the cloves and blanch for 1 minute.

2. Drain the cloves in a colander. When cool enough to handle, peel them.

3. Place the peeled cloves and olive oil in a small ovenproof casserole dish. Toss to coat with oil. Cover and place in a 400°F oven. Stirring occasionally, roast the cloves until very soft (about 20 minutes).

4. Reserving the oil, remove the cloves and use as directed.

Method 2

This slow-roasting method, which uses very little oil, results in cloves that are savory and melt-in-your-mouth delicious.

15 garlic or shallot cloves, unpeeled

1½ tablespoons extra-virgin olive oil

1. Bring a small saucepan of water to a boil. Add the cloves and blanch for 1 minute.

2. Drain the cloves in a colander. When cool enough to handle, peel them.

3. Brush a 12-inch square of foil with a little olive oil. Place the cloves in the center of the foil and drizzle with the remaining oil. Fold the foil into a sealed packet and place in a 400°F oven.

4. Roast the cloves until very soft (about 20 minutes). Use as directed.

Top: Sausage-n-Cheese
Bottom: New York Pretzel
Piz.

Smoky Feta Pizza

Almost any grilled vegetables are suitable for this pizza, but I especially like the combination given in this recipe—artichoke hearts, tomatoes, sweet onions, and zucchini. Because of its heavy topping, this pizza requires a firm crust.

Yield: *16-inch thin-crust pizza / 8 slices*

Suggested Crusts: *Hard Pretzel,*

Olive Oil, or Whole Wheat.

(See Chapter 2 for recipes.)

8 tablespoons olive oil

2 tablespoons cornmeal

Dough for 16-inch crust (see suggestions)

2 cans (15 ounces each) artichoke hearts, drained

8 ounces (2½ cups) crumbled Feta cheese

2 tablespoons balsamic vinegar

2 cloves garlic, crushed

½ teaspoon liquid hickory smoke flavoring

2 tablespoons minced fresh basil, or 1½ teaspoons dried

1 tablespoon minced fresh oregano, or 1 teaspoon dried

¾ teaspoon sea salt

½ teaspoon ground black pepper

2 large sweet yellow or Vidalia onions, peeled and left whole

4 medium zucchini

4 large medium-ripe tomatoes

1. Preheat the oven to 450°F for 30 minutes. Brush 1 tablespoon of the oil over the surface of a 16-inch pizza pan and sprinkle with cornmeal, shaking out the excess. (If using pizza stones or tiles, place them in the oven before preheating, and heavily flour a pizza paddle.) Pat, stretch, or roll the dough in the prepared pan or on the paddle and set aside.

2. Preheat a gas or charcoal grill to medium.

3. Thread the artichoke hearts on a skewer and set aside. In a small bowl, mash together the Feta cheese and 1½ tablespoons of the oil. In another bowl, combine the remaining oil with the vinegar, garlic, and hickory flavoring. In a third bowl, combine the parsley, basil, oregano, salt, and pepper.

4. When the grill is ready, lightly brush the rack with oil. Liberally brush the artichoke hearts, onions, zucchini, and tomatoes with the flavored oil, and grill them, turning once and basting frequently, until golden brown (5 to 15 minutes).

5. When cool enough to handle, slice the zucchini and onion into thin rounds, cut the artichoke hearts in half, and cut each tomato into 5 or 6 pieces.

6. Arrange the grilled vegetables over the prepared crust and sprinkle with the herb mixture.

7. Bake the pizza 10 minutes, remove from the oven, and top with the cheese mixture. Continue to bake the pizza until the cheese has melted and the crust is golden (6 to 8 minutes).

White Clam Pizza

Yield: *16-inch thin-crust pizza / 8 slices*

Suggested Crusts: *Combo,*

European Milk, Graham, Semolina,

Simple, Speedy, Sponge,

or Whole Wheat.

(See Chapter 2 for recipes.)

3 tablespoons olive oil

2 tablespoons cornmeal

Dough for 16-inch crust (see
   suggestions)

2 cans (6½ ounces each) chopped
   clams, drained

4 scallions, minced

4 cloves garlic, roasted* and crushed

1 tablespoon grated lemon zest

¾ teaspoon sea salt

½ teaspoon ground white pepper

1½ cups *Sea Cream Sauce* (page 76)

8 ounces ripe Brie cheese

* For garlic-roasting information see
page 90.

*This smooth, creamy pizza sauce is brimming with melted Brie,
chopped clams, scallions, and garlic.*

1. Preheat the oven to 450°F for 30 minutes. Brush 1 table-
    spoon of the oil over the surface of a 16-inch pizza pan
    and sprinkle with cornmeal, shaking out the excess. (If
    using pizza stones or tiles, place them in the oven before
    preheating, and heavily flour a pizza paddle.) Pat, stretch,
    or roll the dough in the prepared pan or on the paddle and
    set aside.

2. In a medium-sized bowl, combine the clams, scallions,
    garlic, lemon zest, salt, pepper, and the remaining oil. Set
    aside.

3. Heat the *Sea Cream Sauce* in a medium-sized saucepan
    over low heat. Remove and discard the hard rind from the
    Brie, then cut it into small cubes. Stir the Brie cubes into
    the sauce and heat until the cheese is almost melted (about
    5 minutes).

4. Spread the sauce over the prepared crust, and top with the
    clam mixture.

5. Bake the pizza until the top is bubbly and the crust is
    golden (13 to 18 minutes). Allow the pizza to stand 5 to
    8 minutes before cutting.

5

Pizzas from the Midwest

On the midwestern section of the United States, Chicago's deep-dish pizza is possibly the most popular. First created during the early 1940s, this pizza, with its dense cornmeal-rich crust, comes heaped with mounds of delectable toppings and is usually eaten with a knife and fork.

A typical Chicago-style pizza has a thick, biscuit-like crust that is patted into a deep round pan. Whole milk mozzarella is then arranged atop the dough to keep the crust from becoming soggy. A layer of meat or other filling goes on next. The pizza is then topped with well-drained crushed tomatoes, a sprinkling of herbs, and a handful of grated cheese.

In this chapter, you will find tasty variations of this basic deep-dish pie—savory, thick-crusted creations that are piled high with delectable toppings. Be sure to try the *Deep and Dark Pizza,* oozing with garlicky black beans and cheese, or the chili-laden *Devil's Brew Pizza.* For a rich, savory meal, sample a down-home rustic *Farmland Pizza* or a hearty *St. Louis Pizza.*

All of the pizzas in this chapter, whether reflective of the Midwest's bustling urban areas or quiet farm towns, have captured the warmth and heartiness of this region. So travel through this chapter and enjoy a memorable taste of the Midwest.

Cauliflower Pie

Yield: *12-inch deep-dish pizza / 6 slices*

Suggested Crusts: *Cheese, Combo,*

European Milk, Herb, Rich Egg,

Rosy, Simple, Speedy, Sponge,

or Whole Wheat.

(See Chapter 2 for recipes.)

3 tablespoons olive oil

2 tablespoons cornmeal

Dough for 12-inch crust (see suggestions)

1 large head cauliflower, separated into flowerets

1 large sweet yellow onion, chopped

3 cloves garlic, crushed

2 tablespoons snipped fresh chives or parsley, or 2 teaspoons dried

¾ teaspoon sea salt

½ teaspoon white pepper

¼ teaspoon crushed dried hot red chiles (or to taste)

7 ounces (2 cups) crumbled Feta cheese

6 ounces (1½ cups) shredded Mozzarella cheese

6 ounces (¾ cup) Ricotta cheese

This deep-dish pie oozes with savory cheeses and nutritious vegetables.

1. Preheat the oven to 450°F for 30 minutes.* Brush 1 tablespoon of the oil over the surface of a 12-inch deep-dish pizza pan and sprinkle with cornmeal, shaking out the excess. Pat the dough in the prepared pan and set aside.

2. Steam the cauliflower until just barely tender. Coarsely chop enough of the flowerets to equal 3 cups. Reserve the remaining cauliflower for another use.

3. Heat the remaining oil in a large skillet over medium-low heat. Add the onion and garlic, and sauté until soft (about 4 minutes).

4. Add the cauliflower to the skillet and continue to cook, stirring frequently, until very soft and golden (about 10 minutes).

5. Transfer the cauliflower mixture to a medium-sized bowl and stir in the chives, salt, pepper, chiles, Feta, Mozzarella, and Ricotta. Mix together well, and spread over the prepared crust.

6. Bake the pizza until the top is bubbly and the crust is golden (18 to 22 minutes).

* If using *Rich Egg Dough*, preheat the oven to 400°F.

Deep and Dark Pizza

In this intense pizza, cumin-scented garlicky black beans are part-nered with oozing cheese and spicy tomatoes.

1. Preheat the oven to 450°F for 30 minutes. Brush 1 table-spoon of the oil over the surface of a 12-inch deep-dish pizza pan and sprinkle with cornmeal, shaking out the excess. Pat the dough in the prepared pan and set aside.

2. Heat 2 tablespoons of the oil in a large skillet over medium-low heat. Add the onion, green bell pepper, and garlic, and sauté, stirring frequently, until tender (5 to 7 minutes). Transfer to a medium-sized bowl and stir in the black beans, red bell pepper, scallions, taco seasoning, and cumin.

3. In another bowl, mix together the plum tomatoes, sun-dried tomatoes, cilantro, salt, pepper, and the remaining oil. Set aside.

4. Spread the *Fresh Tomato Sauce* over the prepared crust. Sprinkle with half of the Mozzarella and half of the Monterey Jack cheese. Top with an even layer of the bean mixture and scatter with the plum tomato mixture.

5. Bake the pizza for 15 minutes. Remove from the oven and scatter the remaining cheese on top.

6. Return the pizza to the oven and continue to bake until the cheese has melted and the crust is golden (5 to 8 minutes).

Yield: *12-inch deep-dish pizza / 6 slices*

Suggested Crust: *Olive Oil*

4 tablespoons olive oil

2 tablespoons cornmeal

Prepared *Olive Oil Dough* (page 48)

1 large sweet yellow onion, chopped

1 large green bell pepper, chopped

3 cloves garlic, crushed

4 cups cooked black beans

1 small red bell pepper, minced

4 scallions or shallots, chopped

1 tablespoon taco seasoning

1½ teaspoon ground cumin

3 ripe plum tomatoes, skinned* and chopped

2 oil-packed sun-dried tomatoes, drained and chopped

2 tablespoons chopped fresh cilantro or parsley, or 2 teaspoons dried

¾ teaspoon sea salt

½ teaspoon ground black pepper

1 cup *Fresh Tomato Sauce* (page 68), *Quick Tomato Sauce* (page 70), or commercial pizza sauce

6 ounces (1½ cups) shredded Mozzarella cheese

6 ounces (1½ cups) shredded Monterey Jack cheese with jalapeños

* For tomato-skinning information, see page 68.

Devil's Brew Pizza

Yield: *12-inch deep-dish pizza / 6 slices*

Suggested Crusts: *Cheese, Combo,*

Garlic, Graham, Greek, Olive Oil,

Rye, or Whole Wheat.

(See Chapter 2 for recipes.)

1 tablespoon olive oil

2 tablespoons cornmeal

Dough for 12-inch crust (see
    suggestions)

12 ounces (4 cups) shredded sharp
    Cheddar cheese

CHILI

2 tablespoons olive oil

2 pounds lean beef, cut into $\frac{1}{2}$-inch
    cubes

2 medium-sized sweet yellow onions,
    chopped

$\frac{1}{2}$ teaspoon crushed dried hot red
    chiles (or to taste)

2 tablespoons ground cumin

1 tablespoon chili powder

2 cloves garlic, crushed

1 teaspoon sea salt

$\frac{1}{4}$ teaspoon ground black pepper

2 cups beef broth

1 cup flat beer

1 large ripe tomato, skinned* and
    chopped

1 tablespoon fresh oregano, chopped,
    or 1 teaspoon dried

2 teaspoons cider vinegar

1 tablespoon masa harina or cornmeal

* For tomato-skinning information, see
page 68.

This pizza is topped with a distinguished chili that develops more character if it sits a day before it is used. Be sure to serve this four-alarm pizza with icy mugs of beer to quench the fire.

1. To make the chili, heat the oil in a large saucepan over medium heat. Add the beef and sauté, turning frequently, until cooked (about 8 minutes). Stir in the onions, chiles, cumin, chili powder, garlic, salt, and pepper. Add the beef broth and bring to a boil. Reduce the heat to low and simmer, uncovered, until the beef is almost tender (1 to $1\frac{1}{2}$ hours).

2. To the simmering beef, add $\frac{1}{2}$ cup of the beer, the tomato, oregano, and vinegar. Bring to a boil, then reduce the heat to low. Simmer uncovered for 30 minutes, stirring frequently.

3. In a small cup, stir the masa harina into the remaining beer, then add it to the chili. Simmer 15 minutes more until the meat is very tender and the sauce has thickened.**

4. When ready to assemble the pizza, preheat the oven to 450°F for 30 minutes. Brush the oil over the surface of a 12-inch deep-dish pizza pan and sprinkle with cornmeal, shaking out the excess. Pat the dough in the prepared pan and set aside.

5. Scatter 2 cups of the Cheddar cheese over the prepared crust, top with the chili, and sprinkle with the remaining Cheddar.

6. Bake the pizza until the cheese has melted and the crust is golden (15 to 22 minutes).

** The chili must have the right consistency (moist but not runny) to top the pizza. If the chili is too thick, add 1 or 2 tablespoons of water, broth, or beer. If the chili is too thin, continue to cook it, uncovered, until it thickens. Or dissolve 1 or 2 tablespoons of masa harina in a little water and add it to the chili.

Farmland Pizza

For this rustic pizza, I mix a savory blend of spices with ground chicken and pair it with oven-baked eggplant and creamy mozzarella cheese.

1. Place the eggplant in a colander and sprinkle with salt. Let drain for 30 minutes, rinse well, and pat dry with paper towels. Use 2 tablespoons of the oil to brush both sides of the eggplant slices, and arrange them in a single layer on a baking sheet.

2. Preheat the oven to 450°F for 30 minutes. Brush 1 tablespoon of the oil over the surface of a 12-inch deep-dish pizza pan and sprinkle with cornmeal, shaking out the excess. Pat the dough in the prepared pan and set aside.

3. While the oven is heating, place the eggplant slices in the oven. Bake, turning once, until the slices are soft and turning golden (about 15 minutes). Remove from the oven and set aside.

4. Heat the remaining olive oil in a large skillet over medium heat. Add the chicken, scallions, and garlic, and sauté, stirring, until browned. Pour off any oil that accumulates, then transfer the chicken to a large bowl. Stir in the parsley, rosemary, thyme, sage, pepper, and the remaining teaspoon of sea salt. Combine well and set aside.

5. Spread the *Fresh Tomato Sauce* over the prepared crust and top with the eggplant slices. Mix together the Mozzarella and chicken mixture, then spread it evenly over the eggplant.

6. Bake the pizza until the cheese has melted and the crust is golden (15 to 22 minutes).

Yield: *12-inch deep-dish pizza / 6 slices*

Suggested Crusts: *California, Cheese, Combo, Greek Garlic, Herb, Semolina, Simple, Speedy, or Sponge.*

(See Chapter 2 for recipes.)

1 large eggplant, peeled and cut into ¼-inch slices

2 tablespoons plus 1 teaspoon sea salt

4 tablespoons olive oil

2 tablespoons cornmeal

Dough for 12-inch crust (see suggestions)

1 pound ground chicken

8 scallions, minced

2 cloves garlic, crushed

3 tablespoons chopped fresh parsley, or 3 teaspoons dried

1 tablespoon snipped fresh rosemary, or 1 teaspoon dried

2 teaspoons snipped fresh thyme, or ¾ teaspoon dried

1½ tablespoons chopped fresh sage, or 1½ teaspoons dried

½ teaspoon ground black pepper

1 cup *Fresh Tomato Sauce* (page 68), *Quick Tomato Sauce* (page 70), or commercial pizza sauce

8 ounces (2 cups) shredded Mozzarella cheese

Hundreds of Onions Pizza

Yield: *12-inch deep-dish pizza / 6 slices*

Suggested Crusts: *Basil-Rosemary,*

California, Cheese, Combo, Herb,

Olive Oil, Rosy, Simple, Speedy,

Sponge, or Whole Wheat.

(See Chapter 2 for recipes.)

¼ cup plus 1 tablespoon olive oil

2 tablespoons cornmeal

Dough for 12-inch crust (see
   suggestions)

¼ cup dry white wine

2½ pounds onions (any combination
   of yellow, red, Vidalia, leeks,
   scallions, shallots, chives), thinly
   sliced

3 cloves garlic, crushed

4 large ripe tomatoes, skinned* and
   coarsely chopped

¼ cup chopped fresh basil, or
   1⅓ tablespoons dried

1 tablespoon snipped fresh rosemary,
   or 1 teaspoon dried

2 teaspoons chopped fresh oregano,
   or ¾ teaspoon dried

¾ teaspoon sea salt

½ teaspoon ground black pepper

1 cup sliced Kalamata or other
   imported black olives

4 ounces (1 cup) grated Parmesan,
   Grana Padano, or
   Pecorino-Romano cheese (optional)

* For tomato-skinning information, see
page 68.

Hundreds of onions may be an exaggeration, but the idea of combining many types of onions for a luscious pizza topping is a terrific one.

1. Preheat the oven to 450°F for 30 minutes. Brush 1 tablespoon of the oil over the surface of a 12-inch deep-dish pizza pan and sprinkle with cornmeal, shaking out the excess. Pat the dough in the prepared pan and set aside.

2. Heat the remaining oil and the wine in a large skillet over medium-low heat. Toss in the onions and garlic, and combine well. Cover the skillet, reduce the heat to low, and cook the onions, stirring occasionally, until golden brown (about 30 minutes).

3. Add the tomatoes, basil, rosemary, oregano, salt, and pepper to the cooked onions. Stir together and bring to a simmer. Reduce the heat to low, cover, and cook for 10 minutes. Uncover and continue to cook, stirring frequently, until most of the liquid has evaporated (about 10 minutes).

4. Spread the onion-tomato mixture evenly over the prepared crust, scatter the olives on top, and sprinkle with the grated cheese (if using).

5. Bake the pizza until the crust is golden (18 to 22 minutes).

Pizza Blues

There are many types of blue cheese. For this cauliflower pizza, be sure to use a well-aged blue cheese, such as Bleu de Bresse, Danablue, Maytag Blue, Norwegian Blue, Roquefort, or Saga Blue.

Yield: *12-inch deep-dish pizza / 6 slices*

Suggested Crusts: *Combo, Semolina, Simple, Speedy, Sponge, or Whole Wheat.*

(See Chapter 2 for recipes.)

4 tablespoons olive oil

2 tablespoons cornmeal

Dough for 12-inch crust (see suggestions)

1 small head cauliflower, separated into flowerets

15 ounces (2 cups) Ricotta cheese

6 ounces (1½ cups) crumbled blue cheese

4 scallions, chopped

2 tablespoons snipped fresh chives or parsley, or 2 teaspoons dried

¾ teaspoon sea salt

½ teaspoon white pepper

8 ounces (2 cups) shredded Mozzarella cheese

1. Preheat the oven to 450°F for 30 minutes. Brush 1 tablespoon of the oil over the surface of a 12-inch deep-dish pizza pan and sprinkle with cornmeal, shaking out the excess. Pat the dough in the prepared pan and set aside.

2. Steam the cauliflower until just barely tender. When cool enough to handle, cut each floweret into 3 or 4 thin slices, and set aside.

3. Heat the remaining oil in a large skillet over medium heat. Add the cauliflower and sauté, stirring frequently, until it begins to get crisp and turn brown (about 10 minutes).

4. While the cauliflower is sautéing, stir together the Ricotta and blue cheese in a medium-sized bowl.

5. Spread the cheese mixture on the prepared crust, top with cauliflower, and scatter with scallions, chives, salt, and pepper.

6. Bake the pizza for 10 minutes. Remove from the oven and top with Mozzarella cheese.

7. Return the pizza to the oven and continue to bake until the cheese has melted and the crust is golden (8 to 12 minutes).

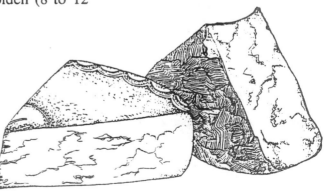

Rustic Pizza

Yield: _12-inch deep-dish pizza / 6 slices_

Suggested Crusts: _Combo, Graham, Rye, Semolina, Simple, Speedy, Sponge, or Whole Wheat._

(See Chapter 2 for recipes.)

4 tablespoons olive oil

2 tablespoons cornmeal

Dough for 12-inch crust (see suggestions)

4 large ripe tomatoes, skinned* and chopped

4 scallions or shallots, chopped

2 cloves garlic, crushed

1 tablespoon chopped fresh basil, or 1 teaspoon dried

3/4 teaspoon sea salt

1/2 teaspoon ground black pepper

2 ounces (1/2 cup) shredded Mozzarella cheese

1 ounce (1/4 cup) grated Parmesan, Asiago, or Pecorino-Romano cheese

8 ounces thinly sliced pepperoni

2 large roasted red or yellow bell peppers,** cut into thin strips

1/2 cup sliced Kalamata or other imported black olives

* For tomato-skinning information, see page 68.
** For pepper-roasting information, see page 75.

Spicy pepperoni is paired with roasted red peppers, fresh tomatoes, black olives, and a scattering of melted cheese in this robust pizza.

1. Preheat the oven to 450°F for 30 minutes. Brush 1 tablespoon of the oil over the surface of a 12-inch deep-dish pizza pan and sprinkle with cornmeal, shaking out the excess. Pat the dough in the prepared pan and set aside.

2. In a medium-sized bowl, combine the tomatoes with the remaining oil, the scallions, garlic, basil, salt, and black pepper, and set aside. In another bowl, combine the Mozzarella and grated cheese.

3. Spread the tomato mixture over the prepared crust and top with pepperoni. Arrange the roasted peppers on top, and scatter with olives.

4. Bake the pizza for 10 minutes, remove from the oven, and sprinkle with the cheese mixture.

5. Return the pizza to the oven and continue to bake until the cheese has melted and the crust is golden (8 to 12 minutes).

Scalloped Pizza

Layers of thinly sliced potatoes and creamy cheese make this pizza a hearty, flavorful meal.

1. Preheat the oven to 450°F for 30 minutes. Brush 1 tablespoon of the oil over the surface of a 12-inch deep-dish pizza pan and sprinkle with cornmeal, shaking out the excess. Pat the dough in the prepared pan and set aside.

2. Bring a large shallow pan of water to a boil. Peel and thinly slice the potatoes, add them to the boiling water, and cook until almost tender (6 to 8 minutes). With a slotted spoon, carefully remove the potato slices to a colander and cool.

3. While the potatoes are cooking, heat 3 tablespoons of the oil in a skillet over medium-low heat. Add the onion and garlic, and sauté, stirring frequently, until soft (about 8 minutes). Set aside.

4. Cut the tomatoes into thin rounds. Place on paper towels to drain.

5. In a small bowl, combine the bread crumbs with ½ cup of the Jarlsberg cheese and set aside. In another bowl, combine the remaining Jarlsberg with the Mozzarella cheese. In a third bowl, combine the thyme, rosemary, salt, and pepper.

6. Arrange half of the potato slices on the prepared crust, sprinkle with half of the herb mixture, and top with half of the onions. Scatter with half of the cheese mixture. Repeat the layering. Top with tomato slices, sprinkle with bread crumb mixture, and drizzle with the remaining oil.

7. Bake the pizza until the crust is golden (18 to 22 minutes).

Yield: *12-inch deep-dish pizza / 6 slices*

Suggested Crusts: *Basil-Rosemary, California, Cheese, Combo, Greek Garlic, Herb, Simple, Speedy, or Sponge.*

(See Chapter 2 for recipes.)

8 tablespoons olive oil

2 tablespoons cornmeal

Dough for 12-inch crust (see suggestions)

5 large russet potatoes

1 large sweet yellow onion, minced

4 scallions (including 2 inches of green tops), minced

2 cloves garlic, crushed

2 large medium-ripe tomatoes, skinned*

½ cup toasted bread crumbs

8 ounces (2¾ cups) shredded Jarlsberg cheese

8 ounces (2 cups) shredded Mozzarella cheese

1 tablespoon snipped fresh thyme, or 1 teaspoon dried

2 teaspoons snipped fresh rosemary, or ¾ teaspoon dried

¾ teaspoon sea salt (or to taste)

½ teaspoon ground black pepper

* For tomato-skinning information, see page 68.

St. Louis Pizza

Yield: *12-inch deep-dish pizza / 6 slices*

Suggested Crusts: *California, Cheese, Combo, Graham, Greek Garlic, Rosy, Rye, Semolina, Simple, Speedy, Sponge, or Whole Wheat.*

(See Chapter 2 for recipes.)

3 tablespoons olive oil

2 tablespoons cornmeal

Dough for 12-inch crust (see suggestions)

1 large sweet yellow or Vidalia onion, chopped

1 large red bell pepper, chopped

2 cloves garlic, crushed

1 pound lean ground beef

1¼ cups *Fresh Tomato Sauce* (page 68), *Quick Tomato Sauce* (page 70), or commercial pizza sauce

1 teaspoon sea salt

1 teaspoon ground black pepper

¼ teaspoon crushed dried hot red chiles (or to taste)

8 ounces (2 cups) crumbled Stilton cheese or full-bodied blue

8 ounces (1 cup) soft cream cheese or farmer cheese

¼ cup minced fresh chives, or 1½ tablespoons dried

I created this hearty pizza one cold, snowy, blustery day in St. Louis. To me, it signifies everything that a warm, filling comfort dish should be.

1. Preheat the oven to 450°F for 30 minutes. Brush 1 tablespoon of the oil over the surface of a 12-inch deep-dish pizza pan and sprinkle with cornmeal, shaking out the excess. Pat the dough in the prepared pan and set aside.

2. Heat the remaining oil in a large skillet over medium-low heat. Add the onion, bell pepper, and garlic, and sauté, stirring frequently, until soft (about 8 minutes). Transfer to a large bowl and set aside.

3. Place the ground beef in the skillet and sauté, stirring frequently, until brown. Pour off the oil as it accumulates. Drain the cooked beef well and add it to the onion mixture along with ¼ cup of the *Fresh Tomato Sauce*, the salt, pepper, and chiles. Stir the ingredients together well.

4. In another bowl, mash together the Stilton and cream cheese, and add the chives.

5. Spread the remaining *Fresh Tomato Sauce* over the prepared crust, and top with the beef. Drop spoonfuls of the cheese evenly on top.

6. Bake the pizza until the crust is golden (18 to 22 minutes).

Sundown Pizza

I often enjoy this colorful pizza on warm evenings as I sit on my terrace, sip a cool refreshing drink, and watch the evening sky turn red and gold.

Yield: *12-inch deep-dish pizza / 6 slices*

Suggested Crusts: *European Milk, Rich Egg, Semolina, Simple, Speedy, Sponge, or Whole Wheat.*

(See Chapter 2 for recipes.)

5 tablespoons olive oil

2 tablespoons cornmeal

Dough for 12-inch crust (see suggestions)

1 large sweet yellow or Vidalia onion, thinly sliced

1 large red bell pepper, thinly sliced

1 cup corn kernels

1 cup cooked black beans

2 cloves garlic, crushed

$\frac{1}{4}$ cup minced fresh chives, or 1$\frac{1}{2}$ tablespoons dried

$\frac{1}{4}$ cup vermouth or dry white wine

1 teaspoon ground black pepper

$\frac{1}{4}$ teaspoon crushed dried hot red chiles (or to taste)

6 ounces (2 cups) crumbled Feta cheese

8 ounces (2 cups) shredded Mozzarella cheese

1. Preheat the oven to 450°F for 30 minutes.* Brush 1 tablespoon of the oil over the surface of a 12-inch deep-dish pizza pan and sprinkle with cornmeal, shaking out the excess. Pat the dough in the prepared pan and set aside.

2. Heat 2 tablespoons of the oil in a large skillet over medium-low heat. Add the onions and bell pepper, and sauté, stirring frequently, until soft (about 8 minutes).

3. In another skillet, mix together the corn, black beans, garlic, chives, vermouth, black pepper, and chiles. Bring to a low boil, then reduce the heat to low and simmer, stirring frequently, until the liquid evaporates (about 5 minutes). Remove from the heat and toss in the Feta cheese, mixing well. Set aside.

4. Scatter the Mozzarella cheese over the prepared crust, and top with the onion-pepper mixture. Add a layer of the corn-bean mixture, and drizzle with the remaining oil.

5. Bake the pizza until the crust is golden (18 to 22 minutes).

* If using *Rich Egg Dough*, preheat the oven to 400°F.

6

West Coast Creations

When nouvelle cuisine—a contemporary style of French cooking characterized by light, healthy ingredients—hit California, it gave birth to the West Coast's version of pizza. Lighter and more sophisticated than its eastern counterparts, California-style pizza is distinguished by its light, chewy crusts and intriguing topping combinations. Reflecting California's characteristic approach to healthy eating, West Coast pizzas are often topped with nontraditional ingredients that have unusual flavors or textures. Goat cheese, tofu, sun-dried tomatoes, salmon, capers, chiles, or alfalfa sprouts commonly crown a thin-crusted California-style pie.

This chapter offers a variety of delicious, though somewhat unusual pizzas. Feeling adventurous? Don't pass up the opportunity to try the lively taste sensations of a *White Bean Pesto Pizza* or a *Goat Cheese and Spinach Pizza*. If you have a passion for mushrooms, the *Wild Mushroom Pizza* is a perfect choice. In the mood for something different? Try the rich, smoky goodness of a *Roasted Feta Pizza*. The choices go on and on.

Enjoy all of the pizza creations in this chapter. You will find that each and every one has captured the light-hearted spirit of the West Coast.

Baby Calzones

Yield: 8 small calzones

Suggested Crusts: California, Cheese, Combo, European Milk, Herb, Rich Egg, Rosy, Semolina, Simple, Speedy, Sponge, or Whole Wheat. (See Chapter 2 for recipes.)

6 tablespoons olive oil

2 tablespoons cornmeal

Dough for crust (see suggestions)

3 cups (about 12 small) diced new potatoes

5 shallots or scallions, minced

2 cloves garlic, minced

8 ounces ripe Camembert or Brie cheese

4 ounces (1 cup) shredded Mozzarella cheese

2 tablespoons snipped fresh chives or parsley, or 2 teaspoons dried

¾ teaspoon sea salt

½ teaspoon white pepper

1 egg yolk

These exquisite packages are bursting with tiny new potatoes, fragrant shallots, and the melting goodness of Camembert cheese.

1. Preheat the oven to 450°F for 30 minutes.* Brush 1 tablespoon of the oil over the surface of a large baking sheet, and sprinkle with cornmeal, shaking out the excess. (If using pizza stones or tiles, place them in the oven before preheating, and heavily flour a pizza paddle.)

2. On a floured surface, divide the dough into 8 equal pieces. With a floured rolling pin, roll each piece into a 4-inch circle and set aside.

3. Heat 4 tablespoons of the remaining oil in a large skillet over medium-low heat. Add the potatoes, shallots, and garlic, and reduce the heat to low. Cook the vegetables, stirring frequently, until the potatoes are tender and golden (8 to 10 minutes).

4. After cutting away any hard rind, cube the Camembert and place in a medium-sized bowl. Add the Mozzarella, chives, salt, pepper, and potato mixture, and blend well.

5. In a small bowl, beat together the egg yolk and the remaining oil. Set aside.

6. Place an equal amount of the cheese-potato mixture on half of each circle of dough, leaving a ½-inch border.

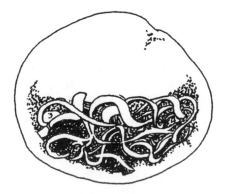

7. Fold each circle in half and press the edges together.

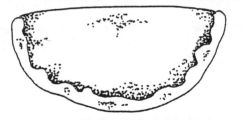

8. Seal the edges with the tines of a floured fork.

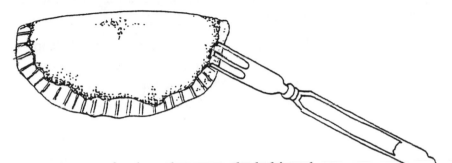

9. With a spatula, transfer the calzones to the baking sheet or pizza paddle. Brush the tops with the beaten egg mixture.

10. Bake the calzones until golden brown (10 to 14 minutes).

* If using *Rich Egg Dough*, preheat the oven to 400°F, and bake the calzones for 14–18 minutes.

Black and White Pizza

Yield: *16-inch thin-crust pizza / 8 slices*

Suggested Crusts: *California,*

Combo, Simple, Speedy, Sponge,

or Whole Wheat.

(See Chapter 2 for recipes.)

3 tablespoons olive oil

2 tablespoons cornmeal

Dough for 16-inch crust (see suggestions)

2 cups cooked black beans

2 medium-sized ripe tomatoes, skinned* and chopped

2 cloves garlic, crushed

3 scallions, minced

1½ tablespoons minced fresh basil, or 1½ teaspoons dried

1 tablespoon minced fresh oregano, or 1 teaspoon dried

1 teaspoon sea salt

½ teaspoon ground black pepper

¼ teaspoon white pepper

15 ounces (2 cups) Ricotta cheese

2 ounces (½ cup) grated Parmesan, Pecorino-Romano, or Asiago cheese

6 ounces (1 cup) diced Provolone cheese

* For tomato-skinning information, see page 68.

The colors in this wonderful pie come from ripe red tomatoes, fresh green herbs, and plump black beans, all nestled beneath a blanket of creamy white cheese.

1. Preheat the oven to 450°F for 30 minutes. Brush 1 tablespoon of the oil over the surface of a 16-inch pizza pan and sprinkle with cornmeal, shaking out the excess. (If using pizza stones or tiles, place them in the oven before preheating, and heavily flour a pizza paddle.) Pat, stretch, or roll the dough in the prepared pan or on the paddle and set aside.

2. In a medium-sized bowl, combine 1 tablespoon of the oil, the black beans, tomatoes, garlic, scallions, basil, oregano, salt, and black pepper. Mix well. In another bowl, mix together the Ricotta cheese, grated cheese, and white pepper. Set aside.

3. Brush the prepared crust with the remaining oil and cover with an even layer of the Ricotta mixture. Top with the bean mixture.

4. Bake the pizza for 12 minutes, remove from the oven, and top with the Provolone cheese.

5. Return the pizza to the oven and continue to bake until the cheese has melted and the crust is golden (6 to 8 minutes).

Double-Trouble Tofu Pizza

The exciting, very sharp English Cheddar called for in this recipe is riddled with minced onions and chives. If you cannot find it, a good English Stilton or a sharp aged Cheddar are excellent substitutes.

1. Preheat the oven to 450°F for 30 minutes. Brush 1 tablespoon of the oil over the surface of an 8-inch deep-dish pizza pan and sprinkle with cornmeal, shaking out the excess.

2. Roll out or stretch ⅓ of the dough to a 9-inch circle and set aside (this will be the top crust). Roll out or stretch the remaining dough to a 13-inch circle. Fit the larger circle of dough into the prepared pan, allowing the excess to hang over the sides. Set aside.

3. Heat 2 tablespoons of the oil in a large skillet over medium-low heat. Add the onion and garlic, and sauté until soft (3 to 5 minutes).

4. Place the flour in a shallow dish. Coat the tofu with the flour and set aside.

5. Push the sautéed vegetables to one side of the skillet and add the remaining oil. Increase the heat to medium. When the oil is hot, add the tofu in a single layer, and sauté until golden brown and crisp on both sides (5 minutes per side).

6. Scatter half of the Cheddar in the bottom of the prepared crust, and top with the tofu and onions.

Yield: *8-inch double-crust pizza / 4 wedges*

Suggested Crusts: *Basil-Rosemary,*

California, Combo, Herb, Semolina,

Simple, Speedy, or Whole Wheat.

(See Chapter 2 for recipes.)

5 tablespoons olive oil

2 tablespoons cornmeal

Dough for 8-inch double crust (see suggestions)

1 large sweet yellow onion, thinly sliced

3 cloves garlic, crushed

¼ cup whole wheat flour

1 pound extra firm tofu, drained and cut into ¼-inch slices

8 ounces (2¾ cups) shredded English Cheddar with onions and chives

1 large egg, beaten

7. Toss the remaining cheese over the tofu, and top with the reserved circle of dough.

8. Fold the hanging edges of dough onto itself and crimp. Brush the top with egg.

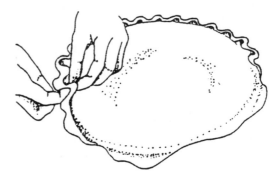

9. Bake the pie until the top is golden (18 to 22 minutes).

10. Allow the pie to sit for 15 minutes before cutting.

Goat Cheese and Spinach Pizza

Although I believe there are few cheeses more wonderful than soft goat cheese, I do realize that it is an acquired taste. In this first-class pizza, the flavor of goat cheese is just noticeable.

1. Preheat the oven to 450°F for 30 minutes. Brush 1 tablespoon of the oil over the surface of a 16-inch pizza pan and sprinkle with cornmeal, shaking out the excess. (If using pizza stones or tiles, place them in the oven before preheating, and heavily flour a pizza paddle.) Pat, stretch, or roll the dough in the prepared pan or on the paddle and set aside.

2. Heat the remaining oil in a large skillet over medium-low heat. Add the onion and garlic, and sauté until soft (about 3 minutes).

3. Add the spinach to the sautéed onions and mix well. Heat for 2 minutes, then transfer to a medium-sized bowl. Stir in the farmer cheese, chives, salt, and pepper, combining well.

4. Scatter the Mozzarella over the prepared crust and top with the spinach mixture.

5. Bake the pizza for 10 minutes, remove from the oven, and top with the Montrachet cheese.

6. Return the pizza to the oven and continue to bake until the cheese has melted and the crust is golden (4 to 8 minutes).

Yield: *16-inch thin-crust pizza / 8 slices*

Suggested Crusts: *Combo, Hard Pretzel, Semolina, Simple, Speedy, Sponge, or Whole Wheat.*

(See Chapter 2 for recipes.)

3 tablespoons olive oil

2 tablespoons cornmeal

Dough for 16-inch crust (see suggestions)

1 large sweet yellow onion, minced

4 cloves garlic, crushed

2 packages (10 ounces each) frozen chopped spinach, thawed and squeezed dry

8 ounces (1 cup) soft farmer cheese or cream cheese

¼ cup minced fresh chives, or 1½ tablespoons dried

¾ teaspoon sea salt

½ teaspoon ground black pepper

8 ounces (2 cups) shredded Mozzarella cheese

5 ounces Montrachet or other soft imported goat cheese, crumbled

Pacific Coast Pizza

Yield: *16-inch thin-crust pizza / 8 slices*

Suggested Crusts: *Cheese, Combo,*

European Milk, Greek Garlic, Olive Oil,

Rich Egg, Simple, Speedy, or Sponge.

(See Chapter 2 for recipes.)

5 tablespoons olive oil

2 tablespoons cornmeal

Dough for 16-inch crust (see
    suggestions)

2 large red onions, thinly sliced

2 cloves garlic, minced

2 poblano or 4 Anaheim chile
    peppers, seeded and sliced

1 teaspoon sea salt

½ teaspoon ground black pepper

4 ounces (1 cup) shredded Monterey
    Jack cheese

8 ounces ripe Brie cheese

⅔ cup sliced black or green olives

4 oil-packed sun-dried tomatoes,
    slivered

Sun-dried tomatoes add an interesting touch to this fresh-tasting pizza pie.

1. Preheat the oven to 450°F for 30 minutes.* Brush 1 tablespoon of the oil over the surface of a 16-inch pizza pan and sprinkle with cornmeal, shaking out the excess. (If using pizza stones or tiles, place them in the oven before preheating, and heavily flour a pizza paddle.) Pat, stretch, or roll the dough in the prepared pan or on the paddle and set aside.

2. Heat 2 tablespoons of the oil in a large skillet over medium-low heat. Add the onions, garlic, and chiles, and sauté until soft (about 10 minutes). Stir in the salt and black pepper.

3. After removing and discarding any hard rind from the Brie, cube it and set aside.

4. Brush the remaining oil over the prepared crust, and top with the onion mixture and Monterey Jack cheese. Scatter with the Brie and olives, and arrange the sun-dried tomatoes on top.

5. Bake the pizza until the cheese has melted and the crust is golden (13 to 18 minutes).

* If using *Rich Egg Dough*, preheat the oven to 400°F.

Roasted Feta Pizza

Did you know that you can roast firm, relatively dry cheeses, such as Feta and Kasseri, on an outdoor grill? The resulting smoky flavor is really quite special.

1. Preheat the oven to 450°F for 30 minutes. Brush 1 tablespoon of the oil over the surface of a 16-inch pizza pan and sprinkle with cornmeal, shaking out the excess. (If using pizza stones or tiles, place them in the oven before preheating, and heavily flour a pizza paddle.) Pat, stretch, or roll the dough in the prepared pan or on the paddle and set aside.

2. Preheat a gas or charcoal grill to medium. Place a mesh grill tray** on the grates.

3. When the grill is ready, lightly brush the grill tray with oil. Liberally brush the tomatoes and Feta slices with oil, and grill them, basting frequently, until the Feta is golden brown and the tomatoes begin to soften (5 to 7 minutes).

4. Crumble the Feta, and coarsely chop the tomatoes.

5. Brush any remaining oil over the prepared crust and top with the tomatoes. Add the Feta, and sprinkle with the garlic, basil, and black pepper.

6. Bake the pizza until the crust is golden (13 to 18 minutes).

** Because small foods and foods that crumble easily (such as the Feta cheese called for in this recipe) can fall through a standard grill rack, a mesh grill tray is recommended. These trays, which fit right on top of the grates, are available wherever grills are sold.

Yield: *16-inch thin-crust pizza / 8 slices*

Suggested Crusts: *Combo, European Milk, Herb, Rich Egg, Semolina, Simple, Speedy, Sponge, or Whole Wheat.*

(See Chapter 2 for recipes.)

⅓ cup olive oil

2 tablespoons cornmeal

Dough for 16-inch crust (see suggestions)

4 large ripe tomatoes

1 pound Feta cheese, cut into 1½-inch-thick slices

4 cloves garlic, roasted* and crushed

2 tablespoons chopped fresh basil, or 2 teaspoons dried

½ teaspoon ground black pepper

* For garlic-roasting information, see page 90.

Seaside Clam Pizza

Yield: *16-inch thin-crust pizza / 8 slices*

Suggested Crusts: *California,*

Cheese, Combo, Greek Garlic,

Rosy, Semolina, Simple, Speedy,

Sponge, or Whole Wheat.

(See Chapter 2 for recipes.)

4 tablespoons olive oil

2 tablespoons cornmeal

Dough for 16-inch crust (see suggestions)

3 cans (6½ ounces each) chopped clams, drained

6 cloves garlic, roasted* and crushed

2 tablespoons minced fresh parsley, or 2 teaspoons dried

1½ tablespoons minced fresh basil, or 1½ teaspoons dried

1 tablespoon minced fresh oregano, or 1 teaspoon dried

¾ teaspoon sea salt

½ teaspoon ground black pepper

3 large ripe tomatoes, skinned** and cubed

4 small hot cherry peppers (or to taste), roasted*** and slivered

4 ounces (1 cup) shredded Mozzarella cheese

* For garlic-roasting information, see page 90.
** For tomato-skinning information, see page 68.
*** For pepper-roasting information, see page 75.

You can almost feel the warm Gulf breezes as you enjoy this garlicky clam pizza.

1. Preheat the oven to 450°F for 30 minutes. Brush 1 tablespoon of the oil over the surface of a 16-inch pizza pan and sprinkle with cornmeal, shaking out the excess. (If using pizza stones or tiles, place them in the oven before preheating, and heavily flour a pizza paddle.) Pat, stretch, or roll the dough in the prepared pan or on the paddle and set aside.

2. Place the clams, garlic, parsley, basil, oregano, salt, and black pepper in a medium-sized bowl. Add the remaining oil and stir well.

3. Scatter the tomatoes over the prepared crust and top with the clam mixture. Arrange the hot peppers on top.

4. Bake the pizza for 10 minutes, remove from the oven, and scatter the Mozzarella on top.

5. Return the pizza to the oven and continue to bake until the cheese has melted and the crust is golden (4 to 8 minutes).

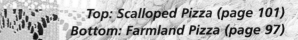

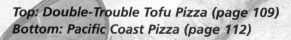

Top: Double-Trouble Tofu Pizza (page 109)
Bottom: Pacific Coast Pizza (page 112)

Tofu or Not Tofu Pizza

Before you declare your aversion to tofu, try this pizza. The protein-rich, nutritious tofu is almost undetectable.

1. Preheat the oven to 450°F for 30 minutes.* Brush the oil over the surface of a 16-inch pizza pan and sprinkle with cornmeal, shaking out the excess. (If using pizza stones or tiles, place them in the oven before preheating, and heavily flour a pizza paddle.) Pat, stretch, or roll the dough in the prepared pan or on the paddle and set aside.

2. In a medium-sized bowl, whisk together the sour cream, egg, garlic, thyme, pepper, and salt until well combined. Stirring gently, add the Montrachet and tofu.

3. Spread the *Onion Sauce* over the prepared crust and top with the tofu mixture. Scatter the scallions on top.

4. Bake the pizza until the crust is golden (15 to 20 minutes).

* If using *Rich Egg Dough*, preheat the oven to 400°F.

Yield: *16-inch thin-crust pizza / 8 slices*

Suggested Crusts: *Cheese, Combo, European Milk, Greek Garlic, Rich Egg, Simple, Speedy, or Whole Wheat.*

(See Chapter 2 for recipes.)

1 tablespoon olive oil

2 tablespoons cornmeal

Dough for 16-inch crust (see suggestions)

½ cup sour cream

1 large egg, beaten

2 cloves garlic, crushed

1 tablespoon snipped fresh thyme, or 1 teaspoon dried

½ teaspoon white pepper

½ teaspoon sea salt

11 ounces Montrachet or other soft mild goat cheese, crumbled

10 ounces firm tofu, drained and cut into small cubes

1 cup *Onion Sauce* (page 78)

4 scallions or shallots, minced

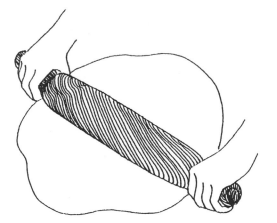

White Bean Pesto Pizza

Yield: *16-inch thin-crust pizza / 8 slices*

Suggested Crusts: *Combo,*

European Milk, Rich Egg, Semolina,

Simple, Speedy, or Whole Wheat.

(See Chapter 2 for recipes.)

4 tablespoons olive oil

2 tablespoons cornmeal

Dough for 16-inch crust (see
  suggestions)

5 scallions or shallots, minced

2 cloves garlic, crushed

2 cups cooked navy or other small
  white beans

½ teaspoon sea salt

½ teaspoon white pepper

1 cup *Pizza Pesto* (page 71), or
  commercial pesto

4 ounces (1 cup) grated Parmesan,
  Asiago, or Pecorino-Romano cheese

A simple pesto pizza is a wonderful treat. Adding small white beans, onions, and garlic turns it into a protein-rich first-class pizza oozing with goodness in every bite.

1. Preheat the oven to 450°F for 30 minutes.* Brush 1 tablespoon of the oil over the surface of a 16-inch pizza pan and sprinkle with cornmeal, shaking out the excess. (If using pizza stones or tiles, place them in the oven before preheating, and heavily flour a pizza paddle.) Pat, stretch, or roll the dough in the prepared pan or on the paddle and set aside.

2. Heat the remaining oil in a small skillet over medium-low heat. Add the scallions and garlic, and sauté until soft (about 4 minutes). Transfer to a medium-sized bowl, and stir in the beans, salt, and pepper.

3. Spread the *Pizza Pesto* over the prepared crust and top with the bean mixture.

4. Bake the pizza for 10 minutes, remove from the oven, and sprinkle with the grated cheese.

5. Return the pizza to the oven and continue to bake until the crust is golden (4 to 8 minutes).

* If using *Rich Egg Dough*, preheat the oven to 400°F.

Wild Mushroom Pizza

Although easily prepared on top of the stove, this mushroom medley gains an incomparable flavor when grilled. Use whatever assortment of mushrooms you can find. Portabella, Crimini, oyster, and shiitake mushrooms are excellent choices.

Yield: *16-inch thin-crust pizza / 8 slices*

Suggested Crusts: *Basil-Rosemary, California, Cheese, Combo, Greek Garlic, Herb, Semolina, Simple, Speedy, Sponge, or Whole Wheat.*

(See Chapter 2 for recipes.)

1 tablespoon olive oil

2 tablespoons cornmeal

Dough for 16-inch crust (see suggestions)

1½ pounds white domestic mushrooms, wiped clean

1 pound wild mushrooms, wiped clean

4 shallots, minced

4 ounces (1 cup) grated Parmesan, Pecorino-Romano, or Asiago cheese

MARINADE

¼ cup olive oil

¼ Cognac or good-quality brandy

¾ teaspoon sea salt

½ teaspoon ground black pepper

½ teaspoon sage

¼ teaspoon nutmeg

1. Preheat the oven to 450°F for 30 minutes. Brush 1 tablespoon of the oil over the surface of a 16-inch pizza pan and sprinkle with cornmeal, shaking out the excess. (If using pizza stones or tiles, place them in the oven before preheating, and heavily flour a pizza paddle.) Pat, stretch, or roll the dough in the prepared pan or on the paddle and set aside.

2. Preheat a gas or charcoal grill to medium. Place a mesh grill tray* on the grates.

3. In a medium-sized bowl, whisk together the marinade ingredients. Add all of the mushrooms to the marinade and combine gently.

4. When the grill is ready, lightly brush the grill tray with oil. Spread the mushrooms over the tray and cook them, basting frequently with the marinade, until brown on all sides (8 to 10 minutes). When the mushrooms are cool enough to handle, cut them into uniform slices and set aside.

5. Place the remaining marinade in a small pot, add the shallots, and bring to a boil. Reduce the heat to low and simmer until the marinade has been reduced to 2 tablespoons.

6. Sprinkle half of the grated cheese over the prepared crust and add the mushrooms in an even layer. Top with the shallots and the remaining grated cheese and drizzle with the marinade.

7. Bake the pizza until the crust is golden (13 to 18 minutes).

* Because mushrooms shrink as they cook and can easily fall through a standard grill rack, a mesh grill tray is recommended for this recipe. These trays, which fit right on top of the grates, are available wherever grills are sold.

7

The Great Southwest

One of the more intriguing regional variations of pizza hails from the area in and around Texas, Arizona, and New Mexico. Strongly influenced by Mexican cooking, this southwestern cuisine is typically referred to as Tex-Mex. And when it comes to pizza, get ready for something really special! Pizzas from this part of the country bear little resemblance to traditional Neapolitan pies. Their crusts vary from ultra-thin and crisp to dense and chewy, while their toppings include typical south-of-the-border ingredients and seasonings. Combinations of fiery red and green chiles, beans of every shape and color, chilis brimming with beef and beans, and thick and chunky tomato salsas are often paired with smooth melting cheeses before being piled high atop a typical Southwestern-style pie. Commonly seasoned with cumin, garlic, chili powder, and coriander, these regional pizzas are some of the most delicious, unusual, and spicy ones to spring forth from American cuisine.

You can almost see the sparks fly with each bite of a fiery *Southwestern Black Bean* or a *Bordertown Pizza*. For those with somewhat conservative tastebuds, the *Potato Jack* and *Triple Bean Pizza* are more appropriate choices. Better wear a sombrero before trying a *Mexican Pizza*. One taste will instantly transport you south of the border.

So get ready for a tasty adventure as you sample these delectable pizza treats inspired by the great Southwest.

A Bit of the Bird Pizza

Yield: *16-inch thin-crust pizza / 8 slices*

Suggested Crusts: *Combo,*

European Milk, Semolina, Simple,

Speedy, or Whole Wheat.

(See Chapter 2 for recipes.)

4 tablespoons olive oil

2 tablespoons cornmeal

Dough for 16-inch crust (see
  suggestions)

1 tablespoon minced fresh basil, or
  1 teaspoon dried

½ teaspoon ground cumin

¾ teaspoon sea salt

½ teaspoon white pepper

2 cloves garlic, crushed

1 cup plus 3 tablespoons *Zesty
  Barbecue Sauce* (page 72), or
  commercial barbecue sauce

1½ pounds boneless, skinless chicken
  breasts

½ teaspoon cayenne pepper (or to
  taste)

3 large ripe tomatoes, skinned* and
  sliced

4 scallions, chopped

6 ounces (1½ cups) shredded
  Mozzarella cheese

* For tomato-skinning information, see
page 68.

A fairly spicy barbecue sauce dresses up this formidable grilled chicken pizza. For a milder sauce, adjust the amount of cayenne pepper, or eliminate it altogether.

1. Preheat the oven to 450°F for 30 minutes. Brush 1 tablespoon of the oil over the surface of a 16-inch pizza pan and sprinkle with cornmeal, shaking out the excess. (If using pizza stones or tiles, place them in the oven before preheating, and heavily flour a pizza paddle.) Pat, stretch, or roll the dough in the prepared pan or on the paddle and set aside.

2. Preheat a gas or charcoal grill to medium.

3. In a small bowl, combine the basil, cumin, salt, and white pepper, and set aside. In another small bowl, make a baste by combining the remaining oil with the garlic and 3 tablespoons of *Zesty Barbecue Sauce.*

4. When the grill is ready, lightly oil the rack. Grill the chicken breasts, turning once and basting frequently, until the breast juices run clear when pierced with a fork (12 to 15 minutes). Transfer to a cutting board and slice into thin strips.

5. Stir the cayenne pepper into the remaining *Zesty Barbecue Sauce* and spread it over the prepared crust. Add a layer of tomato slices and scatter with scallions and Mozzarella cheese. Top with the grilled chicken and sprinkle with the herb mixture.

6. Bake the pizza until the cheese has melted and the crust is golden (13 to 18 minutes).

Bordertown Pizza

This pizza combines a fiery interior with a more mellow topping.

1. Preheat the oven to 450°F for 30 minutes.* Brush the oil over the surface of a 16-inch pizza pan and sprinkle with cornmeal, shaking out the excess. (If using pizza stones or tiles, place them in the oven before preheating, and heavily flour a pizza paddle.) Pat, stretch, or roll the dough in the prepared pan or on the paddle and set aside.

2. In a medium-sized bowl, combine the Ricotta, Mozzarella, and grated cheese, and set aside.

3. In a medium-sized saucepan, combine the beans, beer, onion, garlic, chile, chili powder, oregano, salt, and black pepper. Bring to a boil, reduce the heat to low, and simmer, uncovered and stirring frequently, until the liquid has evaporated (about 10 minutes). Stir in the olives.

4. Spoon the *Mexican Chile Sauce* over the prepared crust and top with an even layer of the bean mixture. Using a rubber spatula, spread the cheese mixture on top.

5. Bake the pizza until the crust is golden (15 to 20 minutes).

* If using *Rich Egg Dough*, preheat the oven to 400°F.

Yield: *16-inch thin-crust pizza / 8 slices*

Suggested Crusts: *California, Combo, European Milk, Olive Oil, Rich Egg, Simple, Speedy, Sponge, or Whole Wheat .*

(See Chapter 2 for recipes.)

1 tablespoon olive oil

2 tablespoons cornmeal

Dough for 16-inch crust (see suggestions)

15 ounces (2 cups) Ricotta cheese

4 ounces (1 cup) shredded Mozzarella cheese

4 ounces (1 cup) grated Parmesan, Sardo, or Pecorino-Romano cheese

2 cups cooked pinto beans or pink beans

½ cup dark flat beer (not stout)

1 medium-sized sweet yellow onion, chopped

3 cloves garlic, chopped

1 serrano chile (or to taste), chopped

1 tablespoon chili powder

1 tablespoon chopped fresh oregano, or 1 teaspoon dried

½ teaspoon sea salt

⅓ teaspoon ground black pepper

1 cup chopped green olives

1 cup *Mexican Chile Sauce* (page 76), or commercial enchilada sauce

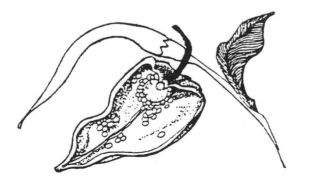

Pizza Con Queso

Yield: *16-inch thin-crust pizza / 8 slices*

Suggested Crusts: *Combo,*

European Milk, Rosy, Simple,

Speedy, Sponge, or Whole Wheat.

See Chapter 2 for recipes.)

3½ tablespoons olive oil

2 tablespoons cornmeal

Dough for 16-inch crust (see
    suggestions)

1 large sweet yellow onion, chopped

1 jalapeño chile (or to taste), minced

2 cloves garlic, crushed

3 large ripe tomatoes, skinned* and
    chopped

1 tablespoon commercial taco
    seasoning

¼ teaspoon sea salt

½ teaspoon ground black pepper

8 ounces (2 cups) shredded Monterey
    Jack cheese

4 ounces (1¼ cups) shredded sharp
    Cheddar cheese

1 cup *Fresh Tomato Sauce* (page 68),
    Quick Tomato Sauce (page 70), or
    commercial pizza sauce

* For tomato-skinning information, see
page 68.

*Con queso means "with cheese" in Spanish, which is exactly what
this Mexican-inspired pizza is all about.*

1. Preheat the oven to 450°F for 30 minutes. Brush 1 table-
    spoon of the oil over the surface of a 16-inch pizza pan
    and sprinkle with cornmeal, shaking out the excess. (If
    using pizza stones or tiles, place them in the oven before
    preheating, and heavily flour a pizza paddle.) Pat, stretch,
    or roll the dough in the prepared pan or on the paddle and
    set aside.

2. Heat the remaining oil in a medium-sized skillet over
    medium-low heat. Add the onion, jalapeño chile, and
    garlic, and sauté until soft (about 4 minutes).

3. Add the tomatoes, taco seasoning, salt, and pepper to the
    skillet. Continue to cook, stirring frequently, for 5 min-
    utes. Transfer to a medium-sized bowl and combine with
    the Monterey Jack and Cheddar cheese.

4. Spread the *Fresh Tomato Sauce* over the prepared crust
    and top with the cheese mixture.

5. Bake the pizza until the cheese has melted and the crust
    is golden (13 to 18 minutes).

Herb Cheese Pizza

It is really quite simple to prepare your own herb cheese for this pizza. You can, however, use a commercial variety, such as Boursin or Rondele, and get the same delectable results.

1. Preheat the oven to 450°F for 30 minutes. Brush 1 tablespoon of the oil over the surface of a 16-inch pizza pan and sprinkle with cornmeal, shaking out the excess. (If using pizza stones or tiles, place them in the oven before preheating, and heavily flour a pizza paddle.) Pat, stretch, or roll the dough in the prepared pan or on the paddle and set aside.

2. Heat the remaining oil in a large skillet over medium heat. Add the bell peppers and onion, and sauté until soft and golden (about 8 minutes).

3. To make the herb cheese, mash together the farmer cheese, garlic, parsley, oregano, thyme, salt, black pepper, and lemon juice in a small bowl. Set aside.

4. Spread the *Fresh Tomato Sauce* over the prepared crust. Add the Mozzarella cheese and the pepper-onion mixture. Drop spoonfuls of the herb cheese on top.

5. Bake the pizza until the cheese has melted and the crust is golden (13 to 18 minutes).

Yield: *16-inch thin-crust pizza / 8 slices*

Suggested Crusts: *California, Cheese, Combo, Herb, Simple, Speedy, Sponge, or Whole Wheat.*

(See Chapter 2 for recipes.)

4 tablespoons olive oil

2 tablespoons cornmeal

Dough for 16-inch crust (see suggestions)

1 red or yellow bell pepper, julienned

1 green bell pepper, julienned

1 large sweet yellow onion, thinly sliced

1 cup *Fresh Tomato Sauce* (page 68), *Quick Tomato Sauce* (page 70), or commercial pizza sauce

6 ounces (1½ cups) shredded Mozzarella cheese

HERB CHEESE

16 ounces (2 cups) soft farmer cheese

3 cloves garlic, crushed

2 tablespoons minced fresh parsley, or 2 teaspoons dried

1 tablespoon minced fresh oregano, or 1 teaspoon dried

1½ teaspoons snipped fresh thyme, or ½ teaspoon dried

¾ teaspoon sea salt

1 teaspoon white pepper

1 teaspoon lemon juice

Mexican Pizza

Yield: *16-inch thin-crust pizza / 8 slices*

Suggested Crusts: *Combo,*

Hard Pretzel, Simple, Speedy,

or Whole Wheat.

(See Chapter 2 for recipes.)

1 tablespoon olive oil

2 tablespoons cornmeal

Dough for 16-inch crust (see
   suggestions)

2 cups cooked red kidney beans

½ cup dry sherry

2 cloves garlic, chopped

1 tablespoon paprika

1 teaspoon chili powder

1 teaspoon ground cumin

½ teaspoon sea salt

⅓ teaspoon ground black pepper

1 medium-sized sweet yellow onion,
   finely chopped

1 small green bell pepper, finely
   chopped

1 jalapeño chile (or to taste), minced

1 cup *Fresh Tomato Sauce* (page 68),
   Quick Tomato Sauce (page 70), or
   commercial pizza sauce

8 ounces (2 cups) shredded
   Mozzarella cheese (optional)

Spicy red beans that have been simmered with chili powder, cumin, and oregano top this hearty, nutrient-rich pizza. Perfect to serve with chilled mugs of ice-cold Mexican beer.

1. Preheat the oven to 450°F for 30 minutes. Brush the oil over the surface of a 16-inch pizza pan and sprinkle with cornmeal, shaking out the excess. (If using pizza stones or tiles, place them in the oven before preheating, and heavily flour a pizza paddle.) Pat, stretch, or roll the dough in the prepared pan or on the paddle and set aside.

2. In a medium-sized saucepan, combine the beans, sherry, garlic, paprika, chili powder, cumin, salt, and black pepper. Bring to a boil, reduce the heat to low, and simmer uncovered, stirring frequently, until the liquid has evaporated (about 10 minutes).

3. In a medium-sized bowl, combine the onion, bell pepper, and jalapeño chile, and set aside.

4. Spread the *Fresh Tomato Sauce* over the prepared crust, and scatter with Mozzarella (if using). Add the bean mixture and top with the onion-pepper-chile combination.

5. Bake the pizza until the crust is golden (13 to 18 minutes).

Pepper⊄Pepper Pizza

This powerful pizza, which is crowned with an assortment of both sweet and hot peppers, is uncomplicated, yet amazingly savory.

1. Preheat the oven to 450°F for 30 minutes. Brush 1 tablespoon of the oil over the surface of a 16-inch pizza pan and sprinkle with cornmeal, shaking out the excess. (If using pizza stones or tiles, place them in the oven before preheating, and heavily flour a pizza paddle.) Pat, stretch, or roll the dough in the prepared pan or on the paddle and set aside.

2. Roast the bell peppers and chiles,* remove the skins, and cut into thin strips. Set aside.

3. While the peppers are roasting, combine the remaining oil with the oregano, garlic, salt, and black pepper in a small bowl.

4. Arrange the pepper slices on the prepared crust and scatter with olives. Drizzle with the flavored oil.

5. Bake the pizza until the crust is golden (13 to 18 minutes). Remove from the oven, sprinkle with the grated cheese (if using), and serve immediately.

* For pepper-roasting information, see page 75.

Yield: *16-inch thin-crust pizza / 8 slices*

Suggested Crusts: *Cheese, Combo, European Milk, Greek Garlic, Olive Oil, Simple, Speedy, or Sponge.*

(See Chapter 2 for recipes.)

¼ cup plus 1 tablespoon olive oil

2 tablespoons cornmeal

Dough for 16-inch crust (see suggestions)

6 large bell peppers (any combination of colors), halved and seeded

2 poblano or 4 Anaheim chiles, halved and seeded

2 jalapeño, Fresno, serrano, or yellow banana chiles, halved and seeded

1½ tablespoons minced fresh oregano, or 1½ teaspoons dried

2 cloves garlic, minced

1 teaspoon sea salt

½ teaspoon ground black pepper

1 cup sliced green olives

2 ounces (½ cup) grated Parmesan, Asiago, or Pecorino-Romano cheese (optional)

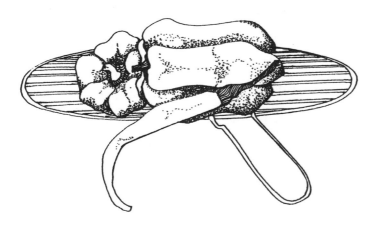

Potato Jack Pizza

Yield: *16-inch thin-crust pizza / 8 slices*

Suggested Crusts: *Combo,*

European Milk, Herb, Rich Egg,

Simple, Speedy, or Sponge.

(See Chapter 2 for recipes.)

6 tablespoons olive oil

2 tablespoons cornmeal

Dough for 16-inch crust (see suggestions)

2 large new potatoes, scrubbed and thinly sliced

4 cups water

1½ tablespoons minced fresh basil, or 1½ teaspoons dried

2 teaspoons snipped fresh rosemary, or ¾ teaspoon dried

1½ teaspoons sea salt

1 teaspoon ground black pepper

1 large Vidalia or other sweet yellow onion, thinly sliced

2 cloves garlic, crushed

8 ounces (2 cups) shredded Monterey Jack cheese with jalapeños

This luscious pizza is topped with thin slices of new potatoes and jalapeño-laced Monterey Jack cheese.

1. Preheat the oven to 450°F for 30 minutes.* Brush 1 tablespoon of the oil over the surface of a 16-inch pizza pan and sprinkle with cornmeal, shaking out the excess. (If using pizza stones or tiles, place them in the oven before preheating, and heavily flour a pizza paddle.) Pat, stretch, or roll the dough in the prepared pan or on the paddle and set aside.

2. In a deep skillet, bring the potatoes and water to a boil. Reduce the heat to low, and simmer the potatoes until just tender (about 8 minutes). Carefully drain the potatoes and place on a plate. Drizzle with 2 tablespoons of the oil, and set aside.

3. In a small bowl, combine the basil, rosemary, salt, and pepper, and set aside.

4. Heat 1 tablespoon of the oil in a large skillet over medium-low heat. Add the onion and garlic, and sauté until soft and golden (about 5 minutes).

5. Scatter the Monterey Jack cheese over the prepared crust, and arrange the potato slices on top in circular rows. Sprinkle the herb mixture over the potatoes, spoon the onions on top, and drizzle with the remaining oil.

6. Bake the pizza until the crust is golden (13 to 18 minutes).

* If using *Rich Egg Dough*, preheat the oven to 400°F.

Southwestern Black Bean Pizza

This pizza can be as mild or fiery as you wish, depending on the type of salsa and the number of jalapeños you use.

Yield: *16-inch thin-crust pizza / 8 slices*

Suggested Crusts: *Cheese, Combo, Greek Garlic, Hard Pretzel, Simple, Speedy, or Sponge.*

(See Chapter 2 for recipes.)

5 tablespoons olive oil

2 tablespoons cornmeal

Dough for 16-inch crust (see suggestions)

4 scallions, chopped

2 cloves garlic, crushed

1 jalapeño chile (or to taste), minced

2 cups cooked black beans

¼ cup dry sherry

1½ tablespoons taco seasoning mix

½ teaspoon ground cumin

½ cup *Fresh Tomato Sauce* (page 68), *Quick Tomato Sauce* (page 70) or commercial pizza sauce

½ cup medium-hot chunky salsa

8 ounces (2 cups) shredded Mozzarella cheese

1. Preheat the oven to 450°F for 30 minutes. Brush 1 tablespoon of the oil over the surface of a 16-inch pizza pan and sprinkle with cornmeal, shaking out the excess. (If using pizza stones or tiles, place them in the oven before preheating, and heavily flour a pizza paddle.) Pat, stretch, or roll the dough in the prepared pan or on the paddle and set aside.

2. Heat 2 tablespoons of the oil in a large skillet over medium-low heat. Add the scallions, garlic, and jalapeño chile, and sauté until soft (about 5 minutes).

3. To the skillet, add the black beans, sherry, taco seasoning, and cumin. Continue to cook, stirring frequently, until the liquid evaporates (about 3 minutes).

4. Combine the *Fresh Tomato Sauce* with the salsa, and spread over the prepared crust. Scatter with Mozzarella cheese and top with the bean mixture. Drizzle with the remaining oil.

5. Bake the pizza until the cheese has melted and the crust is golden (13 to 18 minutes).

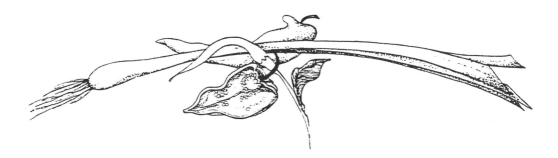

Tex∕Mex Beef Pizza

Yield: *12-inch deep-dish pizza / 6 slices*

Suggested Crusts: *Basil-Rosemary,*

California, Cheese, Combo,

Greek Garlic, Herb, Olive Oil, Rosy,

Simple, Speedy, or Whole Wheat.

(See Chapter 2 for recipes.)

3 tablespoons olive oil

2 tablespoons cornmeal

Dough for 12-inch crust (see
   suggestions)

1 large sweet yellow onion, chopped

1 large leek, white bulb cleaned and
   chopped

3 cloves garlic, minced

1 jalapeño chile (or to taste), seeded
   and minced

1 cup cooked red kidney beans

1 tablespoon chopped fresh oregano,
   or 1 teaspoon dried

1 teaspoon ground cumin

¾ teaspoon sea salt

¾ teaspoon chili powder

½ teaspoon ground black pepper

1 pound lean ground beef

4 ounces (1¼ cups) shredded
   Cheddar cheese

4 ounces (1 cup) shredded Monterey
   Jack cheese

1 cup *Fresh Tomato Sauce* (page 68),
   Quick Tomato Sauce (page 70), or
   commercial pizza sauce

1 cup thinly sliced roasted red peppers

Due to the weight and moistness of the topping, I find this pizza is best when prepared in a deep-dish pan.

1. Preheat the oven to 450+F for 30 minutes. Brush 1 tablespoon of the oil over the surface of a 12-inch deep-dish pizza pan and sprinkle with cornmeal, shaking out the excess. (If using pizza stones or tiles, place them in the oven before preheating, and heavily flour a pizza paddle.) Pat, stretch, or roll the dough in the prepared pan or on the paddle and set aside.

2. Heat the remaining oil in a small skillet over medium-low heat. Add the onion, leek, garlic, and jalapeño chile, and sauté until soft (about 8 minutes). Transfer to a large bowl and stir in the beans, oregano, cumin, salt, chili powder, and black pepper. Set aside.

3. Add the ground beef to the skillet and cook, stirring occasionally, until browned. Drain the cooked beef and add it to the bean mixture along with the Cheddar and Monterey Jack cheese. Combine the ingredients well.

4. Spread the *Fresh Tomato Sauce* over the prepared crust and top with the beef-bean mixture. Arrange the roasted peppers in a decorative fashion on top.

5. Bake the pizza until the cheese has melted and the crust is golden (15 to 20 minutes).

Triple-Bean Pizza

Any combination of legumes can be used to create this nutritious and delightful-tasting pizza.

1. Preheat the oven to 450°F for 30 minutes. Brush 1 tablespoon of the oil over the surface of a 16-inch pizza pan and sprinkle with cornmeal, shaking out the excess. (If using pizza stones or tiles, place them in the oven before preheating, and heavily flour a pizza paddle.) Pat, stretch, or roll the dough in the prepared pan or on the paddle and set aside.

2. Heat the remaining oil in a small skillet over medium-low heat. Add the leek and garlic, and sauté until soft (about 8 minutes). Transfer to a medium-sized bowl and stir in the pinto beans, black beans, navy beans, sage, salt, and pepper.

3. Spread the *Fresh Tomato Sauce* over the prepared crust and top with the bean mixture.

4. Bake the pizza for 10 minutes, remove from the oven, and scatter with the Brick cheese. Arrange the pepper strips on top in a decorative fashion.

5. Return the pizza to the oven and continue to bake until the cheese has melted and the crust is golden (4 to 8 minutes).

Yield: *16-inch thin-crust pizza / 8 slices*

Suggested Crusts: *Basil-Rosemary, California, Cheese, Combo, Greek Garlic, Herb, Rosy, Simple, Speedy, or Whole Wheat.*

(See Chapter 2 for recipes.)

3 tablespoons olive oil

2 tablespoons cornmeal

Dough for 16-inch crust (see suggestions)

1 large leek, white bulb cleaned and thinly sliced

2 cloves garlic, minced

2 cups cooked pinto beans

2 cups cooked black beans

2 cups cooked navy or other small white beans

¼ cup chopped fresh sage, or 1 tablespoon dried

¾ teaspoon sea salt

½ teaspoon ground black pepper

1 cup *Fresh Tomato Sauce* (page 68), *Quick Tomato Sauce* (page 70), or commercial pizza sauce

8 ounces (2¾ cups) shredded Brick or Colby cheese

1 cup thinly sliced roasted red peppers

8

The Italian Pizza Oven

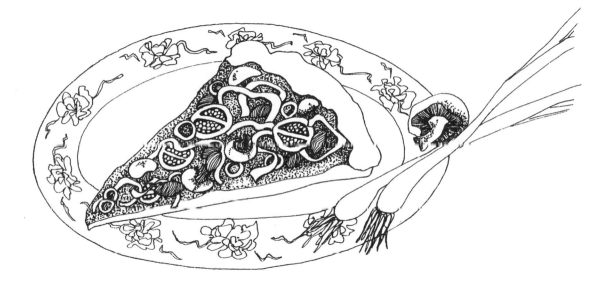

Pizza's origin can be traced back centuries to the Neopolitan region of Italy. There, a flatbread called focaccia became the surface used to form an early version of pizza. Focaccia was first topped simply with oils, herbs, and cheese. Tomatoes, which were brought to the Italian shores by explorers, quickly became a popular addition to this delicious flavored bread.

This chapter offers Italian-style pizzas that range from the simple *Classic Neopolitan* to pies that include a diverse assortment of traditional Italian ingredients in unusual combinations. Enjoy the marriage of heavenly pesto and smooth Gorgonzola cheese in a *Primo Pesto Pizza*, or try the *Pizza Melanzane* with its layers of crisp eggplant, bell peppers, olives, and Provolone cheese. For cheese lovers, the *Pizza Con Fromaggi* is a four-star choice, while the *Pizza de la Casa*, bursting with sausage, pepperoni, and a host of vegetables, is sure to satisfy the heartiest of appetites.

You will find many other luscious, savory choices that are sure to please whenever you crave a little bit of Italy and a lot of pizza!

Classic Neopolitan Pizza

Yield: *16-inch thin-crust pizza / 8 slices*

Suggested Crusts: *Combo,*

Semolina, Simple, Speedy,

Sponge, or Whole Wheat.

(See Chapter 2 for recipes.)

¼ cup plus 1 tablespoon olive oil

2 tablespoons cornmeal

Dough for 16-inch pizza (see suggestions)

8 ripe tomatoes, skinned* and sliced

3 scallions, chopped

2 tablespoons chopped fresh oregano, or 2 teaspoons dried

2 cloves garlic, minced

¾ teaspoon sea salt

½ teaspoon ground black pepper

* For tomato-skinning information, see page 68.

The Neapolitans make a simple pizza topped with vine-ripened tomatoes, olive oil, and herbs. It is a classic pizza that is striking in its utter simplicity.

1. Preheat the oven to 450°F for 30 minutes. Brush 1 tablespoon of the oil over the surface of a 16-inch pizza pan and sprinkle with cornmeal, shaking out the excess. (If using pizza stones or tiles, place them in the oven before preheating, and heavily flour a pizza paddle.) Pat, stretch, or roll the dough in the prepared pan or on the paddle and set aside.

2. Place the tomatoes in a medium-sized bowl and stir in the remaining oil, the scallions, oregano, garlic, salt, and pepper. Spread this tomato mixture over the prepared dough.

3. Bake the pizza until the crust is golden (13 to 18 minutes).

Pizza de la Casa

Sweet Italian sausage, spicy pepperoni, and a host of sautéed vegetables abound in this hearty pizza. It can be easily prepared as a single-crust, deep-dish, or double-crust pie.

1. Preheat the oven to 450°F for 30 minutes. Brush 1 tablespoon of the oil over the surface of a 16-inch pizza pan and sprinkle with cornmeal, shaking out the excess. (If using pizza stones or tiles, place them in the oven before preheating, and heavily flour a pizza paddle.) Pat, stretch, or roll the dough in the prepared pan or on the paddle and set aside.

2. Heat the remaining oil in a large skillet over medium heat. Pierce the sausage links with a fork and add to the skillet. Reduce the heat to low, cover the skillet, and cook the sausage, turning frequently and piercing occasionally, for 10 minutes. Uncover and continue to cook until golden brown on all sides (5 to 7 minutes). Transfer the sausage to paper towels. When cool, slice into thin rounds.

3. Remove all but 3 tablespoons of oil from the skillet. Add the onion, bell peppers, and chilé, and sauté over medium-low heat for 5 minutes. Toss in the mushrooms and garlic, increase the heat to medium, and sauté, stirring frequently, until the mushrooms are golden brown (about 10 minutes). Stir in the basil, fennel, salt, and pepper, and set aside.

4. Scatter the Mozzarella cheese over the pizza crust and top with the sautéed vegetables. Arrange the sausage and pepperoni slices over the vegetables, and drizzle with tomato sauce. Top with olives.

5. Bake the pizza until the cheese has melted and the crust is golden (13 to 18 minutes).

Yield: *16-inch thin-crust pizza / 8 slices*

Suggested Crusts: *California, Cheese, Combo, Graham, Herb, Rye, Semolina, Simple, Speedy, Sponge, or Whole Wheat.*

(See Chapter 2 for recipes.)

---

3 tablespoons olive oil

2 tablespoons cornmeal

Dough for 16-inch crust (see suggestions)

1 pound sweet Italian sausage links

1 large sweet yellow onion, thinly sliced

1 large green or yellow bell pepper, julienned

1 large red bell pepper, julienned

1 hot red or green chile, minced (or to taste)

1 pound fresh mushrooms, wiped clean and sliced

4 cloves garlic, chopped

2 tablespoons minced fresh basil, or 2 teaspoons dried

½ teaspoon crushed fennel seeds

¾ teaspoon sea salt

½ teaspoon ground black pepper

8 ounces (2 cups) shredded Mozzarella cheese

12 ounces pepperoni, thinly sliced

1 cup *Fresh Tomato Sauce* (page 68), *Quick Tomato Sauce* (page 70), or commercial pizza sauce

1 cup sliced Kalamata or other imported black olives

Primo Pesto Pizza

Yield: *16-inch thin-crust pizza / 8 slices*

Suggested Crusts: *Combo,*

Semolina, Simple, Speedy,

Sponge, or Whole Wheat.

(See Chapter 2 for recipes.)

3 tablespoons olive oil

2 tablespoons cornmeal

Dough for 16-inch crust (see suggestions)

1 pound medium-sized raw shrimp, peeled and deveined

4 shallots, roasted* and mashed

4 cloves garlic, roasted* and mashed

¾ teaspoon sea salt

½ teaspoon ground black pepper

1 cup *Pizza Pesto* (page 71), or commercial pesto

8 ounces (1½ cups) crumbled Gorgonzola cheese

* For garlic- and shallot-roasting information, see page 90.

This utterly decadent creation joins an exciting basil pesto with fresh shrimp, roasted garlic and shallots, and creamy Gorgonzola cheese. Served with a chilled bottle of white wine, this pizza is a sensational meal.

1. Preheat the oven to 450°F for 30 minutes. Brush 1 tablespoon of the oil over the surface of a 16-inch pizza pan and sprinkle with cornmeal, shaking out the excess. (If using pizza stones or tiles, place them in the oven before preheating, and heavily flour a pizza paddle.) Pat, stretch, or roll the dough in the prepared pan or on the paddle and set aside.

2. Heat the remaining oil in a large skillet over medium heat. Add the shrimp and stir-fry until they begin to curl and are no longer translucent (2 to 3 minutes). Transfer the shrimp to a bowl and stir in the shallots, garlic, salt, and pepper. Set aside.

3. Bake the prepared crust for 5 minutes then remove it from the oven. Spread the pesto on top, then return to the oven for another 5 minutes. Remove once more and top with the shrimp and Gorgonzola cheese.

4. Return the pizza to the oven and bake until the cheese has melted and the crust is golden (3 to 8 minutes).

Pizza Con Fromaggi

This four-cheese pizza is heady stuff, filled with a combination of outstanding Italian cheeses.

1. Preheat the oven to 450°F for 30 minutes. Brush the oil over the surface of a 16-inch pizza pan and sprinkle with cornmeal, shaking out the excess. (If using pizza stones or tiles, place them in the oven before preheating, and heavily flour a pizza paddle.) Pat, stretch, or roll the dough in the prepared pan or on the paddle and set aside.

2. In a medium-sized bowl, mix together the Ricotta, Gorgonzola, and pepper, and set aside. In another bowl, combine the Mozzarella and Fontina.

3. Spread the Ricotta-Gorgonzola mixture on the prepared crust. Scatter with garlic and shallots, and top with the Mozzarella-Fontina mixture.

4. Bake the pizza until the cheese has melted and the crust is golden (13 to 18 minutes.)

Yield: *16-inch thin-crust pizza / 8 slices*

Suggested Crusts: *Basil-Rosemary, California, Cheese, Combo, Herb, Pesto, Semolina, Simple, Speedy, Sponge, or Whole Wheat.*

(See Chapter 2 for recipes.)

1 tablespoon olive oil

2 tablespoons cornmeal

Dough for 16-inch crust (see suggestions)

8 ounces (1 cup) Ricotta cheese

6 ounces (1 cup) crumbled Gorgonzola cheese

4 ounces (1 cup) shredded fresh Mozzarella or Bufalina cheese

4 ounces (¾ cup) diced Fontina cheese

1 teaspoon ground black pepper

4 cloves garlic, roasted* and mashed

4 shallots, roasted* and mashed

* For garlic- and shallot-roasting information, see page 90.

Prosciutto Pizza Perfecto

Yield: *16-inch thin-crust pizza / 8 slices*

Suggested Crusts: *California, Cheese, Combo, Herb, Semolina, Simple, Speedy, Sponge, or Whole Wheat.*

(See Chapter 2 for recipes.)

3 tablespoons olive oil

2 tablespoons cornmeal

Dough for 16-inch crust (see suggestions)

4 ripe tomatoes, skinned* and sliced

2 tablespoons chopped fresh oregano, or 2 teaspoons dried

2 cloves garlic, minced

3 shallots or scallions, minced

½ teaspoon ground black pepper

¼ teaspoon sea salt

8 ounces prosciutto, cut into thin strips

4 ounces (¾ cup) diced Fontina cheese

* For tomato-skinning information, see page 68.

Prosciutto, a salted, air-cured ham, is available in Italian food stores and many delis. If you can't find prosciutto, Smithfield ham is a good substitute.

1. Preheat the oven to 450°F for 30 minutes. Brush 1 tablespoon of the oil over the surface of a 16-inch pizza pan and sprinkle with cornmeal, shaking out the excess. (If using pizza stones or tiles, place them in the oven before preheating, and heavily flour a pizza paddle.) Pat, stretch, or roll the dough in the prepared pan or on the paddle and set aside.

2. Place the tomatoes in a medium-sized bowl and stir in the remaining oil, the oregano, garlic, shallots, pepper, and salt.

3. Spread the tomato mixture on the prepared dough and bake 10 minutes. Remove from the oven and top with the prosciutto and Fontina.

4. Return the pizza to the oven and continue to bake until the cheese has melted and the crust is golden (4 to 8 minutes).

Spinach Calzones

These wonderful Italian turnovers encase an oozingly sensuous spinach and cheese filling.

Yield: *4 large calzones*

Suggested Crusts: *Combo, Simple, Speedy, Sponge, or Whole Wheat.*

(See Chapter 2 for recipes.)

4 tablespoons olive oil

2 tablespoons cornmeal

Dough for crust (see suggestions)

1 medium-sized sweet yellow onion, chopped

3 cloves garlic, crushed

16 ounces fresh spinach, rinsed well and drained

2 tablespoons snipped fresh dill, or 2 teaspoons dried

1 teaspoon ground black pepper

½ teaspoon sea salt

8 ounces (2 cups) shredded Mozzarella cheese

8 ounces (2½ cups) crumbled Feta cheese

1. Preheat the oven to 450°F for 30 minutes. Brush 1 tablespoon of oil over the surface of a large baking sheet, and sprinkle with cornmeal, shaking out the excess. (If using pizza stones or tiles, place them in the oven before preheating, and heavily flour a pizza paddle.)

2. On a floured surface, divide the dough into 4 equal pieces. With a floured rolling pin, roll each piece into an 8-inch circle and set aside.

3. Heat 2 tablespoons of the oil in a large skillet over medium-low heat. Add the onions and garlic, and sauté until soft (about 3 minutes). Add the spinach and sauté, stirring occasionally, until wilted (3 to 5 minutes).

4. Transfer the spinach mixture to a colander, press out the excess moisture with the back of a spoon, and place in a bowl. Stir in the dill, pepper, and salt. Set aside. In another bowl, combine the Mozzarella and Feta cheese.

5. Place an equal amount of the cheese mixture on half of each circle of dough, leaving a ½-inch border. Press the cheese lightly into the dough and top with the spinach mixture.

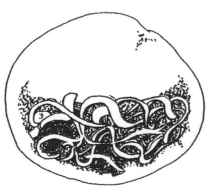

6. Fold each circle in half and press the edges together.

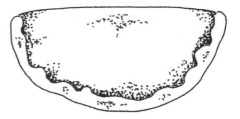

7. Seal with the tines of a floured fork.

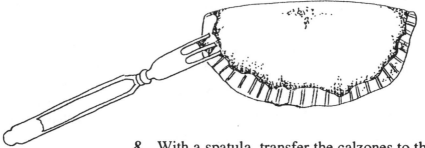

8. With a spatula, transfer the calzones to the baking sheet or pizza paddle. Brush the tops with the remaining oil.

9. Bake the calzones until golden brown (12 to 16 minutes).

Top: Triple-Bean Pizza (page 129)
Bottom: Pepper-Pepper Pizza (page 125)

Top: *Primo Pesto Pizza (page 134)*
Bottom: *Italian Salad Pizza (page 140)*

Amalfi Shrimp Pizza

This luscious pizza is topped with shrimp that have been marinated in oil, garlic, and herbs. Outstanding!

1. Preheat the oven to 450°F for 30 minutes. Brush 1 table-spoon of the oil over the surface of a 16-inch pizza pan and sprinkle with cornmeal, shaking out the excess. (If using pizza stones or tiles, place them in the oven before preheating, and heavily flour a pizza paddle.) Pat, stretch, or roll the dough in the prepared pan or on the paddle and set aside.

2. Place the remaining oil in a large bowl, and toss in the shrimp, garlic, basil, salt, and pepper. Refrigerate for 30 minutes.

3. Using a slotted spoon, transfer the shrimp to another bowl.

4. Brush the oil mixture over the prepared crust and bake for 5 minutes. Remove the crust from the oven and top with the shrimp.

5. Return the pizza to the oven and continue to bake until the shrimp have curled and turned pink, and the crust is golden (8 to 13 minutes).

Yield: *16-inch thin-crust pizza / 8 slices*

Suggested Crusts: *Basil-Rosemary, California, Cheese, Combo, Greek Garlic, Herb, Semolina, Simple, Speedy, or Whole Wheat.*

(See Chapter 2 for recipes.)

4 tablespoons olive oil

2 tablespoons cornmeal

Dough for 16-inch crust (see suggestions)

1 pound medium-sized raw shrimp, peeled and deveined

3 cloves garlic, minced

2 tablespoons minced fresh basil, or 2 teaspoons dried

¾ teaspoon sea salt

½ teaspoon ground black pepper

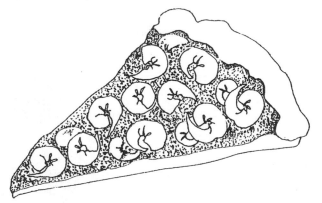

Italian Salad Pizza

Yield: *16-inch thin-crust pizza / 8 slices*

Suggested Crusts: *Basil-Rosemary, California, Cheese, Combo, Herb, Pesto, Semolina, Simple, Speedy, or Whole Wheat.*

(See Chapter 2 for recipes.)

½ cup olive oil

2 tablespoons cornmeal

Dough for 16-inch crust (see suggestions)

2 tablespoons white wine vinegar

1 teaspoon Dijon-style mustard

1 teaspoon sea salt

½ teaspoon ground black pepper

¼ teaspoon crushed dried hot red chiles (or to taste)

1 cup *Fresh Tomato Sauce* (page 68), *Quick Tomato Sauce* (page 70), or commercial pizza sauce

2 large ripe tomatoes, skinned* and chopped

3 ounces (½ cup) diced Fontina cheese

3 ounces (¾ cup) shredded Mozzarella cheese

1 cup stale Italian or French bread cubes (approximately 1-inch cubes)

1 large red onion, diced

3 tablespoons minced fresh basil, or 1 tablespoon dried

* For tomato-skinning information, see page 68.

Many European and Middle Eastern salads feature bread as part of the dish. This pizza recipe, which calls for herbed bread cubes, was inspired by those salads.

1. Preheat the oven to 450°F for 30 minutes. Brush 1 tablespoon of the oil over the surface of a 16-inch pizza pan and sprinkle with cornmeal, shaking out the excess. (If using pizza stones or tiles, place them in the oven before preheating, and heavily flour a pizza paddle.) Pat, stretch, or roll the dough in the prepared pan or on the paddle and set aside.

2. Place the remaining oil in a bowl, whisk in the vinegar, mustard, salt, pepper, and chiles, and set aside for 30 minutes. In another bowl, combine the tomato sauce and the fresh tomatoes. In a third bowl, combine the Fontina and Mozzarella cheese. And in a fourth bowl, toss together the bread cubes, onions, and basil.

3. Spread the tomato mixture over the prepared crust, and scatter the cheese on top. Arrange the bread cubes on the cheese, and drizzle with the flavored oil.

4. Bake the pizza until the cheese has melted and the crust is golden (13 to 18 minutes).

Pizza Melanzane

This distinctive layered pizza is composed of crisp eggplant slices, bell peppers, scallions, Provolone cheese, and olives.

1. Preheat the oven to 450°F for 30 minutes. Brush 1 table-spoon of the oil over the surface of a 16-inch pizza pan and sprinkle with cornmeal, shaking out the excess. (If using pizza stones or tiles, place them in the oven before preheating, and heavily flour a pizza paddle.) Pat, stretch, or roll the dough in the prepared pan or on the paddle and set aside.

2. Peel the eggplant and cut into ¼-inch-thick slices. Place in a colander, sprinkle with salt, and let drain for 30 minutes. Rinse under cold water and pat dry with paper towels.

3. While the eggplant is draining, heat 2 tablespoons of the oil in a large skillet over medium heat. Add the peppers and scallions, and sauté, stirring frequently, until the peppers are soft and beginning to brown (10 to 12 minutes). Transfer to a plate and set aside.

4. Place the eggs in a shallow bowl and the bread crumbs in another. Dip each eggplant slice into the egg, then coat with bread crumbs.

5. Heat half of the remaining oil in a large skillet over medium-high heat. Add half of the eggplant slices in a single layer and fry, turning once, until golden (about 4 minutes per side). Transfer to paper towels. Heat the remaining oil and fry the remaining eggplant.

6. Arrange the eggplant slices on the prepared pizza crust. Top with Provolone, and sprinkle with oregano and black pepper. Add a layer of peppers and onions, scatter with olives, and drop teaspoons of *Fresh Tomato Sauce* on top.

7. Bake the pizza until the cheese has melted and the crust is golden (13 to 18 minutes).

Yield: *16-inch thin-crust pizza / 8 slices*

Suggested Crusts: *California, Combo, Semolina, Simple, Speedy, Sponge, or Whole Wheat.*

(See Chapter 2 for recipes.)

½ cup plus 2 tablespoons olive oil

2 tablespoons cornmeal

Dough for 16-inch crust (see suggestions)

2 medium-sized eggplants

2 tablespoons sea salt

2 large green or red bell peppers, cut into strips

4 scallions, or 1 small sweet yellow onion, chopped

2 large eggs, beaten

2 cups finely grated bread crumbs

8 ounces (1½ cups) diced Provolone or Caciocavallo cheese

2 tablespoons chopped fresh oregano, or 2 teaspoons dried

½ teaspoon ground black pepper

1 cup sliced green olives

⅓ cup *Fresh Tomato Sauce* (page 68), *Quick Tomato Sauce* (page 70), or commercial pizza sauce

Lotsa Mozza Pizza

Yield: *16-inch thin-crust pizza / 8 slices*

Suggested Crusts: *California,*

Combo, Herb, Pesto, Semolina,

Simple, Speedy, or Sponge.

(See Chapter 2 for recipes.)

¼ cup plus 1 tablespoon olive oil

1½ tablespoons minced fresh
   oregano, or 1½ teaspoons dried

1 tablespoon minced fresh basil, or
   1 teaspoon dried

1 teaspoon ground black pepper

1 small fresh red chile, minced (or to
   taste)

2 cloves garlic, crushed

16 ounces fresh Mozzarella, thinly
   sliced*

2 tablespoons cornmeal

Dough for 16-inch crust (see
   suggestions)

* Bufalina, a type of Mozzarella made from
the milk of the water buffalo, is a wonderful
substitute for fresh Mozzarella. If neither is
available, a packaged top-quality whole-milk
Mozzarella can be used with nearly the
same results.

*Fresh mozzarella that has been marinated in oil and herbs gives
this incredible pizza its delightful flavor.*

1. Make the marinade by combining ¼ cup of the oil, the
   oregano, basil, black pepper, chile, and garlic in a shallow
   bowl. Add the Mozzarella slices and coat well. Cover the
   bowl and refrigerate for 6 hours.

2. When ready to assemble the pizza, preheat the oven to
   450°F for 30 minutes. Brush the remaining tablespoon of
   oil over the surface of a 16-inch pizza pan and sprinkle
   with cornmeal, shaking out the excess. (If using pizza
   stones or tiles, place them in the oven before preheating,
   and heavily flour a pizza paddle.) Pat, stretch, or roll the
   dough in the prepared pan or on the paddle and set aside.

3. Arrange the Mozzarella slices on top of the prepared
   dough and drizzle with any remaining marinade.

4. Bake the pizza until the cheese has melted and the crust
   is golden (13 to 18 minutes).

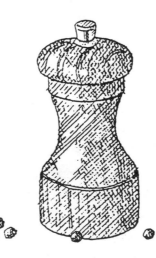

9

Pizza Fantastique!

When one thinks epicurean cuisine, one thinks French cooking. Although French-style cookery has undergone significant changes over the past few years, we still of it as sophisticated and innovative—cuisine prepared by imposing chefs in tall white hats.

In creating pizzas for this chapter, I wanted to preserve this common image of French cuisine. Since pizza isn't traditionally French, I used a good amount of culinary license to create recipes that reflected the tastes of this lovely country. The French style of cooking is a cosmopolitan one. Wonderful cheeses, rich sauces,

delicate herbs, and fresh vegetables are used in delicious combinations. I have used these ingredients in wild abandon to create my French-style pizzas.

If you enjoy a crusty crock of bubbling French onion soup, then the delectable *Paris at Night Pizza* is the perfect choice. One taste of a *Pizza Versailles* and you will find yourself sitting at a sidewalk cafe on the Champs Élysées. The combination of goat cheese and pesto in the *Goatherder's Pizza* will evoke impressions of the rolling French hillsides. Be assured, no matter which pizza you choose from this chapter, all have been created to transport you into the magical realm of French cuisine.

Asparagus Supreme

Yield: *16-inch thin-crust pizza / 8 slices*

Suggested Crusts: *California, Cheese,*

Combo, Graham, Greek Garlic, Pesto,

Rye, Semolina, Simple, Speedy,

Sponge, or Whole Wheat.

(See Chapter 2 for recipes.)

¼ cup plus 1 tablespoon olive oil

2 tablespoons cornmeal

Dough for 16-inch crust (see
  suggestions)

1 pound fresh asparagus spears,
  scraped and cut into 1½-inch pieces

4 shallots or scallions, minced

1 tablespoon snipped fresh tarragon,
  or 1 teaspoon dried

½ teaspoon sea salt

½ teaspoon white pepper

4 ounces (1½ cups) shredded
  Appenzeller, Emmenthaler, or
  other imported Swiss cheese

2 ounces (½ cup) shredded
  Mozzarella cheese

8 ounces prosciutto or other smoked
  ham, sliced into thin strips

2 ounces (½ cup) grated Parmesan,
  Asiago, or Grana Padano cheese

This lovely French pizza showcases tender spears of fresh asparagus, slices of smoked ham, and the melting goodness of an imported Swiss cheese.

1. Preheat the oven to 450°F for 30 minutes. Brush 1 tablespoon of the oil over the surface of a 16-inch pizza pan and sprinkle with cornmeal, shaking out the excess. (If using pizza stones or tiles, place them in the oven before preheating, and heavily flour a pizza paddle.) Pat, stretch, or roll the dough in the prepared pan or on the paddle and set aside.

2. Steam the asparagus until tender-crisp (about 5 minutes). In a small bowl, combine the remaining oil with the shallots, tarragon, salt, and pepper. In another bowl, combine the Swiss and Mozzarella cheese.

3. Scatter the cheese mixture over the prepared crust. Arrange the asparagus and ham on top, and drizzle with the oil mixture.

4. Bake the pizza for 10 minutes. Remove from the oven and sprinkle with the grated cheese.

5. Return the pizza to the oven and continue to bake until the cheese has melted and the crust is golden (4 to 8 minutes).

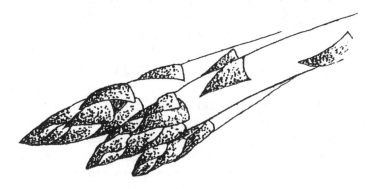

French Beef Pizza

The next time you are barbecuing steaks, throw an extra one on the fire to make this grilled-steak pizza the next day.

1. Preheat the oven to 450°F for 30 minutes. Brush the oil over the surface of a 16-inch pizza pan and sprinkle with cornmeal, shaking out the excess. (If using pizza stones or tiles, place them in the oven before preheating, and heavily flour a pizza paddle.) Pat, stretch, or roll the dough in the prepared pan or on the paddle and set aside.

2. In a small bowl, mash together the Roquefort cheese, cream cheese, shallots, garlic, butter, dry mustard, and Worcestershire sauce. In another bowl, combine the Dijon-style mustard and horseradish sauce.

3. Spoon the Dijon-horseradish sauce on the prepared crust. Arrange the steak slices evenly on the sauce, and top with the cheese mixture.

4. Bake the pizza until the top is bubbly and the crust is golden (13 to 18 minutes).

Yield: *16-inch thin-crust pizza / 8 slices*

Suggested Crusts: *Basil-Rosemary, California, Cheese, Combo, Herb, Semolina, Simple, Speedy, or Sponge. (See Chapter 2 for recipes.)*

1 tablespoon olive oil

2 tablespoons cornmeal

Dough for 16-inch crust (see suggestions)

6 ounces (1½ cups) crumbled Roquefort or other imported blue cheese

6 ounces (¾ cup) soft cream cheese or farmer cheese

3 shallots or scallions, minced

2 cloves garlic, crushed

¼ cup soft unsalted butter or margarine

2 teaspoons dry mustard

⅛ teaspoon white Worcestershire sauce

½ cup Dijon-style mustard

½ cup prepared horseradish sauce*

8 ounces grilled steak, thinly sliced

* Horseradish sauce is found in the condiment section of most supermarkets. To make your own, combine ⅓ cup mayonnaise, 3 tablespoons sour cream, and 1 tablespoon cream-style horseradish.

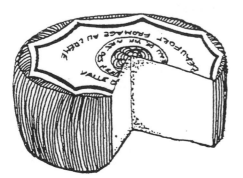

Frenchman's Pizza

Yield: *16-inch thin-crust pizza / 8 slices*

Suggested Crusts: *California, Cheese,*

Combo, Herb, Semolina, Simple,

Speedy, Sponge, or Whole Wheat.

(See Chapter 2 for recipes.)

3 tablespoons olive oil

2 tablespoons cornmeal

Dough for 16-inch crust (see
    suggestions)

3 shallots or scallions, minced

2 cloves garlic, minced

3 slices lean uncooked bacon

1½ cups *Pizza Béchamel Sauce* (page
    69)

4 ounces (1¼ cups) shredded
    Emmenthaler or other imported
    Swiss cheese

1 pound baked or smoked ham, thinly
    sliced and cut into strips

4 ounces (1¼ cups) shredded Gruyère
    cheese

2 tablespoons snipped fresh dill, or
    2 teaspoons dried

Although there is no substitute for the distinct flavor of Gruyère cheese, this pizza can still be enjoyed with Emmenthaler alone.

1. Preheat the oven to 450°F for 30 minutes. Brush 1 tablespoon of the oil over the surface of a 16-inch pizza pan and sprinkle with cornmeal, shaking out the excess. (If using pizza stones or tiles, place them in the oven before preheating, and heavily flour a pizza paddle.) Pat, stretch, or roll the dough in the prepared pan or on the paddle and set aside.

2. Heat the remaining oil in a small skillet over medium-low heat. Add the shallots and garlic, and sauté, stirring frequently, until soft (about 5 minutes). Transfer to a small bowl. Cook the bacon in the skillet until crisp. Drain on paper towels.

3. Crumble the bacon into the bowl with the shallots and garlic. In another bowl, combine the *Pizza Béchamel Sauce* with the Emmenthaler cheese.

4. Spread the cheese mixture over the prepared crust. Arrange the ham strips on top, then sprinkle with dill. Top with the Gruyère and the shallot-bacon mixture.

5. Bake until the cheese has melted and the crust is golden (13 to 18 minutes).

Goatherder's Pizza

For me, this rich, authoritative, and sinfully delicious pizza of goat cheese and basil pesto always evokes memories of rolling French hillsides.

1. Preheat the oven to 450°F for 30 minutes. Brush 1 tablespoon of the oil over the surface of a 16-inch pizza pan and sprinkle with cornmeal, shaking out the excess. (If using pizza stones or tiles, place them in the oven before preheating, and heavily flour a pizza paddle.) Pat, stretch, or roll the dough in the prepared pan or on the paddle and set aside.

2. In a small bowl, combine the remaining oil and the garlic. Set aside.

3. Spread the *Pizza Pesto* on the prepared crust, then add the goat cheese and sun-dried tomatoes. Arrange the basil leaves on top in a spoke-like fashion. Remove the garlic from the olive oil, and drizzle the oil on top of the pizza.

4. Bake the pizza until the crust is golden (13 to 18 minutes).

Yield: *16-inch thin-crust pizza / 8 slices*

Suggested Crusts: *California, Cheese, Combo, Rosy, Simple, Speedy, Sponge, or Whole Wheat.*

(See Chapter 2 for recipes.)

3¼ tablespoons olive oil

2 tablespoons cornmeal

Dough for 16-inch crust (see suggestions)

2 cloves garlic, crushed

1 cup *Pizza Pesto* (page 71), or commercial pesto

2 logs (11 ounces each) Montrachet or other soft mild goat cheese, thinly sliced or crumbled

5 oil-packed sun-dried tomatoes, drained and julienned

8 large fresh basil leaves

Niçoise Potato Pizza

Yield: *16-inch thin-crust pizza / 8 slices*

Suggested Crusts: *Basil-Rosemary,*

California, Cheese, Combo,

Herb, Olive Oil, Semolina, Simple,

Speedy, or Sponge.

(See Chapter 2 for recipes.)

---

4 tablespoons olive oil

2 tablespoons cornmeal

Dough for 16-inch crust (see suggestions)

4 medium-sized (about 1 pound) new potatoes, scrubbed and thinly sliced

4 cloves garlic, roasted*

3 tablespoons chopped fresh parsley, or 1 tablespoon dried

1½ tablespoons snipped fresh thyme, or 1½ teaspoons dried

1 tablespoon chopped fresh marjoram, or 1 teaspoon dried

¾ teaspoon sea salt

½ teaspoon ground black pepper

6 ounces (1½ cups) shredded smoked Mozzarella cheese

1 jar (12 ounces) roasted red peppers, drained and cut into thin strips

6 ounces (1 cup) diced or thinly sliced Provolone cheese

1 large red onion, thinly sliced and separated into rings

1 cup chopped Niçoise or other imported green olives

* For garlic-roasting information, see page 90.

This simple, warming pizza always seems to hit the right cord when I am feeling out of sorts.

1. Preheat the oven to 450°F for 30 minutes. Brush 1 tablespoon of the oil over the surface of a 16-inch pizza pan and sprinkle with cornmeal, shaking out the excess. (If using pizza stones or tiles, place them in the oven before preheating, and heavily flour a pizza paddle.) Pat, stretch, or roll the dough in the prepared pan or on the paddle and set aside.

2. Place the potatoes in a large saucepan and fill with cold water. Bring to a boil, reduce the heat to low, and simmer the potatoes until just barely tender (4 to 6 minutes after the water begins to boil). Remove the potatoes with a slotted spoon and set aside.

3. In a small bowl, combine the remaining oil and the garlic. In another bowl, combine the parsley, thyme, marjoram, salt, and pepper.

4. Scatter the Mozzarella cheese over the prepared crust, add the pepper strips, and top with the potatoes. Drizzle with the garlic oil, sprinkle with half the herb mixture, and top with the Provolone cheese. Add a layer of onion rings, scatter with olives, and sprinkle with the remaining herbs.

5. Bake the pizza until the top is bubbly and the crust is golden (13 to 18 minutes).

Paris at Night Pizza

Combining sautéed onions, garlic, and peppers with a delectable, fully ripened French Brie makes this a most formidable pizza. Serve with a chilled bottle of dry white wine for a divine meal.

1. Preheat the oven to 450°F for 30 minutes. Brush 1 tablespoon of the oil over the surface of a 16-inch pizza pan and sprinkle with cornmeal, shaking out the excess. (If using pizza stones or tiles, place them in the oven before preheating, and heavily flour a pizza paddle.) Pat, stretch, or roll the dough in the prepared pan or on the paddle and set aside.

2. Heat 2½ tablespoons of the oil in a large skillet over medium-low heat. Add the peppers and onions, and sauté, covered, stirring frequently, until very soft and golden (about 25 minutes).

3. Spread the pepper-onion mixture over the crust, and top with the garlic. Arrange the Brie evenly on top and drizzle with the remaining oil.

4. Bake the pizza until the top is bubbly and the crust is golden (13 to 18 minutes).

Yield: *16-inch thin-crust pizza / 8 slices*

Suggested Crusts: *Combo, Semolina, Simple, Speedy, or Sponge.*

(See Chapter 2 for recipes.)

4 tablespoons olive oil

2 tablespoons cornmeal

Dough for 16-inch crust (see suggestions)

2 large red or yellow bell peppers, julienned

1 large green bell pepper, julienned

2 large sweet yellow onions, thinly sliced

15 cloves garlic, roasted*

12 ounces fully ripened herb Brie cheese, cubed

* For garlic-roasting information, see page 90.

Seaport Pesto Pizza

Yield: *16-inch thin-crust pizza / 8 slices*

Suggested Crusts: *Cheese, Combo,*

Greek Garlic, Semolina, Simple,

Speedy, Sponge, or Whole Wheat.

(See Chapter 2 for recipes.)

1 tablespoon olive oil

2 tablespoons cornmeal

Dough for 16-inch crust (see
  suggestions)

1 cup *Pizza Pesto* (page 71), or
  commercial pesto

2 logs (11 ounces each) Montrachet
  or other soft mild goat cheese,
  thinly sliced or crumbled

This pizza joins a mellow yet distinctive Italian basil pesto with a soft, luscious French goat cheese.

1. Preheat the oven to 450°F for 30 minutes. Brush 1 table-spoon of the oil over the surface of a 16-inch pizza pan and sprinkle with cornmeal, shaking out the excess. (If using pizza stones or tiles, place them in the oven before preheating, and heavily flour a pizza paddle.) Pat, stretch, or roll the dough in the prepared pan or on the paddle and set aside.

2. Spread the *Pizza Pesto* over the prepared crust and bake for 10 minutes. Remove the pizza from the oven and top with the cheese.

3. Return the pizza to the oven and bake until the cheese has melted and the crust is golden (4 to 8 minutes.)

Simply French Pizza

The idea for this pizza came from the unassuming and quite exquisite combination of onions, anchovies, tomatoes, olives, and herbs that the French are known to slather on their bread.

1. Preheat the oven to 450°F for 30 minutes. Brush 1 tablespoon of the oil over the surface of a 16-inch pizza pan and sprinkle with cornmeal, shaking out the excess. (If using pizza stones or tiles, place them in the oven before preheating, and heavily flour a pizza paddle.) Pat, stretch, or roll the dough in the prepared pan or on the paddle and set aside.

2. Heat the remaining oil in a large skillet over medium heat. Add the onions and garlic, and sauté, stirring frequently, until soft and pale (about 10 minutes). In a medium-sized bowl, combine the tomatoes, olives, parsley, rosemary, salt, and pepper. Set aside.

3. Spoon the onions over the prepared crust and top with the tomato mixture. Reserving the oil, drain the anchovies and arrange them evenly on the tomatoes. Drizzle with the anchovy oil.

4. Bake the pizza for 10 minutes, remove from the oven, and scatter the cheese on top.

5. Return the pizza to the oven and continue to bake until the cheese has melted and the crust is golden (4 to 8 minutes).

Yield: *16-inch thin-crust pizza / 8 slices*

Suggested Crusts: *Cheese, Combo, Greek Garlic, Rosy, Semolina, Simple, Speedy, or Whole Wheat.*

(See Chapter 2 for recipes.)

4 tablespoons olive oil

2 tablespoons cornmeal

Dough for 16-inch crust (see suggestions)

2 large red onions, chopped

2 large sweet yellow onions, chopped

4 cloves garlic, crushed

3 large ripe tomatoes, skinned* and chopped

1 cup sliced pitted black olives

3 tablespoons chopped fresh parsley, or 1 tablespoon dried

1 tablespoon snipped fresh rosemary, or 1 teaspoon dried

¾ teaspoon sea salt

½ teaspoon ground black pepper

2 cans (2 ounces each) flat anchovy fillets

5 ounces Montrachet or other soft mild goat cheese, crumbled

* For tomato-skinning information, see page 68.

Swiss Mushroom Pizza

Yield: *16-inch thin-crust pizza / 8 slices*

Suggested Crusts: *Combo,*

Olive Oil, Semolina, Simple, Speedy,

Sponge, or Whole Wheat.

(See Chapter 2 for recipes.)

½ cup olive oil

2 tablespoons cornmeal

Dough for 16-inch crust

1 medium-sized sweet yellow or
   Vidalia onion, thinly sliced

3 cloves garlic, crushed

2 pounds fresh mushrooms, wiped
   clean and sliced

2 teaspoons snipped fresh rosemary,
   or ¾ teaspoon dried

1½ teaspoons snipped fresh thyme,
   or ½ teaspoon dried

1 teaspoon sea salt

½ teaspoon ground black pepper

1 cup *Pizza Béchamel Sauce* (page 69)

8 ounces (2¾ cups) shredded
   Emmenthaler, Appenzeller, or
   other imported Swiss cheese

2 ounces (¾ cup) shredded Gruyère
   cheese

Sautéed mushrooms, creamy Béchamel sauce, and mild Swiss cheese are the perfect trio in this sophisticated pie.

1. Preheat the oven to 450°F for 30 minutes. Brush 1 tablespoon of the oil over the surface of a 16-inch pizza pan and sprinkle with cornmeal, shaking out the excess. (If using pizza stones or tiles, place them in the oven before preheating, and heavily flour a pizza paddle.) Pat, stretch, or roll the dough in the prepared pan or on the paddle and set aside.

2. Heat the remaining oil in a large skillet over medium-low heat. Add the onion and garlic, and sauté until soft (about 3 minutes). Toss in the mushrooms and cook, stirring frequently, until they have released their moisture and have turned golden (about 15 minutes). Stir in the rosemary, thyme, salt, and pepper, and set aside.

3. Spread the *Pizza Béchamel Sauce* over the prepared crust. Scatter half of the Emmenthaler cheese on the sauce, then top with the mushroom mixture and the remaining Emmenthaler.

4. Bake the pizza for 10 minutes and remove from the oven. Top with the Gruyère cheese.

5. Return the pizza to the oven and continue to bake until the cheese has melted and the crust is golden (4 to 8 minutes).

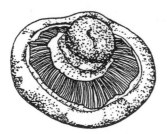

Pizza Versailles

Scraping the asparagus enables it to cook more quickly, retain its color and texture, and become more tender. This pizza spotlights fresh asparagus and mellow French cheese.

Yield: *16-inch thin-crust pizza / 8 slices*

Suggested Crusts: *American Pie, Basil-Rosemary, Cheese, Combo, Herb, Semolina, Simple, Speedy, Sponge, or Whole Wheat.*

(See Chapter 2 for recipes.)

1. Preheat the oven to 450°F for 30 minutes.* Brush 1 tablespoon of the oil over the surface of a 16-inch pizza pan and sprinkle with cornmeal, shaking out the excess. (If using pizza stones or tiles, place them in the oven before preheating, and heavily flour a pizza paddle.) Pat, stretch, or roll the dough in the prepared pan or on the paddle and set aside.

2. Steam the asparagus until tender-crisp (about 5 minutes). Set aside to cool.

3. In a medium-sized skillet, heat the remaining oil over medium-low heat. Add the scallions, garlic, and lemon zest, and sauté, stirring frequently, until soft and golden (about 8 minutes).

4. In a medium-sized bowl, combine the Ricotta, egg, parsley, salt, and pepper.

5. Spread the Ricotta mixture over the prepared crust. Arrange the asparagus evenly on top, and add the scallion mixture. Drizzle with the remaining oil.

6. Bake the pizza for 10 minutes, remove from the oven, and scatter the Port du Salut on top.

7. Return the pizza to the oven and continue to bake until the cheese has melted and the crust is golden (4 to 8 minutes).

¼ cup plus 1 tablespoon olive oil

2 tablespoons cornmeal

Dough for 16-inch crust (see suggestions)

1 pound fresh asparagus, trimmed, scraped, and cut into 1½-inch pieces

6 scallions or shallots, minced

3 cloves garlic, minced

1 tablespoon grated lemon zest

15 ounces (2 cups) Ricotta cheese, drained

1 large egg, beaten

¼ cup minced fresh parsley, or 1½ tablespoons dried

¾ teaspoon sea salt

½ teaspoon white pepper

4 ounces Port du Salut, Brie, or Camembert cheese, diced

* If using *American Pie Dough*, preheat the oven to 400°F. In Step 6, bake the pizza for 20 minutes, remove and top with the cheese, and continue to bake until the crust is golden (4 to 8 minutes). Allow to stand 5 minutes before cutting.

10

European Potpourri

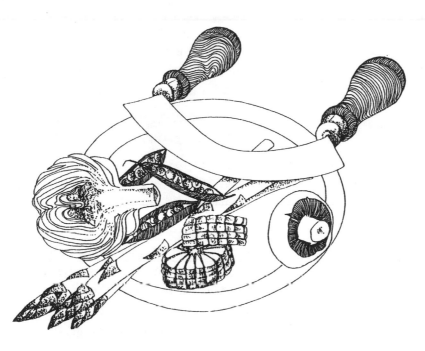

ach country of Europe has its unique identity and cultural heritage. Many of these countries, particularly those in the Mediterranean region, have pizza or pizza-like dishes in their culinary repertoires. For this chapter, I have created my own rendition of these classics. The menus of many other European countries, however, do not include pizza, or dishes like it. For these countries, I have stretched my imagination to create versions of pizza that include flavors and ingredients reflective of these lands. Although my creations may not be authentic, I have tried to keep them faithful to the spirit of the countries they represent.

In the mood for pizza that is overflowing with fresh garden vegetables? Then be sure to try the Spanish-inspired *Gazpacho Pizza*. If seafood is what you crave, the heavenly combination of shrimp and goat cheese found in *Heidi's Pizza* will fill the bill. You may want to sample a *Coventry Gardens Pizza* with its magnificent English Stilton, or the *German Cauliflower Pizza* that begs to be served with steins of ice-cold beer.

Journey through this chapter, making delectable stops along the way. Savor the many flavors and aromas of a Europe that few get to experience. Enjoy the trip.

Pizza el Greco

Yield: *16-inch thin-crust pizza / 8 slices*

Suggested Crusts: *Basil-Rosemary,*

California, Combo, Greek Garlic,

Herb, Semolina, Simple, Speedy,

or Whole Wheat.

(See Chapter 2 for recipes.)

⅓ cup olive oil

2 tablespoons cornmeal

Dough for 16-inch crust (see
    suggestions)

3 tablespoons dry white wine

4 cloves garlic, crushed

2 tablespoons minced fresh mint, or
    2 teaspoons dried

1 teaspoon ground black pepper

2 large eggplants

2 large sweet yellow or Vidalia onions,
    peeled and left whole

½ cup *Fresh Tomato Sauce* (page
    68), *Quick Tomato Sauce* (page
    70), or commercial pizza sauce

2 large ripe tomatoes, skinned* and
    chopped

2 tablespoons toasted sesame seeds

8 ounces (2½ cups) crumbled Feta
    cheese

* For tomato-skinning information, see
page 68.

Slices of marinated, grilled eggplant are married with a fine imported Feta cheese in this very Greek pizza.

1. Preheat the oven to 450°F for 30 minutes. Brush 1 table-spoon of the oil over the surface of a 16-inch pizza pan and sprinkle with cornmeal, shaking out the excess. (If using pizza stones or tiles, place them in the oven before preheating, and heavily flour a pizza paddle.) Pat, stretch, or roll the dough in the prepared pan or on the paddle and set aside.

2. In a large shallow casserole, whisk together the remaining oil, the wine, garlic, mint, and pepper, and set aside.

3. Cut off and discard the ends of the eggplants. Cut the eggplants into ¼-inch-thick slices and add to the flavored oil. Marinate the slices, turning once, for 30 minutes.

4. Heat a gas or charcoal grill to medium, and lightly oil the rack. Grill the eggplant slices and onions, basting and turning frequently until browned (about 15 minutes). Remove from the grill, thinly slice the onion, and set aside. (Instead of grilling, the eggplant and onions can be broiled in a conventional oven.)

5. Spread the tomato sauce over the prepared crust and top with the tomatoes. Arrange the eggplant slices over the tomatoes and sprinkle with sesame seeds. Top with the onions and drizzle with any remaining marinade.

6. Bake the pizza for 10 minutes. Remove from the oven and add the Feta cheese.

7. Return the pizza to the oven and continue to bake until the cheese has melted and the crust is golden (4 to 8 minutes).

Gazpacho Pizza

Summertime and a garden overflowing with tomatoes, peppers, and cucumbers, inspired this pizza, which can be made with or without cheese.

1. Preheat the oven to 450°F for 30 minutes. Brush 1 tablespoon of the oil over the surface of a 16-inch pizza pan and sprinkle with cornmeal, shaking out the excess. (If using pizza stones or tiles, place them in the oven before preheating, and heavily flour a pizza paddle.) Pat, stretch, or roll the dough in the prepared pan or on the paddle and set aside.

2. Heat the remaining oil in a large skillet over medium-low heat. Add the onions and garlic, and sauté until soft (about 3 minutes).

3. Add the peppers to the skillet and toss quickly to coat with oil. Sauté, stirring occasionally, until tender (about 8 minutes). Remove from the heat and stir in the cucumber, parsley, vinegar, salt, cumin, black pepper, and chiles.

4. Spread the *Fresh Tomato Sauce* over the prepared crust. Scatter with Mozzarella cheese, and add the tomatoes. Top with the sautéed pepper mixture.

5. Bake the pizza until the cheese has melted and the crust is golden (13 to 18 minutes).

Yield: *16-inch thin-crust pizza / 8 slices*

Suggested Crusts: *California, Cheese, Combo, Graham, Greek Garlic, Rye, Semolina, Simple, Speedy, Sponge, or Whole Wheat.*

(See Chapter 2 for recipes.)

¼ cup plus 1 tablespoon olive oil

2 tablespoons cornmeal

Dough for 16-inch crust (see suggestions)

1 large sweet yellow onion, chopped

4 cloves garlic, chopped

1 large red bell pepper, chopped

1 large green bell pepper, chopped

1 large yellow, orange, or purple bell pepper, chopped

1 large cucumber, peeled, seeded, and cubed

¼ cup chopped fresh parsley

1 tablespoon white wine vinegar

1 teaspoon sea salt

1 teaspoon ground cumin

½ teaspoon ground black pepper

¼ teaspoon crushed dried hot red chiles (or to taste)

1 cup *Fresh Tomato Sauce* (page 68), *Quick Tomato Sauce* (page 70), or commercial pizza sauce

8 ounces (2 cups) shredded Mozzarella cheese

4 large ripe tomatoes, skinned* and chopped

* For tomato-skinning information, see page 68.

Coventry Gardens Pizza

Yield: *16-inch thin-crust pizza / 8 slices*

Suggested Crusts: *Basil-Rosemary,*

California, Cheese, Combo, Herb,

Semolina, Simple, Speedy, or Sponge.

(See Chapter 2 for recipes.)

½ cup olive oil

1 large sweet yellow or Vidalia onion, chopped

1 large red onion, chopped

2 large leeks, white bulbs cleaned and chopped

6 scallions, chopped

6 cloves garlic, chopped

½ cup snipped fresh chives

¾ teaspoon sea salt

½ teaspoon ground black pepper

Dough for 16-inch crust (see suggestions)

2 tablespoons cornmeal

12 ounces (3 cups) crumbled Stilton cheese

Stilton is a magnificent English cheese whose flavor is a cross between an aged Cheddar and a Roquefort. In this pizza, it is a marvelous accent to a melange of roasted onions and garlic.

1. Preheat the oven to 350°F for 10 minutes. Place all but 1 tablespoon of the oil in a medium-sized oven-proof casserole with a lid. Add the yellow onion, red onion, leeks, scallions, and garlic, tossing well to coat with oil.

2. Cover and roast the vegetables, stirring frequently, for 30 minutes. Remove from the oven, and stir in the chives, salt, and pepper. Set aside to cool.

3. Raise the oven temperature to 450°F. Brush the remaining tablespoon of oil over the surface of a 16-inch pizza pan and sprinkle with cornmeal, shaking out the excess. (If using pizza stones or tiles, place them in the oven before preheating, and heavily flour a pizza paddle.) Pat, stretch, or roll the dough in the prepared pan or on the paddle.

4. Spread the roasted vegetables along with their cooking juices over the prepared crust and bake for 10 minutes. Remove from the oven and scatter the Stilton on top.

5. Return the pizza to the oven and bake until the cheese has melted and the crust is golden (4 to 8 minutes).

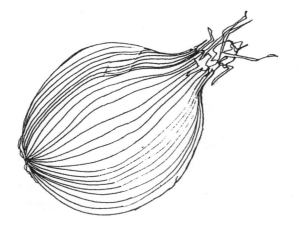

German Cauliflower Pizza

Traditional German salad of cauliflower and bacon inspired this pizza, which just begs to be served with steins of icy cold beer.

1. Preheat the oven to 450°F for 30 minutes. Brush the oil over the surface of a 16-inch pizza pan and sprinkle with cornmeal, shaking out the excess. (If using pizza stones or tiles, place them in the oven before preheating, and heavily flour a pizza paddle.) Pat, stretch, or roll the dough in the prepared pan or on the paddle and set aside.

2. Steam the cauliflower flowerets until tender-crisp (about 5 minutes). Drain, cool, and thinly slice. Set aside.

3. In a large skillet over medium-low heat, cook the bacon until almost crisp. Transfer to absorbent paper towels.

4. Drain all but 3 tablespoons of the bacon oil into a cup, and return the skillet to the stove over medium-low heat. Add the onion and garlic, and sauté until soft and golden brown (about 7 minutes). With a slotted spoon, transfer to a bowl.

5. Add 2 more tablespoons of the reserved bacon oil to the skillet. Increase the heat to medium and add the cauliflower slices. Stir-fry until crisp and golden on both sides (5 to 7 minutes). Transfer to the bowl with the onion and garlic, and add the parsley, vinegar, salt, pepper, and chiles. Mix together.

6. Scatter the Muenster cheese over the prepared crust and top with the cauliflower mixture.

7. Bake the pizza until the cheese has melted and the crust is golden (13 to 18 minutes). Remove from the oven, sprinkle with the grated cheese, and enjoy immediately.

Yield: *16-inch thin-crust pizza / 8 slices*

Suggested Crusts: *California, Cheese, Combo, Graham, Greek Garlic, Rye, Semolina, Simple, Speedy, Sponge, or Whole Wheat.*

(See Chapter 2 for recipes.)

1 tablespoon olive oil

2 tablespoons cornmeal

Dough for 16-inch crust (see suggestions)

1 large head cauliflower, separated into flowerets

1 pound lean uncooked bacon, cut into 1-inch pieces

1 large sweet yellow onion, minced

3 cloves garlic, crushed

$\frac{1}{4}$ cup chopped fresh parsley, or 1$\frac{1}{2}$ tablespoons dried

1 tablespoon white wine vinegar

$\frac{3}{4}$ teaspoon sea salt

$\frac{1}{2}$ teaspoon ground black pepper

$\frac{1}{4}$ teaspoon crushed dried hot red chiles (or to taste)

8 ounces (2 cups) shredded Muenster cheese

2 ounces ($\frac{1}{2}$ cup) grated Parmesan, Pecorino-Romano, or Asiago cheese

Heidi's Pizza

Yield: *16-inch thin-crust pizza / 8 slices*

Suggested Crusts: *Combo,*

Semolina, Simple, Speedy,

Sponge, or Whole Wheat.

(See Chapter 2 for recipes.)

---

8 tablespoons olive oil

2 tablespoons cornmeal

Dough for 16-inch crust (see suggestions)

5 shallots or scallions, minced

4 cloves garlic, crushed

1 pound medium-sized raw shrimp, peeled and deveined

1 tablespoon snipped fresh dill, or 1 teaspoon dried

¾ teaspoon sea salt

½ teaspoon ground black pepper

8 ounces Montrachet or other soft mild goat cheese, crumbled

1 cup *Sauce Americaine* (page 79)

This pizza was inspired by a traditional Swiss dish prepared with shrimp, brandy, and cream.

1. Preheat the oven to 450°F for 30 minutes. Brush 1 tablespoon of the oil over the surface of a 16-inch pizza pan and sprinkle with cornmeal, shaking out the excess. (If using pizza stones or tiles, place them in the oven before preheating, and heavily flour a pizza paddle.) Pat, stretch, or roll the dough in the prepared pan or on the paddle and set aside.

2. Heat the remaining oil in a large skillet over medium-low heat. Add the shallots and garlic, and sauté until soft (about 3 minutes). Spoon 2 tablespoons of the oil into a small cup and reserve.

3. Add the shrimp to the skillet and toss quickly to coat with oil. Sauté, stirring, just until the shrimp begin to curl and turn pink (2 to 3 minutes). Transfer to a bowl, and stir in the dill, salt, and pepper. Set aside.

4. Brush the surface of the prepared crust with the reserved oil, and top with the *Sauce Americaine.* Bake the pizza for 10 minutes, then remove from the oven. Add the shrimp mixture and the goat cheese.

5. Return the pizza to the oven and bake until the cheese has melted and the crust is golden (4 to 8 minutes).

Top: **Pizza el Greco (page 156)**
Bottom: **Scandia Kraut Pizza (page 164)**

Liptauer Pizza

Liptauer Käse is the Hungarian name for a spreadable cheese in which several cheeses have been combined with herbs, onions, and caraway seeds. This pizza reflects the regional cuisine of Hungary and Germany where liptauer is served as an appetizer.

1. Preheat the oven to 450°F for 30 minutes. Brush 1 tablespoon of the oil over the surface of a 16-inch pizza pan and sprinkle with cornmeal, shaking out the excess. (If using pizza stones or tiles, place them in the oven before preheating, and heavily flour a pizza paddle.) Pat, stretch, or roll the dough in the prepared pan or on the paddle and set aside.

2. With a wooden spoon, mash together the farmer cheese, Camembert, and Mozzarella in a medium-sized bowl. Stir in the onion, chives, caraway seeds, paprika, and pepper, and mix until thoroughly combined.

3. In another bowl, combine the artichoke hearts, tomato, capers, dill, garlic powder, salt, and the remaining olive oil.

4. Spread the cheese mixture evenly over the prepared crust and top with the artichoke mixture. Bake the pizza for 10 minutes, remove from the oven, and sprinkle with the grated cheese.

5. Return the pizza to the oven and bake until the cheese has melted and the crust is golden (4 to 8 minutes).

Yield: *16-inch thin-crust pizza / 8 slices*

Suggested Crusts: *Combo, Graham, Rye, Semolina, Simple, Speedy, Sponge, or Whole Wheat.*

(See Chapter 2 for recipes.)

3 tablespoons olive oil

2 tablespoons cornmeal

Dough for 16-inch crust (see suggestions)

12 ounces (1½ cups) soft farmer cheese or cream cheese

12 ounces ripe Camembert cheese, cubed

6 ounces (1½ cups) shredded Mozzarella cheese

1 medium-sized sweet yellow onion, minced

¼ cup snipped fresh chives

2 tablespoons caraway seeds

1 tablespoon sweet Hungarian paprika

1 teaspoon ground black pepper

1 can (16 ounces) artichoke hearts, drained and chopped

1 large ripe tomato, skinned,* diced, and drained on paper towels

2 tablespoons capers

1½ tablespoons snipped fresh dill, or 1½ teaspoons dried

1 teaspoon garlic powder

¾ teaspoon sea salt

2 ounces (½ cup) grated Parmesan, Pecorino-Romano, or Asiago cheese

* For tomato-skinning information, see page 68.

Norwegian Cheese-Onion Pizza

Yield: *16-inch thin-crust pizza / 8 slices*

Suggested Crusts: *Basil-Rosemary,*

Cheese, Combo, European Milk,

Herb, Rich Egg, Semolina, Simple,

Sponge, or Whole Wheat.

(See Chapter 2 for recipes.)

---

4 tablespoons olive oil

2 tablespoons cornmeal

Dough for 16-inch crust (see suggestions)

3 tablespoons unsalted butter or margarine

3 large sweet yellow or Vidalia onions, chopped

1 large leek, white bulb cleaned and chopped

5 scallions or shallots, chopped

8 ounces (2¾ cups) shredded Jarlsberg cheese

4 ounces (1 cup) shredded Mozzarella cheese

3 ounces (⅓ cup) cubed cream cheese or farmer cheese

2 large eggs, beaten

¼ cup snipped fresh chives, or 1½ tablespoons dried

1 tablespoon white Worcestershire sauce

1 teaspoon sea salt

½ teaspoon ground black pepper

4 ounces (1 cup) grated Parmesan, Asiago, or Pecorino-Romano cheese

---

This pizza, inspired by a classic Norwegian tart, highlights velvety cheese and an assortment of sweet sautéed onions.

1. Preheat the oven to 450°F for 30 minutes.* Brush 1 tablespoon of the oil over the surface of a 16-inch pizza pan and sprinkle with cornmeal, shaking out the excess. (If using pizza stones or tiles, place them in the oven before preheating, and heavily flour a pizza paddle.) Pat, stretch, or roll the dough in the prepared pan or on the paddle and set aside.

2. Heat the butter and the remaining oil in a large skillet over medium-low heat. Add the onions, leek, and scallions, and sauté, stirring frequently, until very soft and pale (about 10 minutes). Transfer to a large bowl and stir in 1 cup of the Jarlsberg, the Mozzarella, cream cheese, eggs, chives, Worcestershire, salt, and pepper.

3. Spread the onion mixture over the prepared crust and bake for 10 minutes. Remove from the oven and sprinkle with the remaining Jarlsberg, and top with the grated cheese.

4. Return the pizza to the oven and continue to bake until the cheese has melted and the crust is golden (4 to 8 minutes).

* If using *Rich Egg Dough,* preheat the oven to 400°F.

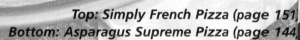

Top: *Simply French Pizza* (page 151)
Bottom: *Asparagus Supreme Pizza* (page 144)

Piroshki Pizza Pie

Potatoes and onions are common ingredients in the cuisines of Poland and Hungary. This pizza features these vegetables layered atop pesto sauce on a rich yeasted egg-dough crust. Unlike most other pizzas, this one should not be baked in an oven hotter than 400°F, or it will burn.

Yield: *16-inch thin-crust pizza / 8 slices*

Suggested Crust: *Rich Egg*

8 tablespoons olive oil

2 tablespoons cornmeal

Prepared *Rich Egg Dough* (page 57)

2 pounds potatoes, peeled and cubed

2 large sweet yellow onions, chopped

2 cloves garlic, chopped

4 ounces (½ cup) Ricotta cheese, well drained

4 ounces (1 cup) grated Parmesan, Asiago, or Pecorino-Romano cheese

¼ cup snipped fresh chives, or 1½ tablespoons dried

3 tablespoons chopped fresh parsley, or 1 tablespoon dried

¾ teaspoon sea salt

½ teaspoon ground black pepper

1 cup *Pizza Pesto* (page 71), or commercial pesto sauce

1. Preheat the oven to 400°F for 15 minutes. Brush 1 table-spoon of the oil over the surface of a 16-inch pizza pan and sprinkle with cornmeal, shaking out the excess. (If using pizza stones or tiles, place them in the oven before preheating, and heavily flour a pizza paddle.) Roll, stretch, or pat the dough in the prepared pan or on the paddle and set aside.

2. In a large saucepan, bring the potatoes and 2 quarts of water to a boil. Reduce the heat and simmer the potatoes until just tender (6 to 8 minutes). Drain well and transfer to a large bowl.

3. Heat the remaining oil in a large skillet over medium-low heat. Add the onions and garlic, and sauté, stirring frequently, until soft and beginning to turn golden (about 10 minutes). Transfer the sautéed onions and garlic to the bowl with the potatoes and gently stir together. Add the Ricotta cheese, half of the grated cheese, the chives, parsley, salt, and pepper. Combine well.

4. Spread the *Pizza Pesto* over the prepared crust, and top with the potato mixture. Sprinkle with the remaining grated cheese.

5. Bake until the top is bubbly and the crust is golden (30 to 35 minutes).

Scandia Kraut Pizza

Yield: *16-inch thin-crust pizza / 8 slices*

Suggested Crusts: *Cheese, Combo,*

Greek Garlic, Semolina, Simple,

Speedy, Sponge, or Whole Wheat.

(See Chapter 2 for recipes.)

¼ cup plus 1 tablespoon olive oil

2 tablespoons cornmeal

Dough for 16-inch crust (see
   suggestions)

2 medium-sized sweet yellow onions,
   chopped

4 cloves garlic, crushed

2 cans (10½ ounces each) sauerkraut,
   drained well

¼ cup vermouth or dry white wine

½ teaspoon sea salt

½ teaspoon ground black pepper

4 ounces (1 cup) shredded Mozzarella
   cheese

8 ounces (2¾ cups) diced Havarti
   cheese

In this notable pizza, sauerkraut gets a well-deserved starring role.

1. Preheat the oven to 450°F for 30 minutes. Brush 1 table-spoon of the oil over the surface of a 16-inch pizza pan and sprinkle with cornmeal, shaking out the excess. (If using pizza stones or tiles, place them in the oven before preheating, and heavily flour a pizza paddle.) Pat, stretch, or roll the dough in the prepared pan or on the paddle and set aside.

2. Heat the remaining oil in a large skillet over medium-low heat. Add the the onions and garlic, and sauté until soft (about 3 minutes).

3. Add the sauerkraut to the skillet and toss quickly to coat with oil. Sauté, stirring, for 5 minutes. Add the vermouth, bring to a boil, then reduce the heat to low. Cook, stirring frequently, until the liquid has evaporated (about 10 minutes). Stir in the salt and pepper, and set aside.

4. Sprinkle the Mozzarella cheese over the prepared crust. Spread half of the sauerkraut over the Mozzarella. Stir 1 cup of the Havarti cheese into the remaining sauerkraut and add to the crust.

5. Bake the pizza for 10 minutes. Remove from the oven and top with the remaining Havarti.

6. Return the pizza to the oven and continue to bake until the cheese has melted and the crust is golden (6 to 8 minutes).

European White Pizza

This deep-dish quiche-like pizza is filled with some exciting European cheeses—Port du Salut and Boursin from France, and Berkgäse from Austria.

Yield: *12-inch deep-dish pizza / 6 slices*

Suggested Crusts: *Basil-Rosemary, California, Cheese, Combo, Herb, Semolina, Simple, Speedy, or Sponge.*

(See Chapter 2 for recipes.)

1. Preheat the oven to 450°F for 30 minutes. Brush 1 table-spoon of the oil over the surface of a 12-inch deep-dish pizza pan and sprinkle with cornmeal, shaking out the excess. Pat the dough in the prepared pan and set aside.

2. Heat the remaining oil in a skillet over medium-low heat. Add the onion, and sauté until soft and pale (about 3 minutes). Stir in the rosemary and set aside.

3. With a wooden spoon, combine the grated cheese, Port du Salut, and Boursin cheese in a large bowl. Add the eggs and pepper, and blend well.

4. Spread the cheese mixture over the prepared crust, and top with the onions.

5. Bake the pizza until the cheese has melted and the crust is golden (15 to 20 minutes).

3 tablespoons olive oil

2 tablespoons cornmeal

Dough for 12-inch crust (see suggestions)

1 medium-sized sweet yellow or Vidalia onion, thinly sliced

1 tablespoon snipped fresh rosemary, or 1 teaspoon dried

4 ounces (1 cup) grated Bergkäse, Parmesan, or Pecorino-Romano cheese

12 ounces (2 cups) diced Port du Salut cheese

8 ounces (1½ cups) Boursin, Boursalt, or other triple crème cheese*

3 large eggs, beaten

½ teaspoon white pepper

* An equal amount of cream cheese (at room temperature) can be substituted for the triple crème cheese.

11

Tastes from Asia

Most countries throughout the world offer dishes that can be considered, even if in broad terms, a type of pizza. By "pizza" I mean a bread of some sort upon which various toppings are added. This is true with many, but not all, of the countries found on the Asian continent. While certainly true of Middle Eastern countries, most regions in the Far East are exceptions to this rule. Countries like China, Japan, Thailand, and Vietnam place their dietary emphasis on rice, fish, vegetables, and fruits, rather than leavened and unleavened bread products. It is in this area where I have taken a great deal of culinary liberty. The Far Eastern-style "pizzas" I have created, though certainly unconventional, are reflective of the tastes common to the Orient.

While you will never find an *Asian Peanut Pizza* or a *Thai Shrimp Pizza* on the menu of an Oriental-style restaurant, you will certainly find them unique and wonderfully flavorful. Moving across the continent, I have also offered pizzas with flavors significant to the Middle East. Try the enchanting *Desert Lands Pizza* or the savory *Moroccan Eggplant Pizza* for a taste that is decidedly Middle Eastern.

Each pizza found in this chapter, whether a subtle unassuming pie with simple toppings, or a commanding melange of spicy flavors and textures, has been created to introduce you to a sampling of the delightfully distinctive ingredients, spices, and aromas of the Asian continent.

Armenian Pizza Pockets

Yield: *4 large calzones*

Suggested Crusts: *California,*

Cheese, Combo, Greek Garlic,

Rice Cake, Semolina, Simple, Speedy,

Sponge, or Whole Wheat.

(See Chapter 2 for recipes.)

4 tablespoons olive oil

2 tablespoons cornmeal

Dough for crust (see suggestions)

1 large new potato, scrubbed and diced

2 cups water

2 large sweet yellow onions, chopped

2 cloves garlic, minced

1 pound lean ground lamb or beef

1/3 cup chopped fresh parsley, or 1 1/2 tablespoons dried

1/4 cup toasted pine nuts

1 teaspoon sea salt

1/2 teaspoon ground black pepper

1/8 teaspoon allspice

1/8 teaspoon ground cinnamon

6 ounces (1 1/2 cups) shredded Mozzarella cheese

1 large egg yolk

Whether you use lamb or beef, you will find these calzones, with their unusual combination of spices, both delicious and quite filling.

1. Preheat the oven to 450°F for 30 minutes. Brush 1 tablespoon of the oil over the surface of a large baking sheet, and sprinkle with cornmeal, shaking out the excess. (If using pizza stones or tiles, place them in the oven before preheating, and heavily flour a pizza paddle.)

2. On a floured surface, divide the dough into 4 equal pieces. With a floured rolling pin, roll each piece into an 8-inch circle and set aside.

3. In a small saucepan, bring the potatoes and 2 cups of water to a boil. Reduce the heat and cook the potatoes until just tender (about 8 minutes). Drain and place in a large bowl.

4. Heat 2 tablespoons of the oil in a large skillet over medium-low heat. Add the onions and garlic, and sauté until soft (about 5 minutes). Transfer to the bowl with the potatoes.

5. Add the ground meat to the skillet and cook, stirring occasionally, until browned. Drain the cooked meat and add it the potato mixture along with the parsley, pine nuts, salt, pepper, allspice, and cinnamon. Combine well.

6. Place an equal amount of the filling on half of each circle of dough, leaving a 1/2-inch border. Top with Mozzarella.

7. Fold each circle in half and press the edges together.

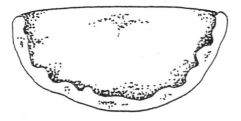

8. Seal with the tines of a floured fork.

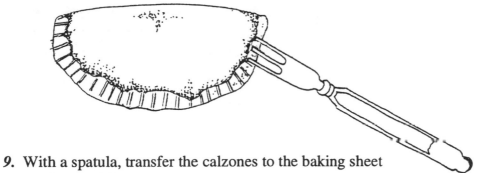

9. With a spatula, transfer the calzones to the baking sheet or pizza paddle.

10. Beat together the egg yolk and the remaining oil. Brush the top of each calzone with this mixture.

11. Bake the calzones until golden brown (12 to 16 minutes). Serve hot.

Arabian Pizza Pie

Yield: *12-inch deep-dish pizza / 6 slices*

Suggested Crusts: *Cheese, Combo,*

Graham, Greek Garlic, Herb,

Rice Cake, Rye, Semolina,

Simple, or Whole Wheat.

(See Chapter 2 for recipes.)

¼ cup plus 1 tablespoon olive oil

2 tablespoons cornmeal

Dough for 12-inch crust (see suggestions)

3 cloves garlic, crushed

3 large sweet yellow onions, thinly sliced

1 can (16 ounces) kidney beans, drained and rinsed

2 large eggs, beaten

1 cup half-n-half or whole milk

⅓ cup minced fresh parsley or chives, or 1⅓ tablespoons dried

½ teaspoon ground cumin

½ teaspoon sea salt

¼ teaspoon ground coriander

¼ teaspoon turmeric

¼ teaspoon cayenne pepper (or to taste)

¼ teaspoon white pepper

8 ounces (2¾ cups) shredded sharp Cheddar cheese

4 ripe tomatoes, skinned* and thinly sliced

2 ounces (½ cup) grated Kefalotiri, Kasseri, or Pecorino-Romano cheese

* For tomato-skinning information, see page 68.

Best when prepared in a deep-dish pan, this pizza is piled high with a spicy topping of beans, tomatoes, and cheese. It is typical of the pastry-lined pies of the Middle East.

1. Preheat the oven to 450°F for 30 minutes. Brush 1 tablespoon of the oil over the surface of a 12-inch deep-dish pizza pan and sprinkle with cornmeal, shaking out the excess. Pat the dough in the prepared pan and set aside.

2. Heat the remaining oil in a large skillet over medium-low heat. Add the garlic and two-thirds of the onions, and sauté, stirring frequently, until soft and just beginning to brown (about 8 minutes). Transfer to a large bowl.

3. Add the remaining onions, the beans, eggs, half-n-half, parsley, cumin, salt, coriander, turmeric, cayenne pepper, and white pepper to the sautéed onions. Stir the ingredients well, then mix in half of the Cheddar cheese.

4. Arrange the tomato slices on the prepared crust and top with the bean mixture.

5. Bake the pizza for 15 minutes, remove from the oven, and scatter with the Kefalotiri cheese and the remaining Cheddar.

6. Return the pizza to the oven and continue to bake until the cheese has melted and the crust is golden (5 to 8 minutes).

Indian Pizza

A melange of noteworthy cheeses and a sampling of Indian-style spices form a flavorful combination that works equally well as a pizza topping or a calzone filling.

1. Preheat the oven to 450°F for 30 minutes. Brush 1 tablespoon of the oil over the surface of a 16-inch pizza pan and sprinkle with cornmeal, shaking out the excess. (If using pizza stones or tiles, place them in the oven before preheating, and heavily flour a pizza paddle.) Pat, stretch, or roll the dough in the prepared pan or on the paddle and set aside.

2. Place the eggs in a large bowl and beat with a wire whisk until frothy. Stir in the remaining ingredients and combine well.

3. Spread the mixture over the prepared crust.

4. Bake the pizza until the cheese has melted and the crust is golden (13 to 18 minutes).

Yield: *16-inch thin-crust pizza / 8 slices*

Suggested Crusts: *Cheese, Combo, Graham, Greek Garlic, Rice Cake, Rosy, Rye, Semolina, Simple, Tandir, or Whole Wheat.*

(See Chapter 2 for recipes.)

2 tablespoons olive oil

2 tablespoons cornmeal

Dough for 16-inch crust (see suggestions)

2 large eggs

12 ounces (3 cups) shredded Muenster cheese

8 ounces (1 cup) soft farmer cheese or cream cheese

4 ounces (1 cup) grated Parmesan, Asiago, or Pecorino-Romano cheese

1/3 cup minced fresh parsley or chives, or 1 1/3 tablespoons dried

3 cloves garlic, crushed

2 teaspoons curry powder

3/4 teaspoon ground cumin

1/2 teaspoon sea salt

1/4 teaspoon turmeric

1/4 teaspoon cayenne pepper (or to taste)

1/4 teaspoon white pepper

Desert Lands Pizza

Yield: *16-inch thin-crust pizza / 8 slices*

Suggested Crusts: *California,*

Cheese, Combo, European Milk,

Greek Garlic, Rice Cake, Rich Egg,

Rosy, Semolina, Simple, Speedy,

Sponge, or Whole Wheat.

(See Chapter 2 for recipes.)

8 tablespoons olive oil

2 tablespoons cornmeal

Dough for 16-inch crust (see suggestions)

1 large sweet yellow onion, finely chopped

3 cloves garlic, crushed

1 large eggplant, unpeeled and cut into ½-inch cubes

1 pound lean ground lamb or beef

2 large ripe tomatoes, skinned* and chopped

2 tablespoons fresh lemon juice

1 tablespoon grated lemon zest

⅓ cup chopped fresh parsley, or 1½ tablespoons dried

1 tablespoon chopped fresh oregano, or 1 teaspoon dried

1 teaspoon ground cinnamon

1 teaspoon sea salt

½ teaspoon ground black pepper

8 ounces (2 cups) shredded Mozzarella cheese

2 ounces (½ cup) grated Parmesan, Asiago, or Pecorino-Romano cheese

* For tomato-skinning information, see page 68.

While I suggest using ground lamb in this enchanted pizza, ground beef can be substituted with equally delicious results.

1. Preheat the oven to 450°F for 30 minutes. Brush 1 tablespoon of the oil over the surface of a 16-inch pizza pan and sprinkle with cornmeal, shaking out the excess. (If using pizza stones or tiles, place them in the oven before preheating, and heavily flour a pizza paddle.) Pat, stretch, or roll the dough in the prepared pan or on the paddle and set aside.

2. Heat the remaining oil in a large skillet over medium-low heat. Add the onion and garlic, and sauté until soft (about 3 minutes). Add the eggplant and continue to sauté for 3 minutes. Transfer to a large bowl.

3. Add the lamb to the skillet and cook, stirring occasionally, until browned. Drain the cooked lamb and add it to the eggplant mixture along with the tomatoes, lemon juice, lemon zest, parsley, oregano, cinnamon, salt, and pepper. Combine well.

4. In another bowl, combine the Mozzarella and Parmesan cheese.

5. Scatter half of the cheese over the prepared crust and top with the eggplant mixture.

6. Bake the pizza for 10 minutes, remove from the oven, and top with the remaining cheese.

7. Return the pizza to the oven and continue to bake until the cheese has melted and the crust is golden (4 to 8 minutes).

Moroccan Eggplant Pizza

This Middle Eastern-style pizza spotlights roasted vegetables and a blend of spices that have also been roasted to intensify their flavors. Serve with plain yogurt for a truly Moroccan taste.

1. Preheat the oven to 450°F.

2. Prick the eggplants with a fork, then place on a baking sheet along with the onions. Roast the vegetables until tender but not mushy (about 45 minutes). After they have been in the oven 15 minutes, add the bell peppers to the baking sheet and roast for the final 30 minutes.

3. While the vegetables are roasting, brush the oil over the surface of a 16-inch pizza pan and sprinkle with cornmeal, shaking out the excess. (If using pizza stones or tiles, place them in the oven before preheating, and heavily flour a pizza paddle.) Pat, stretch, or roll the dough in the prepared pan or on the paddle and set aside.

4. Remove the roasted vegetables from the oven. Place the peppers in a clean paper bag and close it tightly. Let the peppers stream in the bag for 10 minutes before removing their blackened skin and cutting them into 1½-inch pieces. Place in a large bowl.

5. When cool enough to handle, chop the onions and place in the bowl. Peel the eggplants, cut into 1½-inch cubes and add to the bowl with the peppers and onions.

6. Roast the cumin, paprika, salt, black pepper, and cayenne pepper in a small skillet over medium heat. Shake the skillet frequently until the spices are dark and aromatic (about 5 minutes). Add the roasted spices to the eggplant mixture along with the garlic and lemon zest. Mix well.

7. Reserving the oil, drain the roasted red peppers (from the jar), slice into thin strips, and set aside.

8. Scatter the Mozzarella cheese over the prepared crust, arrange the tomato slices on top, and sprinkle with the

Yield: *16-inch thin-crust pizza / 8 slices*

Suggested Crusts: *Combo,*

Greek Garlic, Olive Oil, Rice Cake,

Semolina, Simple, Sponge,

Tandir, or Whole Wheat.

(See Chapter 2 for recipes.)

2 large eggplants

2 large sweet yellow onions

4 large bell peppers (any combination of colors)

1 tablespoon olive oil

2 tablespoons cornmeal

Dough for 16-inch crust (see suggestions)

1 tablespoon ground cumin

2 teaspoons paprika

1 teaspoon sea salt

½ teaspoon ground black pepper

¼ teaspoon cayenne pepper (or to taste)

3 cloves garlic, crushed

1 tablespoon grated lemon zest

1 jar (12 ounces) roasted red peppers

8 ounces (2 cups) shredded Mozzarella cheese

3 large ripe tomatoes, skinned,* sliced, and placed on paper towels to drain

¼ cup chopped fresh parsley (do not use dried)

1½ tablespoons chopped fresh mint, or 1½ teaspoons dried

2 cups plain yogurt (optional)

* For tomato-skinning information, see page 68.

parsley and mint. Drizzle 1½ tablespoons of the reserved pepper oil over the tomatoes. Top with an even layer of the eggplant mixture, arrange the roasted peppers on top, and drizzle with another 1½ tablespoons of oil.

9. Bake the pizza until the crust is golden (13 to 18 minutes). If desired, top each slice with a dollop of yogurt before serving.

Sesame⁄Zucchini Pizza

Yield: *4 individual 8-inch pizzas*

Suggested Crust: *Scallion Pancakes*

When served with a ginger-soy dipping sauce, scallion pancakes are delightful appetizers. In this recipe, however, I use them as crusts for these exceptional "Oriental" pizzas.

4 prepared *Scallion Pancakes* (page 62)

3 tablespoons canola, safflower, or sunflower oil

3 medium-sized zucchini, scrubbed and julienned

2 medium-sized sweet yellow onions, thinly sliced

3 cloves garlic, crushed

2½ teaspoons tamari or other soy sauce

1½ teaspoons black bean garlic sauce

1 teaspoon toasted sesame oil

1½ teaspoons ground black pepper

6 ounces (1½ cups) shredded Mozzarella cheese

1. Preheat the oven to 400°F for 10 minutes. Arrange the scallion pancakes, crisper sides up, on an ungreased baking sheet and set aside.

2. Heat the oil in a wok or skillet over medium-low heat. Add the zucchini, onions, and garlic, and sauté, stirring frequently, until soft and golden (about 10 minutes).

3. Add the soy sauce, black bean garlic sauce, sesame oil, and pepper. Simmer, stirring, until the liquid evaporates.

4. Top each pancake with the Mozzarella cheese and the vegetables.

5. Bake the pizzas until the crusts are crisp (12 to 15 minutes).

Asian Peanut Pizza

Tender strips of broiled chicken and a spicy peanut butter sauce give this pizza its decidedly Far Eastern flavor.

1. Preheat the oven to broil. Whisk together the baste ingredients in a small bowl.

2. Brush the chicken breasts with the baste and place in the broiler, 10 inches from the heat source. Broil the chicken, basting frequently and turning once, until the breast juices run clear when pierced with a fork (5 to 6 minutes per side).

3. Transfer the cooked breasts to a cutting board and slice into thin strips. Place the strips on a plate and drizzle with any remaining baste.

4. Reduce the oven heat to 450°F. Brush 1 tablespoon of the oil over the surface of a 16-inch pizza pan and sprinkle with cornmeal, shaking out the excess. (If using pizza stones or tiles, place them in the oven before preheating, and heavily flour a pizza paddle.) Pat, stretch, or roll the dough in the prepared pan or on the paddle and set aside.

5. Heat the remaining oil in a large skillet over medium-low heat. Add the onion, bell pepper, and carrots, and sauté, stirring frequently, until tender (8 to 10 minutes).

6. To make the peanut sauce, blend together the peanut butter, broth, cumin, curry, and lime juice in a blender or food processor until smooth.

7. Spread the peanut sauce over the prepared crust. Scatter with the Mozzarella, and add the sautéed vegetables. Top with the chicken strips.

8. Bake the pizza until the cheese has melted and the crust is golden (13 to 18 minutes).

Yield: *16-inch thin-crust pizza / 8 slices*

Suggested Crust: *Rice Cake*

1½ pounds boneless, skinless chicken breasts

¼ cup plus 1 tablespoon olive oil

2 tablespoons cornmeal

Prepared *Rice Cake Dough* (page 63)

1 large sweet yellow onion, thinly sliced

1 medium-sized red bell pepper, julienned

2 medium-sized carrots, scraped and thinly sliced

4 ounces (1 cup) shredded Mozzarella cheese

BASTE

2 cloves garlic, crushed

1 teaspoon powdered ginger root

3 tablespoons olive oil

PEANUT SAUCE

⅔ cup creamy peanut butter (do not use freshly ground)

½ cup chicken broth

1 teaspoon ground cumin

1 teaspoon curry powder

2 tablespoons fresh lime juice

Pork Barbecue Pizza

Yield: *16-inch thin-crust pizza / 8 slices*

Suggested Crusts: *Combo, Rice Cake,*

Semolina, Simple, Sponge, Tandir,

or Whole Wheat.

(See Chapter 2 for recipes.)

5 tablespoons canola, safflower, or
  sunflower oil

2 tablespoons cornmeal

Dough for 16-inch crust (see
  suggestions)

1 cup shredded green or Chinese
  cabbage

6 scallions, chopped

1 package (10 ounces) frozen green
  peas, thawed

8 ounces raw bean sprouts

1 pound lean boneless pork, thinly
  sliced

1 teaspoon dry sherry

½ teaspoon Chinese five-spice powder

1 cup *Zesty Barbecue Sauce* (page
  72), or commercial barbecue sauce

1 tablespoon tamari or other soy sauce

1 teaspoon hoisin sauce

¼ teaspoon crushed dried hot red
  chiles (or to taste)

A blend of soy sauce and hoisin sauce gives this savory pizza of boneless pork strips and stir-fried vegetables an exotic Oriental touch.

1. Preheat the oven to 450°F for 30 minutes. Brush 1 table-spoon of the oil over the surface of a 16-inch pizza pan and sprinkle with cornmeal, shaking out the excess. (If using pizza stones or tiles, place them in the oven before preheating, and heavily flour a pizza paddle.) Pat, stretch, or roll the dough in the prepared pan or on the paddle and set aside.

2. Heat 2 tablespoons of the oil in a wok or large skillet over medium-high heat. Add the cabbage and stir-fry for 4 minutes, then transfer to a large bowl.

3. Heat another tablespoon of oil in the wok. Add the scallions and peas, and stir-fry for 2 minutes. Add the bean sprouts and stir-fry another minute. Transfer to the bowl with the cabbage.

4. Heat the remaining oil in the wok. Add the pork and stir-fry until no longer pink (3 to 4 minutes). Transfer the cooked pork, sherry, and Chinese five-spice powder to the vegetables. Combine well.

5. In a small bowl, combine the *Zesty Barbecue Sauce* with the soy sauce, hoisin sauce, and chiles.

6. Spread the sauce over the prepared crust, and top with the pork-vegetable mixture.

7. Bake the pizza until the crust is golden (13 to 18 minutes).

Stir-Fried Veggie Pizza

In this pizza, Asian vegetables are stir-fried, placed atop a rice-cake crust, and drizzled with spicy sesame oil.

Yield: 16-inch thin-crust pizza / 8 slices

Suggested Crust: Rice Cake

1. Preheat the oven to 450°F for 30 minutes. Brush 1 tablespoon of the oil over the surface of a 16-inch pizza pan and sprinkle with cornmeal, shaking out the excess. (If using pizza stones or tiles, place them in the oven before preheating, and heavily flour a pizza paddle.) Pat, stretch, or roll the dough in the prepared pan or on the paddle and set aside.

2. Place the noodles and dried mushrooms in a large bowl, cover with boiling water, and soak for 30 minutes. Drain. Cut the noodles into 2-inch lengths and the mushrooms into thin strips. Place in a large bowl.

3. Heat 1 tablespoon of the oil in a wok or large skillet over medium-high heat. Add the tofu and stir fry until golden brown (about 10 minutes). Transfer to a plate.

4. Add the remaining oil to the wok, reduce the heat to medium, and add the leeks, carrots, and green beans. Stir-fry until tender-crisp (about 3 minutes). Combine with the noodles and mushrooms.

5. In a small bowl, stir together the sesame oil, soy sauce, garlic, ginger root, and chiles, and set aside.

6. Scatter the Mozzarella cheese over the prepared crust. Add the tofu, bamboo shoots, and straw mushrooms. Drizzle with the sesame oil mixture, and top with sesame seeds.

7. Bake the pizza until the crust is golden (13 to 18 minutes).

4 tablespoons canola, safflower, or sunflower oil

2 tablespoons cornmeal

Prepared *Rice Cake Dough* (page 63)

2 ounces cellophane noodles

5 dried Oriental mushrooms

8 ounces extra-firm tofu, drained and cut into small cubes

2 large leeks, white bulbs cleaned and thinly sliced

2 medium-sized carrots, scraped and thinly sliced

8 ounces fresh green beans, julienned

2 tablespoons toasted sesame oil

2 teaspoons tamari or other soy sauce

3 cloves garlic, crushed

½ teaspoon minced ginger root

¼ teaspoon crushed dried hot red chiles (or to taste)

6 ounces (1½ cups) shredded Mozzarella cheese

½ cup bamboo shoots, julienned

1 can (8 ounces) straw mushrooms, drained

2 tablespoons toasted sesame seeds

Thai Shrimp Pizza

Yield: *16-inch thin-crust pizza / 8 slices*

Suggested Crusts: *Rice Cake*

1/3 cup canola, safflower, or sunflower oil

2 tablespoons cornmeal

Prepared *Rice Cake Dough* (page 63)

6 scallions, chopped

4 cloves garlic, minced

3 tablespoons sesame seeds

1 pound medium-sized raw shrimp, peeled and deveined

2 tablespoons Oriental fish sauce

2 tablespoons minced fresh cilantro, or 2 teaspoons dried

1/2 teaspoon sea salt

1/4 teaspoon crushed dried hot red chiles (or to taste)

2/3 cup tahini (sesame seed paste)

3 tablespoons fish broth or bouillon

2 tablespoons fresh lemon juice

1 tablespoon hoisin sauce

1 tablespoon dry sherry

1 teaspoon toasted sesame oil

1 teaspoon tamari or other soy sauce

4 ounces (1 cup) shredded Monterey Jack or Mozzarella cheese

This unique, tasty pizza is crowned with a spicy shrimp-filled topping.

1. Preheat the oven to 450°F for 30 minutes. Brush 1 tablespoon of the oil over the surface of a 16-inch pizza pan and sprinkle with cornmeal, shaking out the excess. (If using pizza stones or tiles, place them in the oven before preheating, and heavily flour a pizza paddle.) Pat, stretch, or roll the dough in the prepared pan or on the paddle and set aside.

2. Heat 2 tablespoons of the oil in a wok or large skillet over medium-high heat. Add the scallions and garlic, and stir-fry until lightly browned (about 3 minutes). Transfer to a large bowl.

3. Heat another tablespoon of oil in the wok. Add the sesame seeds and stir-fry until toasted (2 to 3 minutes). Add to the bowl.

4. Heat the remaining oil in the wok. Toss in the shrimp and stir-fry until they turn pink and begin to curl. Add to the scallion mixture, along with the fish sauce, cilantro, salt, and chiles. Combine well and set aside.

5. In a medium-sized bowl, whisk together the tahini, fish broth, lemon juice, hoisin sauce, sherry, sesame oil, and soy sauce until smooth.

6. Spread the sauce over the prepared crust and scatter with the Monterey Jack cheese.

7. Bake the pizza for 10 minutes, remove from the oven, and top with the shrimp mixture.

8. Return the pizza to the oven and continue to bake until the top is hot and bubbly and the crust is golden (4 to 8 minutes).

12

Tropical Pizzas

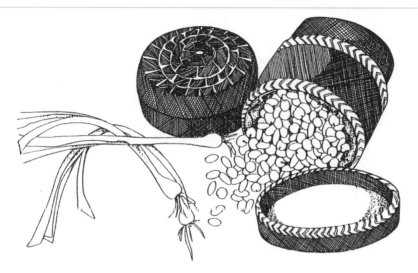

South America and the islands that dot its surrounding waters feature a cuisine that somewhat resembles North America's regional Creole cooking. Fresh, protein-rich foods often flavored with intense spices and herbs are characteristic.

What the menus of the Caribbean and South America do not have is pizza. What they do have, however, is the empanada. Closely resembling calzones, empanadas are pastry turnovers filled with delicious, savory fillings. Commonly served as entrées, empanadas are also offered as snacks and appetizers.

To create pizzas that reflect the cuisines of South America and the islands in and around the Caribbean, I looked to some traditional empanada recipes for inspiration. I then extended this starting point to include some unconventional ingredient combinations,

which translated into exciting, out-of-the-ordinary pizzas. For instance, traditional beef and pork empanadas were direct inspirations for my *Argentinean Steak Pizza*—paper-thin beef slices with vegetables and cheese piled high upon a crisp crust, and my *Chilean Pizza*—a combination of roasted pork cubes, bell peppers, onions, and cheese. For pizzas with more of an "island" flair, I combined some popular island ingredients and transformed them into exciting pizzas with a tropical twist. For instance, be sure to try the *Martinique Goat Cheese Pizza* or the *Caribbean Shrimp and Edam Pizza* for a divine taste of the tropics.

Any one of the exotic pizzas from this chapter will transport you to a sun-drenched tropical island, where you can almost feel the warm breezes and hear the relaxing sound of steel drums.

Argentinean Steak Pizza

Yield: *16-inch thin-crust pizza / 8 slices*

Suggested Crusts: *Cheese, Combo,*

Greek Garlic, Olive Oil, Semolina,

Simple, or Whole Wheat.

(See Chapter 2 for recipes.)

1½ pounds lean round or flank steak, thinly sliced*

4 tablespoons olive oil

2 tablespoons cornmeal

Dough for 16-inch crust (see suggestions)

3 carrots, scraped and julienned

3 cloves garlic, crushed

1 pound fresh spinach, rinsed well and patted dry

6 ounces (1½ cups) shredded Mozzarella cheese

4 ounces (1¼ cups) crumbled Feta cheese

½ teaspoon sea salt

¼ teaspoon ground black pepper

1 cup cooked fresh peas

2 tablespoons minced fresh parsley, or 2 teaspoons dried

1½ tablespoons snipped fresh thyme, or 1½ teaspoons dried

MARINADE

¼ cup red wine vinegar

¼ cup olive oil

2 tablespoons minced fresh parsley, or 2 teaspoons dried

1½ tablespoons snipped fresh thyme, or 1½ teaspoons dried

1 medium-sized sweet yellow onion, chopped

½ teaspoon sea salt

¼ teaspoon ground black pepper

*For easiest slicing, first chill the beef in the freezer until firm.

Combine wafer-thin slices of marinated beef with layers of vegetables and cheese for a splendid version of Latin American pizza.

1. Combine all of the marinade ingredients in a medium-sized bowl. Add the beef and toss to coat well. Cover and refrigerate at least 12 hours.

2. Preheat the oven to 450°F for 30 minutes. Brush 1 tablespoon of the oil over the surface of a 16-inch pizza pan and sprinkle with cornmeal, shaking out the excess. (If using pizza stones or tiles, place them in the oven before preheating, and heavily flour a pizza paddle.) Pat, stretch, or roll the dough in the prepared pan or on the paddle and set aside.

3. Heat 2 tablespoons of the oil in a large skillet over medium-low heat. Add the carrots and garlic, and sauté, stirring, until the carrots are tender (6 to 8 minutes). Transfer to a plate.

4. Add the spinach to the skillet, and sauté until the leaves are wilted (2 to 3 minutes). Place the spinach in a colander and press out any excess moisture. Transfer to a cutting board and chop.

5. In a medium-sized bowl, combine the Mozzarella and Feta cheese, and set aside.

6. Heat the remaining oil in the skillet over medium heat. Add the marinated beef and stir-fry until no longer pink (2 to 3 minutes).

7. Scatter the cheese mixture over the prepared crust and top with the spinach. Sprinkle with salt and pepper, and add the carrots. Arrange the beef strips in a spoke design on top. Scatter with the peas, parsley, and thyme.

8. Bake the pizza until the crust is golden (13 to 18 minutes).

Caribbean Shrimp and Edam Pizza

Seafood is the natural harvest of the Caribbean islands. In this lively pie, succulent shrimp is briefly marinated before it is grilled and paired with smooth Edam cheese.

Yield: *16-inch thin-crust pizza / 8 slices*

Suggested Crusts: *Cheese, Combo, Graham, Greek Garlic, Olive Oil, Rosy, Rye, Semolina, Simple, or Whole Wheat.*

(See Chapter 2 for recipes.)

1½ pounds medium-sized raw shrimp, peeled and deveined

¼ cup olive oil

1 large ripe tomato, skinned* and chopped

2 tablespoons cornmeal

Dough for 16-inch crust (see suggestions)

12 ounces (2 cups) cubed Edam cheese

MARINADE

2 tablespoons olive oil

1 medium-sized sweet yellow onion, chopped

2 cloves garlic, chopped

1 fresh hot chile (or to taste), seeded and finely chopped

½ cup fresh lime juice

½ teaspoon sea salt

½ teaspoon ground black pepper

* For tomato-skinning information, see page 68.

1. Combine all of the marinade ingredients in a medium-sized bowl. Add the shrimp and toss to coat well. Refrigerate 30 minutes.

2. Preheat the oven to 450°F for 30 minutes. Brush 1 table-spoon of the oil over the surface of a 16-inch pizza pan and sprinkle with cornmeal, shaking out the excess. (If using pizza stones or tiles, place them in the oven before preheating, and heavily flour a pizza paddle.) Pat, stretch, or roll the dough in the prepared pan or on the paddle and set aside.

3. Preheat a gas or charcoal grill to medium.

4. Thread the marinated shrimp onto skewers, and pour the marinade into a saucepan. Heat the marinade over medium-low heat, add the tomato, and cook, stirring occasionally, until thick (about 5 minutes). Set aside.

5. When the grill is ready, lightly brush the rack with oil. Liberally brush the shrimp with oil and grill them, turning frequently, just until they begin to curl and turn pink (3 to 4 minutes). Remove the cooked shrimp from the skewers and set aside.

6. Scatter the Edam cheese over the prepared crust. Bake for 10 minutes, remove from the oven, and arrange the shrimp on top. Drop spoonfuls of marinade over the shrimp.

7. Return the pizza to the oven and continue to bake until the crust is golden (4 to 8 minutes).

Chilean Pizza

Yield: *16-inch thin-crust pizza / 8 slices*

Suggested Crusts: *Combo,*

European Milk, Graham, Olive Oil,

Rich Egg, Rosy, Rye, Semolina,

Simple, or Whole Wheat.

(See Chapter 2 for recipes.)

1 pound boneless pork loin, cut into
   1-inch cubes

6 tablespoons olive oil

2 tablespoons cornmeal

Dough for 16-inch crust (see
   suggestions)

1 large sweet yellow onion, thinly
   sliced

1 large red bell pepper, julienned

6 ounces (1 1/2 cups) shredded
   Mozzarella cheese

2 ounces (1/2 cup) grated Parmesan,
   Asiago, or Pecorino-Romano cheese

MARINADE

1/2 cup white wine vinegar

1 teaspoon crushed dried hot red
   chiles

1 medium-sized sweet yellow onion,
   chopped

2 cloves garlic, crushed

1 teaspoon sea salt

1/2 teaspoon ground white pepper

1/4 teaspoon cayenne pepper (or to
   taste)

Small cubes of boneless pork are marinated, roasted, and then placed atop a chewy crust in this spicy pizza.

1. Combine all of the marinade ingredients in a medium-sized bowl. Add the pork cubes and toss to coat well. Cover and refrigerate 1 hour.

2. After the pork has marinated 45 minutes, preheat the oven to 450°F.* Brush 1 tablespoon of the oil over the surface of a 16-inch pizza pan and sprinkle with cornmeal, shaking out the excess. (If using pizza stones or tiles, place them in the oven before preheating, and heavily flour a pizza paddle.) Pat, stretch, or roll the dough in the prepared pan or on the paddle and set aside.

3. Preheat a gas or charcoal grill to medium.

4. Thread the marinated pork onto skewers. When the grill is ready, lightly brush the rack with oil. Grill the pork, basting with the marinade and turning occasionally, until no pink remains (8 to 10 minutes). Remove the cooked pork from the skewers and set aside.

5. Heat the remaining oil in a large skillet over medium-low heat. Add the onion and bell pepper, and sauté, stirring frequently, until soft and tender (about 10 minutes).

6. Combine the Mozzarella and grated cheese, and scatter over the prepared crust. Cover with the sautéed onions and peppers, and arrange the pork cubes on top.

7. Bake the pizza until the cheese has melted and the crust is golden (13 to 18 minutes).

* If using *Rich Egg Dough*, preheat the oven to 400°F.

Cuban Pizza Pie

Black beans, a staple on the island of Cuba, stand center stage in this spicy pizza. For an authentic Cuban taste, use Queso Blanco, a white cheese available in some supermarkets and most Spanish grocery stores, in place of the Monterey Jack.

1. Preheat the oven to 450°F for 30 minutes. Brush 1 tablespoon of the oil over the surface of a 16-inch pizza pan and sprinkle with cornmeal, shaking out the excess. (If using pizza stones or tiles, place them in the oven before preheating, and heavily flour a pizza paddle.) Pat, stretch, or roll the dough in the prepared pan or on the paddle and set aside.

2. Heat 2 tablespoons of the oil in a large skillet over medium-low heat. Add the peppers, sliced onions, and two-thirds of the minced garlic, and sauté until soft and beginning to turn golden (about 10 minutes).

3. In a blender or food processor, combine the remaining garlic and all but ½ cup of the beans. Process until smooth then transfer to a medium-sized bowl. Stir in the remaining beans, the chiles, wine, grated onion, half of the cilantro, the salt, black pepper, cumin, and cayenne pepper.

4. Arrange half of the Monterey Jack slices over the prepared crust and cover with the black bean mixture. Add the remaining cheese and top with the sautéed peppers and onions. Sprinkle the remaining cilantro on top and drizzle with the remaining oil.

5. Bake the pizza until the cheese has melted and the crust is golden (13 to 18 minutes).

Yield: *16-inch thin-crust pizza / 8 slices*

Suggested Crusts: *Cheese, Combo,*

European Milk, Garlic Greek,

Olive Oil, Semolina, Simple,

or Whole Wheat.

(See Chapter 2 for recipes.)

⅓ cup olive oil

2 tablespoons cornmeal

Dough for 16-inch crust (see suggestions)

2 large red and/or green bell peppers, sliced

1 large sweet yellow onion, sliced

3 cloves garlic, minced

2 cans (16 ounces each) black beans, drained

1 can (4 ounces) chopped green chiles, drained

3 tablespoons dry red wine

1 small sweet yellow onion, grated

¼ cup minced fresh cilantro or parsley (do not use dried)

1 teaspoon sea salt

½ teaspoon ground black pepper

½ teaspoon ground cumin

¼ teaspoon cayenne pepper (or to taste)

8 ounces (2 cups) thinly sliced Monterey Jack cheese

Shrimp Boat Pizza

Yield: *16-inch thin-crust pizza / 8 slices*

Suggested Crusts: *American Pie,*

Basil-Rosemary, Cheese, Combo,

European Milk, Greek Garlic, Herb,

Olive Oil, Semolina, Simple,

or Whole Wheat.

(See Chapter 2 for recipes.)

1 pound medium-sized raw shrimp, peeled and deveined

1 tablespoon olive oil

2 tablespoons cornmeal

Dough for 16-inch crust (see suggestions)

2 cups fresh corn kernels

1 large red bell pepper, diced

2 green chiles (or to taste), seeded and slivered

4 ounces (1 cup) shredded Monterey Jack cheese

2 ounces ($\frac{1}{2}$ cup) grated Parmesan, Asiago, or Pecorino-Romano cheese

MARINADE

5 tablespoons olive oil

5 shallots or scallions, minced

2 cloves garlic, crushed

1 tablespoon freshly grated lime zest

1 teaspoon sea salt

$\frac{1}{2}$ teaspoon ground black pepper

$\frac{1}{8}$ teaspoon ground nutmeg

This savory pizza has a colorful array of small pink shrimp, yellow sweet corn, green chiles, and red bell pepper.

1. Combine all of the marinade ingredients in a medium-sized bowl. Add the shrimp and toss to coat well. Cover and refrigerate 30 minutes.

2. Preheat the oven to 450°F for 30 minutes.* Brush the oil over the surface of a 16-inch pizza pan and sprinkle with cornmeal, shaking out the excess. (If using pizza stones or tiles, place them in the oven before preheating, and heavily flour a pizza paddle.) Pat, stretch, or roll the dough in the prepared pan or on the paddle and set aside.

3. With a slotted spoon, transfer the marinated shrimp to a bowl and set aside.

4. Heat the marinade in a large skillet over medium heat. Add the shrimp and sauté, stirring constantly until they just start to curl and turn pink. Using a slotted spoon, transfer the shrimp to a bowl.

5. To the skillet, add the corn, bell pepper, and chiles, and sauté until the pepper is tender (about 5 minutes).

6. Scatter the Monterey Jack cheese over the prepared crust and top with the corn mixture.

7. Bake the pizza for 10 minutes, remove from the oven, and arrange the shrimp on top. Sprinkle with the grated cheese.

8. Return the pizza to the oven and continue to bake until the crust is golden (4 to 8 minutes).

* If using *American Pie Dough*, preheat the oven to 400°F. In Step 6, bake the pizza for 20 minutes, remove and top with shrimp and grated cheese, and continue to bake until the crust is golden (4 to 8 minutes). Allow to stand 5 minutes before cutting.

Galician Sausage Pizza

Empanadas, meat-filled turnovers, have long been a favorite Latin American meal. For this pizza, I have combined some popular empanada fillings to create this notable meat-lovers pizza.

1. Preheat the oven to 450°F for 30 minutes.* Brush 1 tablespoon of the oil over the surface of a 16-inch pizza pan and sprinkle with cornmeal, shaking out the excess. (If using pizza stones or tiles, place them in the oven before preheating, and heavily flour a pizza paddle.) Pat, stretch, or roll the dough in the prepared pan or on the paddle and set aside.

2. Heat all but 1 tablespoon of the remaining oil in a large skillet over medium heat. Add the onion and garlic, and sauté until soft and pale (about 5 minutes).

3. To the skillet, add the pork, chorizo, ham, chile, and saffron. Reduce the heat to low and cook, covered, until the meat is tender (about 30 minutes). Remove from the heat, stir in the parsley, oregano, salt, and pepper, and set aside.

4. In a small bowl, blend together the butter and horseradish, then spread it over the prepared crust. Scatter with half of the Monterey Jack cheese, and top with the sausage mixture.

5. Bake the pizza for 10 minutes, remove from the oven, and sprinkle the remaining cheese on top.

6. Return the pizza to the oven and continue to bake until the cheese has melted and the crust is golden (4 to 8 minutes).

* If using *Rich Egg Dough*, preheat the oven to 400°F.

Yield: *16-inch thin-crust pizza / 8 slices*

Suggested Crusts: *California, Cheese, Combo, Greek Garlic, Herb, Rich Egg, Semolina, Simple, Speedy, Sponge, or Whole Wheat.*

(See Chapter 2 for recipes.)

8 tablespoons olive oil

2 tablespoons cornmeal

Dough for 16-inch crust (see suggestions)

1 large sweet yellow onion, chopped

2 cloves garlic, chopped

8 ounces boneless pork, diced

8 ounces chorizo or pepperoni, skinned and diced

8 ounces smoked ham, diced

1 fresh hot red chile (or to taste), chopped

2 threads saffron, or $\frac{1}{8}$ teaspoon ground

2 tablespoons minced fresh parsley, or 2 teaspoons dried

1 tablespoon chopped fresh oregano, or 1 teaspoon dried

1 teaspoon sea salt

$\frac{1}{2}$ teaspoon ground black pepper

4 tablespoons soft butter or margarine

1 tablespoon cream-style horseradish

8 ounces (2 cups) shredded Monterey Jack cheese

Saffron Vegetable Pizza

Yield: *16-inch thin-crust pizza / 8 slices*

Suggested Crusts: *Cheese, Combo,*

European Milk, Graham, Greek Garlic,

Olive Oil, Rye, Semolina, Simple,

or Whole Wheat.

(See Chapter 2 for recipes.)

8 tablespoons olive oil

2 tablespoons cornmeal

Dough for 16-inch crust (see
   suggestions)

1 pound extra firm tofu, drained and
   cut into 1-inch cubes

1 can (16 ounces) artichoke hearts,
   drained and sliced into thirds

1 large sweet yellow onion, diced

1 large green bell pepper, diced

5 cloves garlic, crushed

1 teaspoon paprika

1 teaspoon sea salt

$\frac{1}{2}$ teaspoon ground black pepper

4 threads saffron, or $\frac{1}{4}$ teaspoon
   ground

$\frac{1}{4}$ teaspoon cayenne pepper (or to
   taste)

1 cup fresh peas

2 large ripe tomatoes, skinned* and
   coarsely chopped

2 ounces ($\frac{1}{2}$ cup) grated Parmesan,
   Asiago, or Pecorino-Romano cheese

4 ounces ($\frac{3}{4}$ cup) shredded Roncal,
   smoked Edam, or Gouda cheese

4 ounces (1 cup) shredded Mozzarella
   cheese

* For tomato-skinning information, see
page 68.

As I adore the exquisite flavor and sunny color of saffron, I felt compelled to create a vegetarian pizza that spotlighted this popular Latin American spice.

1. Preheat the oven to 450°F for 30 minutes. Brush 1 tablespoon of the oil over the surface of a 16-inch pizza pan and sprinkle with cornmeal, shaking out the excess. (If using pizza stones or tiles, place them in the oven before preheating, and heavily flour a pizza paddle.) Pat, stretch, or roll the dough in the prepared pan or on the paddle and set aside.

2. Heat 2 tablespoons of the oil in a large skillet over medium heat. Add the tofu and stir-fry until brown and crisp (about 8 minutes). Transfer to a large bowl.

3. Heat another 2 tablespoons of oil in the skillet. Add the artichoke hearts and stir-fry until crisp (about 5 minutes). Add to the tofu.

4. Reduce the heat to medium-low, and heat 2 more tablespoons of oil in the skillet. Add the onions, bell pepper, and garlic, and sauté until golden (about 8 minutes). Gently stir this mixture into the bowl with the tofu and artichoke hearts. Add the paprika, salt, black pepper, saffron, and cayenne pepper.

5. Heat the remaining oil in the skillet over medium heat. Add the peas and quickly stir-fry until lightly crisp (3 to 4 minutes). Remove from the heat, add the tomatoes and grated cheese, and set aside.

6. Combine the Roncal and Mozzarella cheese, and scatter over the prepared crust. Add the tofu-vegetable mixture, and top with the tomato-pea mixture.

7. Bake the pizza until the crust is golden (13 to 18 minutes).

Top: **Sesame-Zucchini Pizza (page 174)**
Bottom: **Asian Peanut Pizza (page 175)**

Top: Rio Carnaval Pizza (page 190)
Bottom: Chilean Pizza (page 182)

Pork Calzones Caribe

These spicy pies of ground pork, eggplant, and cheese make won-derful entrées. Smaller versions can be served as hors d'oeuvres.

1. Place the eggplant in a colander and sprinkle with 2 tablespoons of the salt. Drain for 30 minutes, rinse with cold water, and pat dry. Set aside.

2. While the eggplant is draining, preheat the oven to 450°F for 30 minutes. Brush 1 tablespoon of the oil over the surface of a large baking sheet, and sprinkle with corn-meal, shaking out the excess. (If using pizza stones or tiles, place them in the oven before preheating, and heav-ily flour a pizza paddle.)

3. Divide the dough into 4 equal pieces. With a floured rolling pin, roll each piece into an 8-inch circle.

4. Heat 2 tablespoons of the oil in a large skillet over medium-low heat. Add the onion, mushrooms, and garlic, and sauté until soft (about 5 minutes). Stir in the pork, then transfer the mixture to a large bowl.

5. Heat 2 more tablespoons of oil and sauté the eggplant until tender. Add this to the pork mixture, along with the beaten egg, parsley, oregano, black pepper, and teaspoon of salt. Combine well, then add the Feta cheese.

6. Spread 2 teaspoons of mustard over each circle of dough, leaving a ½-inch border. Place an equal amount of pork mixture on half of each circle.

Yield: *4 large calzones*

Suggested Crusts: *California, Cheese, Combo, European Milk, Greek Garlic, Semolina, Simple, Speedy, Sponge, or Whole Wheat.*

(See Chapter 2 for recipes.)

1 medium eggplant, peeled and cut into small cubes

2 tablespoons plus 1 teaspoon sea salt

6 tablespoons olive oil

2 tablespoons cornmeal

Dough for crust (see suggestions)

1 large sweet yellow onion, chopped

8 ounces fresh mushrooms, wiped clean and sliced

2 cloves garlic, chopped

1 cup cooked ground pork

1 large egg, beaten

2 tablespoons minced fresh parsley, or 2 teaspoons dried

1 tablespoon chopped fresh oregano, or 1 teaspoon dried

½ teaspoon ground black pepper

4 ounces (1¼ cups) crumbled Feta cheese

5 tablespoons plus 1 teaspoon Dijon-style mustard

1 large egg yolk

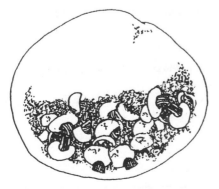

7. Fold each circle in half and press the edges together.

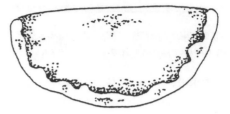

8. Seal with the tines of a floured fork.

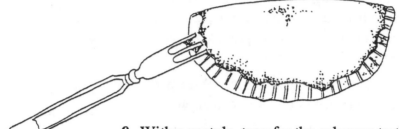

9. With a spatula, transfer the calzones to the baking sheet or pizza paddle. Whisk together the egg yolk and the remaining oil. Brush the tops with this mixture.

10. Bake the calzones until golden brown (12 to 16 minutes).

How to Peel and Seed a Mango

Since the flesh of the mango clings tightly to its large seed, it is helpful to know the proper paring technique. Follow the steps below:

1. With a sharp knife, make shallow lengthwise cuts in the skin.
2. With the knife, pry up the corners of the strips. Slide the knife between the skin and the flesh, and peel away the skin.
3. Slice through both sides of the mango, cutting as close to the to the seed as possible.
4. Angle the knife close to the seed and cut away the flesh. You will have two large pieces. Cut away all the meat that remains around the seed.

Martinique Goat Cheese Pizza

Whether you roast the vegetables on an outdoor grill or in your oven, the taste of this pizza will conjure images of warm tropical beaches and languid summer days.

1. Preheat the oven to 450°F for 30 minutes. Brush 1 tablespoon of the oil over the surface of a 16-inch pizza pan and sprinkle with cornmeal, shaking out the excess. (If using pizza stones or tiles, place them in the oven before preheating, and heavily flour a pizza paddle.) Pat, stretch, or roll the dough in the prepared pan or on the paddle and set aside.

2. Preheat a gas or charcoal grill to medium. When the grill is ready, lightly oil the rack. Brush the tomatoes, bell peppers, and mango with oil and place them on the grill. Cook, turning occasionally, until golden brown but not charred. Remove from the grill.

3. When cool enough to handle, cut the bell peppers in half, remove the seeds and cut into thin strips. Remove the mango flesh from the seed and cut into cubes. Set aside.

4. When the tomatoes have cooled, place them in a colander and coarsely chop, allowing the juices to drain. Place the chopped tomatoes in a saucepan along with the vinegar, garlic, basil, salt, white pepper, and the remaining oil. Heat the mixture, stirring occasionally, over low heat.

5. Scatter the goat cheese over the prepared crust and top with pepper strips and mango.

6. Bake the pizza until the cheese has melted and the crust is golden (13 to 18 minutes). Serve immediately alongside a bowl of the warm tomato sauce.

Yield: *16-inch thin-crust pizza / 8 slices*

Suggested Crusts: *Basil-Rosemary, Cheese, Combo, European Milk, Graham, Greek Garlic, Herb, Olive Oil, Rye, Semolina, Simple, or Whole Wheat.*

(See Chapter 2 for recipes.)

¼ cup plus 1 tablespoon olive oil

2 tablespoons cornmeal

Dough for 16-inch crust (see suggestions)

3 large ripe tomatoes

1 large red bell pepper

1 large green bell pepper

1 large yellow, orange, or purple bell pepper

1 large mango, peeled*

2 tablespoons balsamic or red wine vinegar

2 cloves garlic, crushed

2 tablespoons chopped fresh basil, or 2 teaspoons dried

¾ teaspoon sea salt

½ teaspoon ground white pepper

16 ounces Montrachet or other soft mild goat cheese, crumbled

* For mango-peeling instructions, see page 188.

Rio Carnaval Pizza

Yield: *16-inch thin-crust pizza / 8 slices*

Suggested Crusts: *American Pie,*

Basil-Rosemary, Cheese, Combo,

European Milk, Greek Garlic,

Herb, Olive Oil, Semolina,

Simple, or Whole Wheat.

(See Chapter 2 for recipes.)

6 tablespoons olive oil

2 tablespoons cornmeal

Dough for 16-inch crust (see suggestions)

2 pounds Brussels sprouts, trimmed

1 cup toasted bread crumbs

2 large eggs, beaten

2 tablespoons milk

1 teaspoon sea salt

½ teaspoon ground white pepper

4 ounces (1 cup) shredded Mozzarella cheese

4 ounces (¾ cup) shredded Provolone cheese

1 cup *Catalina Sauce* (page 73)

2 ounces (½ cup) grated Parmesan, Asiago, or Pecorino-Romano cheese

3 tablespoons chopped fresh parsley, or 1 tablespoon dried

Brussels sprouts are breaded and fried before crowning this simple vegetable pizza.

1. Preheat the oven to 450°F for 30 minutes.* Brush 1 tablespoon of the oil over the surface of a 16-inch pizza pan and sprinkle with cornmeal, shaking out the excess. (If using pizza stones or tiles, place them in the oven before preheating, and heavily flour a pizza paddle.) Pat, stretch, or roll the dough in the prepared pan or on the paddle and set aside.

2. Place the Brussels sprouts in a medium-sized saucepan with enough water to cover. Bring to a boil, reduce the heat to low, and simmer until just tender (6 to 10 minutes for small sprouts, 10 to 15 minutes for large ones). Rinse under cold water. Cut each sprout in half and set aside.

3. In a shallow bowl, whisk together the eggs and milk. Place the bread crumbs in another shallow bowl. Dip the Brussels sprouts first into the bread crumbs, then into egg, and then into the bread crumbs again.

4. Heat the remaining oil in a large skillet over medium heat. Fry the Brussels sprouts until golden brown. Transfer to paper towels and sprinkle with salt and pepper.

5. Combine the Mozzarella and Provolone cheese, and scatter half over the prepared crust. Drizzle with the *Catalina Sauce,* then cover with the remaining cheese. Arrange the sprouts in a single layer on top.

6. Bake the pizza for 10 minutes, remove from the oven, and sprinkle with the grated cheese and parsley. Continue to bake until the crust is golden (4 to 8 minutes).

* If using *American Pie Dough,* preheat the oven to 400°F. In Step 6, bake the pizza for 20 minutes, remove and top with cheese and parsley, and continue to bake until the crust is golden (4 to 8 minutes). Allow to stand 5 minutes before cutting.

13

Country Breakfast Pizzas

While most people think of pizza as an easy choice for lunch, dinner, or a snack, others find it equally satisfying as the first meal of the day. Compare a typical breakfast to a typical pizza. What do many people choose for breakfast on those days when a quick bagel or Danish on the run isn't enough? Eggs, bacon, toast, and perhaps potatoes? Then consider whether or not pizza, with its wide variety of nutritious toppings, might not be a better breakfast choice. A simple pizza topped with sauce and cheese contains less fat, more complex carbohydrates, and as much protein as a bacon and egg breakfast.

In this chapter you will find a wide assortment of nutritious and flavorful pizzas to start your day. To save time during the early morning hours, all of these delightful breakfast affairs are made on readily available commercially prepared bread items such as Italian bread shells (boboli), bagels, and pocket breads. Although none of the breakfast pizzas requires a homemade crust, feel free to make one if you have the time and desire to do so. With the exception of the *Hard Pretzel* and *Soft Pretzel* doughs, all of the doughs in Chapter 2 are good choices.

Some of the creations in this chapter, such as my *Breakfast Brie* and *Mushroom Cheese* pizzas, are rich and decadent and oozing with cheese. For those who prefer to start their day with something sweet, *Apple Butter Pizzas* and *Peanut Honeys* are good choices. Looking to satisfy the heartiest of appetites? Try *Pizzas Benedict Arnold* or a *Farmhouse Pizza*. There is even a *Healthy Morning Pizza* for a light, nutritious way to greet the morning. One thing is certain, the variety of breakfast pizzas found in this chapter is sure to please even the most discriminating pizzaholics!

Apple Butter Pizzas

Yield: *4 servings*

- 4 6-inch pizza shells, Italian bread shells (boboli), focaccia, pita bread, naan, bagels, or English muffins*
- 8 ounces lean uncooked bacon, cut into 1-inch pieces
- 1 cup apple butter
- 1 cup creamy peanut butter
- 2 tablespoons date sugar or brown sugar
- ¼ teaspoon ground cinnamon
- ⅛ teaspoon ground nutmeg
- 1 large Granny Smith or other tart apple, peeled, cored, and finely chopped

* If using bagels or English muffins, split them in half before arranging on the baking sheet.

Remember old-fashioned apple butter? Blend it with peanut butter and top with fresh apples for a delightful pizza topping!

1. Preheat the oven to 400°F for 10 minutes. Cook the bacon until just crisp, drain on paper towels, and set aside. In a medium-sized bowl, blend the apple butter and peanut butter. In a small bowl, combine the sugar, cinnamon, and nutmeg.

2. Place the pizza shells on an ungreased pizza pan or baking sheet. Spread the apple-peanut butter mixture on top of each shell. Top with bacon, and scatter with apples. Sprinkle the sugar mixture on top.

3. Bake the pizzas until the tops are bubbly and the crusts are golden (10 to 12 minutes).

Breakfast Brie Pizzas

Yield: *4 servings*

- 4 6-inch pizza shells, Italian bread shells (boboli), focaccia, pita bread, or naan
- 10 ounces ripe Brie cheese, thinly sliced
- 1 cup toasted and chopped cashews, macadamias, pecans, or almonds
- ⅔ cup apricot or peach preserves

This pizza, which makes a perfect, deliciously decadent meal for breakfast, is also a wonderful cocktail party appetizer.

1. Preheat the oven to 400°F for 10 minutes. Place the pizza shells on an ungreased pizza pan or baking sheet. Top with the Brie and sprinkle with nuts.

2. Bake the pizzas until the cheese is bubbly and the crusts are golden (8 to 10 minutes). Remove from the oven and place a dollop of preserves on the center of each. Serve immediately.

Bacon and Cheese Pizzas

When I was growing up, my mother often prepared grilled cheese and bacon sandwiches for lunch, which prompted me to create these breakfast pizzas.

Yield: *4 servings*

1. Preheat the oven to 400°F for 10 minutes. Cook the bacon and onions over medium heat until the bacon is just crisp and the onions are golden (8 to 10 minutes). Reserving a bit of the oil, transfer the bacon and onions to paper towels to drain. In a medium-sized bowl, combine the Mozzarella and goat cheese.

2. Place the pizza shells on an ungreased pizza pan or baking sheet. Brush each pizza shell with some of the reserved oil, and sprinkle the cheese mixture on top. Top with the bacon and onions.

3. Bake the pizzas until the cheese is bubbly and the crusts are golden (12 to 15 minutes).

- 4 6-inch pizza shells, Italian bread shells (boboli), focaccia, pita bread, or naan
- 12 ounces lean uncooked bacon, cut into 1-inch pieces
- 1 medium-sized sweet yellow or Vidalia onion, thinly sliced
- 8 ounces (2 cups) shredded Mozzarella cheese
- 11 ounces Montrachet or other soft mild goat cheese, crumbled

Blueberry Cheese Pizzas

These delicious breakfast pizzas are best with fresh blueberries, although frozen berries can be used as well.

Yield: *4 servings*

1. Preheat the oven to 400°F for 10 minutes. In a medium-sized bowl, blend the Ricotta cheese, date sugar, orange zest, and nutmeg. In another bowl, combine the berries and confectioners' sugar.

2. Place the pizza shells on an ungreased pizza pan or baking sheet. Spread the Ricotta mixture on each shell and top with the berries.

3. Bake the pizzas until the tops are bubbly and the crusts are golden (10 to 12 minutes).

- 4 6-inch pizza shells, Italian bread shells (boboli), focaccia, pita bread, or naan
- 15 ounces (2 cups) whole-milk Ricotta cheese
- ½ cup date sugar or brown sugar
- 1½ tablespoons grated orange zest
- ¼ teaspoon ground nutmeg
- 2 cups fresh blueberries, or frozen blueberries that have been thawed and drained
- ½ cup sifted confectioners' sugar

Farmhouse Pizzas

Yield: *4 servings*

These delicious breakfast noshes can be assembled the night before.

4 6-inch pizza shells, Italian bread shells (boboli), focaccia, pita bread, naan, bagels, or English muffins*

1 pound lean uncooked bacon

8 ounces (2¾ cups) shredded sharp Cheddar cheese

4 large hard-boiled eggs, thinly sliced

1 teaspoon sea salt

½ teaspoon ground black pepper

2 ounces (½ cup) grated Parmesan, Asiago, or Pecorino-Romano cheese

* If using bagels or English muffins, split them in half before arranging on the baking sheet.

1. Preheat the oven to 400° F for 10 minutes. In a large skillet, cook the bacon until crisp. Reserving some of the oil, transfer the bacon to paper towels to drain, then crumble it into large pieces.

2. Place the pizza shells on an ungreased pizza pan or baking sheet. Brush each shell with some of the reserved oil and top with the Cheddar cheese. Add the bacon, and arrange one sliced egg on each. Sprinkle with salt, pepper, and the grated cheese.

3. Bake the pizzas until the cheese is bubbly and the crusts are golden (10 to 12 minutes).

Peanut Honeys

Yield: *4 servings*

These sweet breakfast treats are high in protein and a snap to make.

4 6-inch pizza shells, Italian bread shells (boboli), focaccia, pita bread, naan, bagels, or English muffins*

1 cup peanut butter (any style)

1 cup honey

½ cup golden raisins

⅓ cup sunflower seeds

* If using bagels or English muffins, split them in half before arranging on the baking sheet.

1. Preheat the oven to 400°F for 10 minutes. In a medium-sized bowl blend together the peanut butter, honey, raisins, and sunflower seeds.

2. Place the pizza shells on an ungreased pizza pan or baking sheet. Spread the peanut butter mixture on top of each shell.

3. Bake the pizzas until the tops are bubbly and the crusts are golden (10 to 12 minutes).

4. Sprinkle a few raisins and/or sunflower seeds on top of the pizzas before serving.

Hawaiian Morning Pizzas

These fresh pizzas can be whipped up in a flash and are heavenly first thing in the morning.

1. Preheat the oven to 400°F for 10 minutes. In a medium-sized bowl, blend together the cream cheese, ½ cup of the honey, and the nuts.

2. Place the pizza shells on an ungreased pizza pan or baking sheet. Spread the cream cheese mixture on top of each shell. Top with the pineapple chunks, pressing them lightly into the cheese. Drizzle with the remaining honey.

3. Bake the pizzas until the tops are bubbly and the crusts are golden (10 to 12 minutes).

Yield: *4 servings*

4 6-inch pizza shells, Italian bread shells (boboli), focaccia, pita bread, naan, bagels, or English muffins*

16 ounces (2 cups) whipped or very soft cream cheese

¾ cup honey

1 cup toasted and chopped macadamia nuts or pecans

1 can (10 ounces) pineapple chunks, drained

* If using bagels or English muffins, split them in half before arranging on the baking sheet.

Old Favorites

Although the combination of peanut butter and bananas is certainly not a new idea, it makes a breakfast pizza that is simply divine.

1. Preheat the oven to 400°F for 10 minutes. In a small bowl, blend together the raisins and peanut butter.

2. Place the pizza shells on an ungreased pizza pan or baking sheet. Spread the peanut butter mixture on each shell. Arrange the banana slices on top and sprinkle with coconut. Drizzle honey on top.

3. Bake the pizzas until the tops are bubbly and the crusts are golden (10 to 12 minutes).

Yield: *4 servings*

4 6-inch pizza shells, Italian bread shells (boboli), focaccia, pita bread, naan, bagels, or English muffins*

½ cup golden raisins

1½ cups creamy peanut butter

4 large ripe bananas, sliced into circles

½ cup flaked coconut

¼ cup honey

* If using bagels or English muffins, split them in half before arranging on the baking sheet.

Healthy Morning Pizzas

Yield: *4 servings*

- 4 6-inch pizza shells, Italian bread shells (boboli), focaccia, pita bread, naan, bagels, or English muffins*
- 8 ounces (1 cup) soft farmer cheese or cottage cheese
- 4 ounces (1¼ cups) shredded sharp Cheddar cheese
- 2 medium-sized carrots, scraped and grated
- 1 large celery stalk, finely chopped
- 5 scallions or shallots, finely chopped
- 1 tablespoon snipped fresh dill, or 1 teaspoon dried
- 1 teaspoon sea salt
- ½ teaspoon ground white pepper
- ¼ teaspoon cayenne pepper (or to taste)

* If using bagels or English muffins, split them in half before arranging on the baking sheet.

These are my favorite breakfast pizzas, largely because they are so healthy and full of fresh flavor.

1. Preheat the oven to 400°F for 10 minutes. Place the pizza shells on an ungreased pizza pan or baking sheet and set aside. In a medium-sized bowl, blend together the remaining ingredients.

2. Bake the shells for 8 minutes. Remove from the oven and top each shell with the cheese mixture.

3. Return the pizzas to the oven and bake until the tops are bubbly and the crusts are golden (4 to 6 minutes).

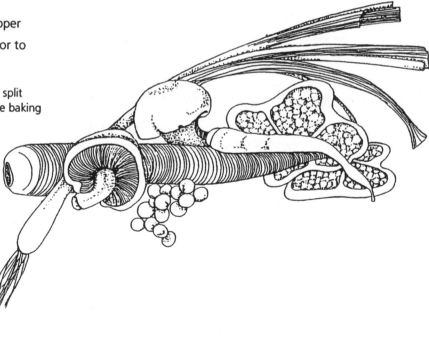

Mushroom Cheese Pizzas

These marvelous creamy smoked pizzas are scrumptious for break-fast or lunch.

1. Preheat the oven to 400°F for 10 minutes. In a large skillet, heat the oil over medium-low heat. Add the scallions and mushrooms and cook, stirring frequently, until the mushrooms have released their moisture and have turned golden brown (about 15 minutes). Sprinkle with salt and pepper and set aside.

2. Place the pizza shells on an ungreased pizza pan or baking sheet. Spread 2 tablespoons of horseradish sauce on each shell. Scatter with the cheese and top with the mushrooms.

3. Bake the pizzas until the cheese has melted and the crusts are golden (12 to 15 minutes).

Yield: *4 servings*

4 6-inch pizza shells, Italian bread shells (boboli), focaccia, pita bread, or naan

1 tablespoon canola, safflower, or sunflower oil

4 scallions or shallots, minced

1 pound fresh mushrooms, wiped clean and sliced

1 teaspoon sea salt

½ teaspoon ground black pepper

½ cup horseradish sauce*

8 ounces (1½ cups) diced smoked Gouda or Edam cheese

* Prepared horseradish sauce is found in the condiment section of most supermarkets. To make your own, combine ⅓ cup of mayonnaise, 3 tablespoons sour cream, and 1 tablespoon cream-style horseradish.

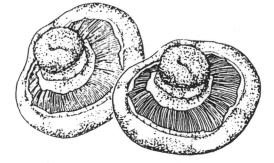
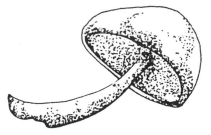

Pizzas Benedict Arnold

Yield: *4 servings*

4 6-inch pizza shells, Italian bread
   shells (boboli), focaccia, pita bread,
   or naan

1 tablespoon canola, safflower, or
   sunflower oil

12 slices Canadian bacon

6 ounces (2 cups) shredded
   Emmenthaler, Appenzeller, or
   other imported Swiss cheese

4 tablespoons butter or margarine, or
   canola, safflower, or sunflower oil

4 large eggs

¼ cup sliced pitted black olives

HOLLANDAISE SAUCE

3 large egg yolks

2 tablespoons fresh lemon juice

½ cup (1 stick) unsalted butter,
   melted and cooled to room
   temperature

½ teaspoon sea salt (or to taste)

½ teaspoon white pepper

Pinch cayenne pepper (or to taste)

After enjoying this unique version of eggs Benedict, you may never go back to the original.

1. Preheat the oven to 375°F for 10 minutes.

2. To make the Hollandaise sauce, fill the bottom of a double boiler with water and bring it to a boil over medium-high heat. Reduce the heat to low so the water is just under a simmer. While the water is heating, whisk together the egg yolks and lemon juice in the top half of the double boiler. When the water is just under a simmer, set the top half of the pot over the bottom, and continue to whisk the yolks until smooth.

3. Gradually whisk the melted butter into the egg yolks in a slow, steady stream. Add the salt, white pepper, and cayenne pepper, and continue to whisk over the hot water until the sauce is thick. Turn off the heat, cover, and keep warm.

4. Heat the oil in a large skillet over medium-low heat. Add the Canadian bacon and cook for 2 minutes on each side. Transfer to paper towels.

5. Place the pizza shells on an ungreased pizza pan or baking sheet. Scatter the cheese on each shell, and bake for 8 minutes.

6. In a large skillet, melt the butter or heat the oil over medium-low heat. Fry the eggs sunny-side up until the whites are firm (do not overcook).

7. Arrange 3 slices of Canadian bacon on each shell. Place an egg in the middle of each, and top with Hollandaise sauce. Sprinkle with olives and return the pizzas to the oven until the sauce begins to bubble and the crusts are golden (3 to 5 minutes). Serve immediately.

Sausage Hash Brown Pizzas

Make your own hash brown potatoes or use one of the many commercial varieties for these substantial and filling pizzas.

Yield: *4 servings*

1. In a large skillet, heat the oil over medium-low heat. Add the sausage and cook until no pink remains. Leaving 2 tablespoons of the oil in the skillet, transfer the sausage to paper towels to drain.

2. To make the hash browns, add the potatoes and onion to the skillet and toss gently to coat with oil. With a spatula, press the potatoes into the skillet and cook without stirring until lightly browned on the bottom. Turn the potatoes over and continue to cook until the other side is golden brown. Sprinkle with salt, pepper, and Cajun seasoning and set aside.

3. While the hash browns are cooking, preheat the oven to 400°F for 10 minutes. Place the pizza shells on an ungreased pizza pan or baking sheet. Top the shells with the Jarlsberg cheese, the hash brown potatoes, and the sausage. Sprinkle with the grated cheese.

4. Bake the pizzas until the tops are bubbly and the crusts are golden (12 to 15 minutes.)

4 6-inch pizza shells, Italian bread shells (boboli), focaccia, pita bread, or naan

1 tablespoon canola, safflower, or sunflower oil

8 ounces Italian sweet sausage, cut into ¼-inch slices

3 large russet potatoes, cooked and thinly sliced

1 small sweet yellow or Vidalia onion, thinly sliced

1 teaspoon sea salt

½ teaspoon ground black pepper

½ teaspoon Cajun seasoning

8 ounces (2¾ cups) shredded Jarlsberg cheese

2 ounces (½ cup) grated Parmesan, Asiago, or Pecorino-Romano cheese

Tuna Eye-Openers

Yield: *4 servings*

- 4 6-inch pizza shells, Italian bread shells (boboli), focaccia, pita bread, or naan

- 2 cans (6 ounces each) water-packed tuna, drained well

- 8 ounces (1 cup) soft cream cheese or farmer cheese

- 4 ounces (1 cup) shredded sharp Cheddar cheese

- 1 large stalk celery, finely chopped

- 5 scallions, or 1 small sweet yellow or Vidalia onion, minced

- 2 tablespoons snipped fresh chives, or 2 teaspoons dried

- ½ teaspoon sea salt (or to taste)

- ½ teaspoon ground white pepper

This breakfast pizza is perfect for those hectic mornings when time is at a premium.

1. Preheat the oven to 400°F for 10 minutes. Place the pizza shells on an ungreased pizza pan or baking sheet.

2. Combine the remaining ingredients in a medium-sized bowl and blend well. Spread this mixture on each shell.

3. Bake the pizzas until the crusts are golden (12 to 15 minutes).

14

International Desserts

Want to really dazzle your family or friends with a truly spectacular dessert? Try one of the outrageous dessert pizzas found in this chapter. Considered "pizzas" in the broadest, most unconventional sense of the word, each creation is a delightful, heavenly treat.

A variety of doughs serve as crusts for these lavish affairs. Most of the recipes in this chapter include instructions for quick-and-easy pastry crusts. Others, such as the *Country Market Apple Pizza,* call for a crust from Chapter 2. Still other recipes, like the fudgy, decadent *Pecan-Chocolate Pizza,* use refrigerated cookie dough as their base.

Keeping with the theme of this book, I have created a number of sweet-treat pizzas that have been influenced by popular desserts from around the world. From the island of Sicily, enjoy a *Cannoli Pizza* with its sweet, creamy Ricotta topping and crisp cookie crust. In the mood for a sugary array of fruit and nuts on a buttery shortcake base? Try the Scottish-inspired *Highland Tart Pizza.* And what could be a more patriotic dessert to serve at a Fourth of July barbecue than a red, white, and blue *American Flag Pizza*?

So the next time you want to serve a dessert that is both unique and sinfully delicious, give one of these sensational sweet-treat pizzas a try. I know you will enjoy serving them as much as I have enjoyed creating them.

American Flag Pizza

Yield: *12-inch pizza / 6 slices*

1 package (20 ounces) refrigerated
   sugar cookie dough

3 cups plain yogurt or sour cream

½ cup honey

½ teaspoon vanilla extract

2 cups fresh blueberries

2 cups pitted fresh or Bing cherries

So named because of its patriotic colors, this pizza features cherries, blueberries, and yogurt atop a crisp cookie crust.

1. Preheat the oven to 350°F for 15 minutes. Lightly oil a 12-inch pizza pan.

2. With floured fingers, tear off small pieces of the cookie dough and press over the surface of the pan, forming a ½-inch-high rim along the edge. Bake the crust until firm and golden (12 to 15 minutes). Cool completely.

3. In a medium-sized bowl, blend together the yogurt, honey, and vanilla. Spread over the cooled crust.

4. Starting at the center and fanning out to the edge, arrange half of the blueberries over one-fourth of the pizza. Create another wedge with half of the cherries. (See illustration below.) Repeat with the remaining blueberries and cherries.

5. Refrigerate the pizza for at least 1 hour before serving.

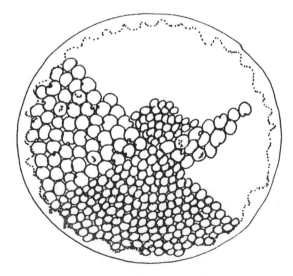

Cannoli Pizza

The cannoli, a crisp cookie tube filled with sweet Ricotta and candied fruit, is one of Sicily's most famous dessert creations and the inspiration for this luscious sweet-treat pizza.

1. Place the flour in a large bowl. With a pastry blender or two knives, cut the butter into the flour until the mixture resembles small peas. Stir in the sugar, coffee, and chocolate, blending well. With a fork, mix in the egg and egg yolk, forming a dough. Gather the dough into a ball, flatten slightly, and wrap in wax paper. Chill for 30 minutes.

2. Preheat the oven to 350°F for 15 minutes. Lightly oil a 12-inch pizza pan and set aside.

3. Place the chilled dough between 2 pieces of wax paper, roll it into a 14-inch circle, then place it over the prepared pan. Fold the overlapping dough onto itself, forming a rim along the edge. With floured fingers, crimp the edges. Bake the crust until crisp (12 to 15 minutes). Cool completely.

4. In a large bowl, combine the Ricotta, sugar, citron, orange peel, vanilla extract, and liqueur, blending well. Spread over the cooled crust and scatter with pistachios.

5. Refrigerate the pizza for at least 1 hour before serving.

Yield: *12-inch pizza / 6 slices*

CRUST

2 cups unbleached flour

1 cup (2 sticks) soft butter or margarine (do not use reduced-calorie)

1½ cups sifted confectioners' sugar

1 tablespoon instant coffee

7 squares (1 ounce each) bittersweet or semi-sweet chocolate, finely chopped (do not use unsweetened chocolate)

1 large egg, beaten

1 large egg yolk

TOPPING

30 ounces (4 cups) whole-milk Ricotta cheese

1¼ cups sifted confectioners' sugar

½ cup minced candied citron

½ cup minced candied orange peel

1 tablespoon vanilla extract

1 tablespoon orange-flavored liqueur

1 cup chopped pistachios

Country Market Apple Pizza

Yield: *16-inch pizza / 8 slices*

Prepared *Sweet Dough* (page 65)

1 tablespoon canola, safflower, or sunflower oil

2 tablespoons cornmeal

1½ cups golden raisins

3 cups boiling water

¾ cup date sugar or brown sugar

⅓ cup rum, orange juice, or apple cider

3 tablespoons arrowroot, or 2 tablespoons cornstarch

3 tablespoons fresh lemon juice

2 teaspoons grated orange zest

1 teaspoon ground cinnamon

¼ teaspoon ground nutmeg

1½ pounds Granny Smith or other tart apple, peeled, cored, and cut into ¼-inch slices

8 ounces (2¾ cups) shredded sharp Cheddar cheese

The rich combination of apple pie and Cheddar cheese is a familiar one in this heavenly dessert pizza. For added decadence, top each slice with a scoop of vanilla ice cream before serving.

1. Preheat the oven to 400°F for 30 minutes. Brush the oil over the surface of a 16-inch pizza pan and sprinkle with cornmeal, shaking out the excess. (If using pizza stones or tiles, place them in the oven before preheating, and heavily flour a pizza paddle.) Pat, stretch, or roll the dough in the prepared pan or on the paddle and set aside.

2. Place the raisins in a large bowl and cover with boiling water. Let soak for 10 minutes, then drain, reserving 1½ cups of the water.

3. Place the reserved water in a large saucepan and whisk in the sugar, rum, arrowroot, lemon juice, orange zest, cinnamon, and nutmeg. Bring to a boil over medium-high heat and cook, stirring, until the mixture begins to thicken (about 3 minutes).

4. Carefully fold the apples and raisins into the thickened mixture, reduce the heat to low, and cook until the apples are almost tender (about 5 minutes).

5. Scatter the Cheddar cheese over the prepared crust and bake for 15 minutes. Remove the pizza from the oven and top with an even layer of the apple mixture.

6. Return the pizza to the oven and bake until the top is bubbly and the crust is golden (12 to 15 minutes).

Highland Tart Pizza

This sweet, rich pizza, was inspired by a generations-old Scottish tart recipe. Its topping of nuts, currants, coconut, and candied fruit adorns a buttery shortbread crust.

Yield: *12-inch pizza / 6 slices*

CRUST

2 cups unbleached flour

1 cup (2 sticks) soft butter or margarine (do not use reduced-calorie)

2 teaspoons grated lemon zest

1½ cups sifted confectioners' sugar

1 large egg

1 large egg yolk

TOPPING

4 large eggs

1½ cups chopped walnuts

1 cup currants

1½ cups flaked coconut

1 cup dried cranberries or cherries

1 cup chopped candied cherries

1½ cups golden raisins

2 cups date sugar or brown sugar

1 cup (2 sticks) butter, melted and cooled

GLAZE

3 cups sifted confectioners' sugar

6 tablespoons orange juice

1. Place the flour in a large bowl. With a pastry blender or two knives, cut the butter into the flour until the mixture resembles small peas. Stir in the lemon zest and sugar, blending well. With a fork, mix in the egg and egg yolk, forming a dough. Gather the dough into a ball, flatten slightly, and wrap in wax paper. Chill for 30 minutes.

2. Preheat the oven to 350°F for 15 minutes. Lightly oil a 12-inch pizza pan and set aside.

3. Place the chilled dough between 2 pieces of wax paper, roll it into a 14-inch circle, and place over the prepared pan. Fold the overlapping dough onto itself, forming a ½-inch-high rim along the edge. With floured fingers, crimp the edges. Bake the crust until it begins to firm (about 8 minutes). Remove and set aside. Increase the oven temperature to 375°F.

4. In a medium-sized bowl, lightly beat the eggs. Add the walnuts, currants, coconut, cranberries, cherries, raisins, date sugar, and melted butter, blending well. Pour into the prepared crust and bake until firm (about 30 minutes).

5. While the pizza bakes, make a glaze by blending together the confectioners' sugar and orange juice until smooth. Drizzle this glaze in a zig-zag pattern over the hot pizza.

6. Cool completely before cutting into wedges and serving.

Italian Ricotta and Chocolate Pizza

Yield: *12-inch pizza / 6 slices*

The combination of Ricotta cheese and chocolate is pure magic in this enchanting dessert pizza.

CRUST

¾ cup (1½ sticks) soft butter or margarine (do not use reduced calorie)

1 cup date sugar or brown sugar

¼ cup cocoa powder

1 egg yolk

1 teaspoon almond extract

2 cups unbleached flour

TOPPING

4 ounces (1 cup) semi-sweet chocolate chips

15 ounces (2 cups) whole-milk Ricotta cheese

6 tablespoons sifted confectioners' sugar

2 tablespoons Amaretto or other almond-flavored liqueur

1 tablespoon grated lemon zest

¼ teaspoon sea salt

SAUCE

1 cup heavy cream

¼ cup honey

1 tablespoon Amaretto or other almond-flavored liqueur

8 ounces (2 cups) semi-sweet chocolate chips

1. Preheat the oven to 350°F for 15 minutes. Lightly oil a 12-inch pizza pan and set aside.

2. In a large bowl, cream together the butter, sugar, and cocoa until fluffy. Beat in the egg yolk and almond extract, then gradually add the flour, blending until a soft dough forms. Gather the dough into a ball and flatten slightly.

3. With floured hands, press the dough over the surface of the prepared pan, forming a ½-inch-high rim along the edge. Bake the crust until crisp and golden (30 to 35 minutes). Cool completely.

4. To make the topping, finely chop the chocolate chips and set aside. Place the Ricotta cheese in a medium-sized bowl, and beat with an electric mixer until smooth. Beat in the confectioners' sugar, Amaretto, lemon zest, and salt. Fold in the chopped chocolate. Spread this Ricotta mixture evenly over the cooled crust.

5. To make the sauce, bring the heavy cream and honey to a boil in a small saucepan. Immediately remove the pan from the heat and add the Amaretto and chocolate chips. Stir until the chocolate melts and the sauce is smooth.

6. Slice the pizza and top each wedge with chocolate sauce. Enjoy immediately.

Pecan-Chocolate Pizza

Even the most discriminating chocoholic will delight in this chewy, extravagant pizza with its deep, dark, delicious fudge topping.

1. Preheat the oven to 350°F for 15 minutes. Lightly oil a 12-inch pizza pan.

2. With floured fingers, tear off small pieces of the cookie dough and press over the surface of the pan, forming a ½-inch-high rim along the edge. Bake the crust until lightly set (8 to 10 minutes). Remove from the oven and set aside. Reduce the oven temperature to 325°F.

3. In a medium-sized saucepan, combine the date sugar, honey, butter, and milk. Cook over medium heat, stirring frequently with a wooden spoon, until the sugar dissolves and the mixture is smooth (about 5 minutes). Remove the pan from the heat and add the chocolate, stirring until melted and smooth.

4. To the chocolate mixture, add the flour, vanilla extract, and rum extract. Gradually add the eggs, stirring until well blended.

5. Pour the filling into the prepared crust and scatter the top with chopped nuts. Sprinkle with superfine sugar.

6. Bake the pizza until a knife inserted near the center comes out clean (about 45 minutes). Cool completely before serving.

Yield: *12-inch pizza / 6 slices*

1 package (20 ounces) refrigerated chocolate-chip cookie dough

2 cups date sugar or brown sugar

⅔ cup honey

⅔ cup (1½ sticks) soft butter or margarine (do not use reduced calorie)

¼ cup milk

4 squares (1 ounce each) unsweetened chocolate, finely chopped

2 tablespoons unbleached flour

1 teaspoon vanilla extract

1 teaspoon rum extract

4 large eggs, lightly beaten

1 cup chopped pecans, toasted

⅓ cup superfine sugar

Scottish Banana Pizza

Yield: *12-inch pizza / 6 slices*

CRUST

2 cups unbleached flour

1 cup (2 sticks) soft butter or
   margarine (do not use
   reduced-calorie)

2 teaspoons grated lemon zest

1½ cups sifted confectioners' sugar

1 large egg, beaten

1 large egg yolk

TOPPING

1½ cups sour cream

9 tablespoons date sugar or brown
   sugar

1 teaspoon grated lemon zest

4 large firm, ripe bananas

Sliced bananas nestled in sugary sour cream adorn a crisp lemony crust in this sensational dessert pizza.

1. Place the flour in a large bowl. With a pastry blender or two knives, cut the butter into the flour until the mixture resembles small peas. Stir in the lemon zest and confectioners' sugar, blending well. With a fork, mix in the egg and egg yolk, forming a dough. Form the dough into a ball, flatten slightly, and wrap in wax paper. Chill for 30 minutes.

2. Preheat the oven to 350°F for 15 minutes. Lightly oil a 12-inch pizza pan and set aside.

3. Place the chilled dough between 2 pieces of wax paper, roll it into a 14-inch circle, and place over the prepared pan. Fold the overlapping dough onto itself, forming a ½-inch-high rim along the edge. With floured fingers, crimp the edges. Bake the crust until crisp (12 to 15 minutes). Cool completely.

4. In a medium-sized bowl, whisk together the sour cream, sugar, and lemon zest until smooth. Spread over the cooled crust. Cut the bananas into ¼-inch slices and arrange on top.

5. Refrigerate the pizza for 30 minutes before serving.*

* As sliced bananas turn brown quickly, this pizza should be served shortly after it is prepared.

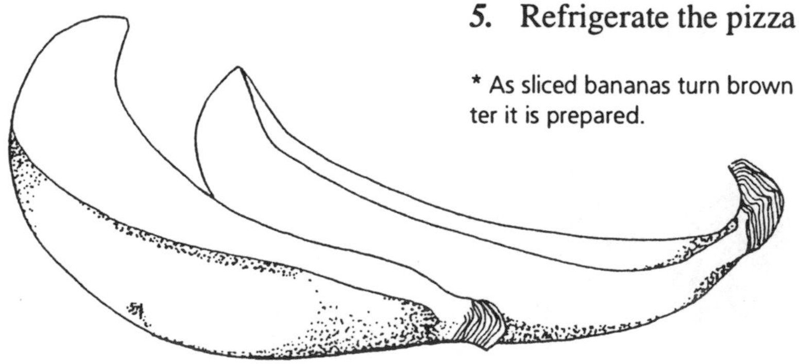

Caramel Cheesecake Pizza

I wish all cheesecake recipes were as easy to prepare as this one. No lengthy baking time, no fussing . . . just a quick and easy dessert created from ingredients you probably already have on hand.

Yield: *12-inch pizza / 6 slices*

1 package (20 ounces) refrigerated sugar cookie dough

12 ounces (1½ cups) soft cream cheese

½ cup granulated sugar

1 tablespoon orange-flavored liqueur or orange juice

1 teaspoon grated orange zest

1 jar (12 ounces) caramel ice-cream topping

1 cup chopped cashews or macadamia nuts

1. Preheat the oven at 350°F for 15 minutes. Lightly oil a 12-inch pizza pan.

2. With floured fingers, tear off small pieces of the cookie dough and press over the surface of the pan, forming a ½-inch-high rim along the edge. Bake the crust until firm and golden (12 to 15 minutes). Cool completely.

3. In a medium-sized bowl, cream together the cream cheese, sugar, liqueur, and orange zest with an electric mixer until smooth. Spread over the cooled crust.

4. Heat the caramel topping in a small saucepan over low heat until just warm and liquidy. Using an oiled knife or spatula, spread this topping evenly over the pizza. Immediately scatter with nuts, pressing them lightly into the caramel.

5. Refrigerate the pizza for at least 1 hour before serving.

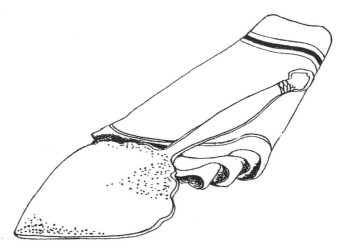

Fruited Pizza Pie

Yield: *12-inch pizza / 6 slices*

CRUST

1 ½ cups unbleached flour

6 tablespoons date sugar or brown sugar

1 ½ teaspoons grated orange zest

½ teaspoon vanilla extract

¾ cup (1 ½ sticks) soft butter or margarine (do not use reduced-calorie)

2 large egg yolks, lightly beaten

TOPPING

1 package (8 ounces) soft cream cheese

½ cup sour cream

2 large ripe bananas, mashed

⅓ cup honey

2 tablespoons orange-flavored liqueur

4 large ripe peaches, skinned and sliced

1 quart fresh strawberries, hulled and sliced

In this luscious dessert pizza, fresh strawberries and peaches are nestled in a bed of banana cream. Yum!

1. Combine the flour, sugar, orange zest, and vanilla extract in a large bowl. With a pastry blender or 2 knives, cut the butter into the flour until the mixture resembles small peas. With a fork, mix in the egg yolks, forming a dough. Gather the dough into a ball, flatten slightly, and wrap in wax paper. Chill for 1 hour.

2. Preheat the oven to 400°F for 15 minutes. Lightly oil a 12-inch pizza pan and set aside.

3. Place the dough between 2 pieces of wax paper, roll it into a 14-inch circle, and place over the prepared pan. Fold the overlapping dough onto itself, forming a ½-inch-high rim along the edge. With floured fingers, crimp the edges. Bake the crust until crisp and golden (10 to 12 minutes). Cool completely.

4. Using an electric mixer, blend the cream cheese, sour cream, bananas, honey, and liqueur until smooth. Spread evenly over the cooled crust.

5. Beginning at the outer edge of the pie, arrange the strawberry slices in an overlapping circle. Working toward the center of the pie, next arrange a circle of peach slices. Continue making alternating circles of strawberries and peaches.

6. Chill the pizza for 30 minutes before serving.

Top: Peanut Honeys (page 194)
Bottom: Farmhouse Pizza (page 194)

Top: *Highland Tart Pizza* (page 205)
Bottom: *Cannoli Pizza* (page 203)

Pineapple Shortbread Pizza

This light, crisp, and oh-so-buttery dessert crust is topped with fresh pineapple then crowned with a golden honey-mint glaze.

1. Preheat the oven to 350°F for 15 minutes. Lightly oil a 12-inch pizza pan and set aside.

2. In a large bowl, cream together the butter and sugar until fluffy. Beat in the egg yolk and vanilla, then gradually add the flour, blending until a soft dough forms. Gather the dough into a ball and flatten slightly.

3. With floured hands, press the dough over the surface of the prepared pan, forming a ½-inch-high rim along the edge. Bake the crust until crisp and golden (30 to 35 minutes). Cool completely.

4. In a small saucepan, heat the honey, lime juice, mint leaves, and mint extract over very low heat. Stir until the ingredients are well blended and the liquid is thin.

5. Arrange the pineapple chunks on the cooled crust. Top with an even coating of the honey glaze.

6. Allow the pizza to stand for 30 minutes before cutting and serving.

Yield: *12-inch pizza / 6 slices*

CRUST

¾ cup (1½ sticks) soft butter or margarine (do not use reduced calorie)

1 cup date sugar or brown sugar

1 egg yolk

1 teaspoon vanilla extract

2 cups unbleached flour

TOPPING

⅔ cup honey

6 tablespoons fresh lime juice

3 tablespoons chopped fresh mint leaves (do not use dried)

½ teaspoon mint extract

6 cups bite-sized fresh pineapple chunks

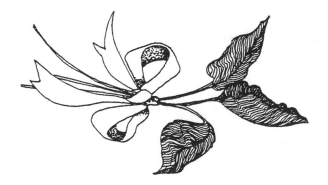

Index